The Fiction of Margaret Atwood

READERS' GUIDES TO ESSENTIAL CRITICISM SERIES

CONSULTANT EDITOR: NICOLAS TREDELL

Published

Thomas P. Adler	Tennessee Williams: *A Streetcar Named Desire/Cat on a Hot Tin Roof*
Pascale Aebischer	Jacobean Drama
Lucie Armitt	George Eliot: *Adam Bede/The Mill on the Floss/Middlemarch*
Dana E. Aspinall	William Shakespeare: *As You Like It*
Simon Avery	Thomas Hardy: *The Mayor of Casterbridge/Jude the Obscure*
Paul Baines	Daniel Defoe: *Robinson Crusoe/Moll Flanders*
Brian Baker	Science Fiction
Annika Bautz	Jane Austen: *Sense and Sensibility/Pride and Prejudice/Emma*
Matthew Beedham	The Novels of Kazuo Ishiguro
Nick Bentley	Contemporary British Fiction
Richard Beynon	D. H. Lawrence: *The Rainbow/Women in Love*
Scott Boltwood	Brian Friel
Peter Boxall	Samuel Beckett: *Waiting for Godot/Endgame*
Claire Brennan	The Poetry of Sylvia Plath
Susan Bruce	Shakespeare: *King Lear*
Sandie Byrne	Jane Austen: *Mansfield Park*
Sandie Byrne	The Poetry of Ted Hughes
Alison Chapman	Elizabeth Gaskell: *Mary Barton/North and South*
Peter Childs	The Fiction of Ian McEwan
Christine Clegg	Vladimir Nabokov: *Lolita*
Jay Corwin	Corwin: *Gabriel García Márquez*
John Coyle	James Joyce: *Ulysses/A Portrait of the Artist as a Young Man*
Martin Coyle	Shakespeare: *Richard II*
Jessica Cox	Victorian Sensation Fiction
Sarah Davison	Modernist Literatures
Sarah Dewar-Watson	Tragedy
Justin D. Edwards	Postcolonial Literature
Robert C. Evans	Philip Larkin
Michael Faherty	The Poetry of W. B. Yeats
Sarah Gamble	The Fiction of Angela Carter
Jodi-Anne George	*Beowulf*
Jodi-Anne George	Chaucer: The General Prologue to *The Canterbury Tales*
Jane Goldman	Virginia Woolf: *To the Lighthouse/The Waves*
Huw Griffiths	Shakespeare: *Hamlet*
Vanessa Guignery	The Fiction of Julian Barnes
Louisa Hadley	The Fiction of A. S. Byatt
Sarah Haggarty and Jon Mee	William Blake: *Songs of Innocence and Experience*
Geoffrey Harvey	Thomas Hardy: *Tess of the d'Urbervilles*
Paul Hendon	The Poetry of W. H. Auden
Terry Hodgson	The Plays of Tom Stoppard for Stage, Radio, TV and Film
William Hughes	Bram Stoker: *Dracula*
Stuart Hutchinson	Mark Twain: *Tom Sawyer/Huckleberry Finn*
Stuart Hutchinson	Edith Wharton: *The House of Mirth/The Custom of the Country*
Betty Jay	E. M. Forster: *A Passage to India*
Aaron Kelly	Twentieth-Century Irish Literature

Elmer Kennedy-Andrews	Nathaniel Hawthorne: *The Scarlet Letter*
Elmer Kennedy-Andrews	The Poetry of Seamus Heaney
Daniel Lea	George Orwell: *Animal Farm/Nineteen Eighty-Four*
Jinqi Ling	Asian American Literature
Rachel Lister	Alice Walker: *The Color Purple*
Sara Lodge	Charlotte Brontë: *Jane Eyre*
Philippa Lyon	Twentieth-Century War Poetry
Merja Makinen	The Novels of Jeanette Winterson
Stephen Marino	Arthur Miller: Death of a Salesman/The Crucible
Britta Martens	The Poetry of Robert Browning
Matt McGuire	Contemporary Scottish Literature
Timothy Milnes	Wordsworth: *The Prelude*
Jago Morrison	The Fiction of Chinua Achebe
Merritt Moseley	The Fiction of Pat Barker
Pat Pinsent	Children's Literature
Carl Plasa	Toni Morrison: *Beloved*
Carl Plasa	Jean Rhys: *Wide Sargasso Sea*
Nicholas Potter	Shakespeare: *Antony and Cleopatra*
Nicholas Potter	Shakespeare: *Othello*
Nicholas Potter	Shakespeare's Late Plays: *Pericles/Cymbeline/The Winter's Tale/The Tempest*
Steven Price	The Plays, Screenplays and Films of David Mamet
Julia Round, Rikke Platz Cortsen and Maaheen Ahmed	Comics and Graphic Novels
Berthold Schoene-Harwood	Mary Shelley: *Frankenstein*
Nicholas Seager	The Rise of the Novel
Nick Selby	T. S. Eliot: *The Waste Land*
Nick Selby	Herman Melville: *Moby Dick*
Nick Selby	The Poetry of Walt Whitman
David Smale	Salman Rushdie: *Midnight's Children/The Satanic Verses*
Enit Steiner	Jane Austen: *Northanger Abbey/Persuasion*
Patsy Stoneman	Emily Brontë: *Wuthering Heights*
Susie Thomas	Hanif Kureishi
Fiona Tolan	The Fiction of Margaret Atwood
Nicolas Tredell	Joseph Conrad: *Heart of Darkness*
Nicolas Tredell	Charles Dickens: *Great Expectations*
Nicolas Tredell	William Faulkner: *The Sound and the Fury/As I Lay Dying*
Nicolas Tredell	F. Scott Fitzgerald: *The Great Gatsby*
Nicolas Tredell	Shakespeare: *A Midsummer Night's Dream*
Nicolas Tredell	Shakespeare: *Macbeth*
Nicolas Tredell	Shakespeare: The Tragedies
Nicolas Tredell	The Fiction of Martin Amis
David Wheatley	Contemporary British Poetry
Michael Whitworth	Virginia Woolf: *Mrs Dalloway*
Martin Willis	Literature and Science
Matthew Woodcock	Shakespeare: *Henry V*
Gillian Woods	Shakespeare: *Romeo and Juliet*
Angela Wright	Gothic Fiction
Andrew Wyllie and Catherine Rees	The Plays of Harold Pinter

The Fiction of Margaret Atwood

Fiona Tolan

BLOOMSBURY ACADEMIC
LONDON · NEW YORK · OXFORD · NEW DELHI · SYDNEY

BLOOMSBURY ACADEMIC
Bloomsbury Publishing Plc
50 Bedford Square, London, WC1B 3DP, UK
1385 Broadway, New York, NY 10018, USA
29 Earlsfort Terrace, Dublin 2, Ireland

BLOOMSBURY, BLOOMSBURY ACADEMIC and the Diana logo are trademarks of
Bloomsbury Publishing Plc

First published in Great Britain 2023
Paperback edition published 2024

Copyright © Fiona Tolan, 2023, 2024

Fiona Tolan has asserted her right under the Copyright, Designs and Patents Act, 1988, to be identified as Author of this work.

Cover design: Rebecca Heselton
Cover image: Margaret Atwood at the Edinburgh International Book Festival 2009 © GL Portrait / Alamy Stock Photo

All rights reserved. No part of this publication may be reproduced or transmitted in any form or by any means, electronic or mechanical, including photocopying, recording, or any information storage or retrieval system, without prior permission in writing from the publishers.

Bloomsbury Publishing Plc does not have any control over, or responsibility for, any third-party websites referred to or in this book. All internet addresses given in this book were correct at the time of going to press. The author and publisher regret any inconvenience caused if addresses have changed or sites have ceased to exist, but can accept no responsibility for any such changes.

A catalogue record for this book is available from the British Library.

Library of Congress Control Number: 2022939013

ISBN: HB: 978-1-3503-3673-5
PB: 978-1-3503-3677-3
ePDF: 978-1-3503-3674-2
eBook: 978-1-3503-3675-9

Typeset by Deanta Global Publishing Services, Chennai, India

To find out more about our authors and books visit www.bloomsbury.com and sign up for our newsletters.

For Cecilia and Aurora – my clever, funny, beautiful girls

Contents

	Introduction	1
	Biography	2
	Organization of this guide	7
1	Early works and early reception: *The Edible Woman* and *Surfacing*	9
	The Edible Woman	10
	Overview	11
	Early reception	13
	The romance plot and fairy-tale gothic	15
	Fairy-tale imagery	17
	Consumption and the body	19
	Surfacing	20
	Overview	20
	Early reception	22
	Feminist readings	24
	A gothic novel	27
	Language and form	28
2	A developing canon and developing themes: *Lady Oracle*, *Life Before Man* and *Bodily Harm*	31
	Lady Oracle	31
	Overview	32
	Gothic romance	34
	Princesses and goddesses	36
	Life Before Man	39
	Overview	41
	Between romance and realism	42
	Consumption and survival	44
	Bodily Harm	46
	Overview	46
	A postcolonial novel?	48
	Touch and responsibility	50
	A healing comedy?	51

3	'Are there any questions?': A focus on *The Handmaid's Tale*	53
	Overview	54
	Early responses	56
	What genre *is* it?	58
	Writing about feminism in the 1980s	61
	Offred's storytelling: Language and narrative	63
	Complicity, victimhood and responsibility	67
	Reading the conclusion	70
4	Spotty-handed villainesses: *Cat's Eye* and *The Robber Bride*	75
	Cat's Eye	77
	Overview	78
	A fictional autobiography?	81
	Women beware women	83
	Art and representation	85
	The Robber Bride	88
	Overview	88
	(Hi)storytellers: Narrative authority	91
	Friendship/sisterhood/feminism	92
	Another gothic tale	94
	The conclusion	96
5	History, memory and recovering the past: *Alias Grace*, *The Blind Assassin* and *The Penelopiad*	99
	Alias Grace	100
	Overview	100
	Readerly desire	101
	Historical fiction	103
	The servant girl	104
	The quilt motif	106
	An anti-detective novel	107
	The Blind Assassin	109
	Overview	109
	A self-conscious storyteller	111
	A gothic tale of victims and villains	113
	The Penelopiad	115
	Overview	115
	Is it a novel?	116
	Reclaiming voices – the twelve hanged maids	117
	Classical revisions and re-readings	119

6	Atwood's dystopian futures: The *MaddAddam* trilogy	121
	Oryx and Crake	123
	Overview	123
	Textual allusions in *Oryx and Crake*	125
	Our post-human future	127
	An ethical novel	129
	The Year of the Flood	131
	Overview	133
	Gendered futures	134
	Humanism/posthumanism	136
	Reading the conclusion	138
	MaddAddam	138
	Overview	138
	Narrative structure: Who speaks?	139
	After the Anthropocene	141
	Conclusion	145
	Stone Mattress: Nine Wicked Tales	146
	The Heart Goes Last	147
	Hag-Seed	148
	The Atwood phenomenon	149
	Notes	153
	Select bibliography	176
	Index	191

Introduction

Margaret Atwood is inarguably one of the most successful and critically acclaimed writers working today. She is commonly described as Canada's most eminent poet and novelist. Since the appearance of *Double Persephone*, a poetry pamphlet she first published with the small press Hawkshead in 1961, she has gone on to produce a phenomenal body of work. This includes, to date, seventeen novels, eight short story collections and eighteen poetry collections. Her extended bibliography encompasses children's books, graphic novels, non-fiction and critical essays, reviews, edited collections and television scripts. This versatility – and the creative pleasure she evidently derives from experimenting with genres and forms – has only gathered pace as her career has developed.

Her first full-length published book was another poetry volume, the 1966 collection *The Circle Game*, for which she received Canada's prestigious Governor General's Award. She remains best known, however, as a novelist. *The Edible Woman*, her first novel, appeared in 1969; a striking darkly comic tale, it views contemporary expectations of women's lives and the familiar romance narrative through an unexpectedly gothic lens. Since then, she has proceeded to produce works that manage to sustain clear, traceable threads of the characteristically 'Atwoodian' (a notion that will recur in this volume) while also persistently challenging readerly expectations. Her work encompasses genre fiction, speculative fiction and adaptations, and her settings stretch from the historic to the contemporary to the imagined future. If anything can be said to unite this diverse body of work, it might perhaps be best defined as both a close careful attention to language and its slippery power and a deeply ethical concern with 'Power Politics' – a phrase she notably adopted as the title of a 1971 poetry collection. Whether examining contemporary gender roles, fairy tales and myths, fundamentalism or multinational corporations, Atwood's writing typically works to examine and expose inequalities, myriad abuses of power and violence in all its forms.

Biography

Margaret Eleanor Atwood was born in November 1939 in Ottawa, Canada, and was raised in Northern Ontario and Quebec. Her father, Carl Atwood, was an entomologist and the family would spend long extended summers in the Canadian bush in makeshift accommodation while he conducted his research. This was a formative period for Atwood; she and her older brother Harold enjoyed the freedom of roaming outdoors and entertaining themselves, largely undisturbed by either formal education or the conservative social niceties of 1940s provincial Canada. Atwood recalls that her mother, Margaret, also 'preferred the bush. She hated hats, tea parties and housework'.[1] Shortly after the end of the Second World War, the family settled permanently in Toronto, with her father taking up a university professorship. This move represented a significant upheaval for the eight-year-old Atwood. Suddenly, school beckoned, and in 1951 her younger sister, Ruth, was born. Later, Atwood would capture something of this shock of transition in her 1988 novel *Cat's Eye*, in which Elaine Risley is similarly abruptly socialized into the world of little girls after a childhood spent living 'like nomads on the far edges of the war' (25). The experience of living in the bush and the influence of her father's scientific interests can also be traced in other works across her canon: from the 1972 novel *Surfacing*, in which the narrator travels up into the lakes of Northern Quebec in search of her missing father, to the story 'The Boys at the Lab', published more recently in *Moral Disorder* (2006).

Atwood went on to study for a BA in English at Victoria College at the University of Toronto and then moved to the United States to study at Radcliffe College in Cambridge, Massachusetts (a women's liberal arts college that later merged with the originally all-male Harvard College). At Radcliffe she studied Victorian and American literature, gaining an MA and commencing a PhD thesis on 'The English Metaphysical Romance' that was never to be completed. Discussing Atwood's time in the United States in her 1996 monograph *Margaret Atwood*, Coral Ann Howells describes the young Canadian's sudden realization that Canada was simply 'invisible' to Americans: a blank space on the map, somewhere cold up north. For Howells, Atwood's experience was 'the common colonial experience of moving to a metropolitan culture where people know nothing and care nothing about one's home place'.[2] Howells locates in this period, and in this sense of cultural erasure, the roots of Atwood's Canadian nationalism, which developed over the 1960s and typically defined Canada in opposition to the nation's more confident, more powerful southern neighbour: an idea that shapes both *Surfacing* and her contemporaneous literary critical work, *Survival*.

Atwood returned to Canada and spent some years taking up temporary posts in various university English departments. In 1967, she married James Polk, but the couple were to divorce in 1973 and Atwood began a long and happy relationship with the writer Graeme Gibson, with whom she has a daughter, Eleanor Jess Gibson, born in 1976. Against a backdrop of studying, teaching and occasional employment across the 1950s and the 1960s (like Marian in *The Edible Woman*, she worked in market research for a time), Atwood was always at work on her true passion: writing. As Heidi Slettedahl Macpherson notes, discussing the formative stages of Atwood's career in *The Cambridge Introduction to Margaret Atwood*, the limited sense, at that time, of a strong canon of Canadian literature made her decision to become a writer 'not only unusual, but improbable (doubly improbable given that she was female too)'.[3] But while the newly staked outfield of 'Can Lit' was yet to fully develop, there was a burgeoning folk and experimental art scene in Canada in the 1960s, and Atwood gave poetry readings in bohemian Toronto coffee houses alongside other young avant-garde poets such as Fred Wah, Al Purdy and bpNichol. In *Writing in Our Time*, Pauline Butling and Susan Rudy document the radical poetry scene in Canada in the 1960s and 1970s, and in the occasional, oblique glimpses of Atwood that the book affords, we get another perspective on the famous novelist as young experimental poet.[4]

By the time Atwood came to publish *The Edible Woman*, the novel which was to bring her to wider critical attention, she had already published three prize-winning collections of poetry. And since these early beginnings, she has continued to write and publish poetry, most recently *Dearly* in 2020. But increasingly, she became primarily known as a novelist and in this guise, she takes her place within a generation of Canadian novelists that came to prominence in the mid-to-late twentieth century, including Margaret Laurence, Michael Ondaatje, Alice Munro, Anne Hébert, Timothy Findlay and Carol Shields.

Many of this new generation of writers were beneficiaries of arts funding from the Canada Council. Established in 1957, the Council's mandate was to support the production of art in Canada by Canadians and to raise the profile of Canadian cultural production. With sudden access to much-needed financial support, literary journals and magazines and small presses sprang up. Indeed, some of Atwood's early work, in keeping with these developments, was published by House of Anansi Press, a small publishing house founded in

1967 with Canada Council support and with a mandate to publish Canadian writers. Paul Groetsch, in an essay on Atwood's Canadian nationalism, notes that this push for a cultural revival was intensified by a sense of economic and political crisis prompted by Quebec separatism and US imperialism, 'which had shown its ugly head in Vietnam and seemed to threaten Canada with an economic and political takeover'.[5] Against this rather anxious backdrop, Atwood published her controversial 1972 study, *Survival: A Thematic Guide to Canadian Literature*.

With *Survival*, Atwood made a leap from being a product of the Canadian cultural renaissance to becoming an instrumental figure in shaping the debate around the nature of Canada's national culture. The book was strongly influenced by the then popular critical mode championed by Northrop Frye, who was teaching at the University of Toronto when Atwood was there. In it, she identifies the patterns and themes that she saw as characterizing and defining Canadian literature in contrast to the national literature of the United States. Canadian literature (and by extension, the Canadian national psyche), she argued, is notably more pragmatic and less optimistic than American literature, and commonly preoccupied with themes of survival and victimhood. The book was challenged on many fronts. Goetsch notes that it annoyed Marxists for its liberal ahistoricism, irritated some nationalists for its pessimistic vision of Canada and its severely limited consideration of French-Canadian literature, and was rejected by others for its failure to acknowledge Canada's multiculturalism and for its erection of a grand thematic meta-narrative at a time when such constructions were being determinedly torn down. At the same time, argues Goetsch, in hindsight, *Survival* is 'a crucial book which fulfilled important functions in the 1970s and met needs of the time'. It opened up a valuable debate, and its hypothesis, he suggests, 'now appears less restrictive than it did at first'.[6] While *Survival* describes a now-dated mode of nationalist literary criticism, and Atwood has acknowledged that she would not write the same book today, in 1985 she declared that she stood by its central premise: 'that Canadian literature is a distinct entity, that it is informed by its colonial or post-colonial status, and that it is worthy of study'.[7]

From her inception as a young poet in Toronto through the early years of developing a reputation as a key figure in Canada's cultural landscape, Atwood's work garnered international critical attention relatively quickly. The first collection of critical essays to address her writing appeared in 1977 in *The Malahat Review: Margaret Atwood: A Symposium*, edited by Linda Sandler. Describing her as 'the presiding genius of Canadian letters', Sandler declares: 'Nothing quite like Atwood has ever happened to Canada before.'[8]

Since then, and across nearly sixty years of literary production, a significant body of secondary critical material has built up around her work. Indeed, there are very few contemporary living writers who have amassed a comparable amount of critical analysis. Some of these analyses are large, authoritative, reception-defining works: from early, exploratory interventions such as Barbara Hill Rigney's *Margaret Atwood* (1987) and Judith McCombs's *Critical Essays on Margaret Atwood* (1988) to more recent, reflective considerations of Atwood's accumulated works such as Reingard Nischik's monumental *Margaret Atwood: Works and Impact* (2000) and Coral Ann Howells's authoritative *The Cambridge Companion to Margaret Atwood* (second edition, 2021). And numerous as these monographs and edited collections are, more Atwood criticism is produced by far in essays, chapters and journal articles. There is also a Margaret Atwood Society 'with whom she has an uneasy relationship'[9] – stemming, one suspects, from a certain discomfort at being the living subject of an association – a *Margaret Atwood Studies* journal (affiliated to the Margaret Atwood Society) and an international network of Atwood scholars, many of whom travel to consult the well-used Margaret Atwood Archive, held at the Thomas Fisher Rare Book Library at the University of Toronto.

Atwood's work has been acknowledged by a host of international bodies. Since winning early accolades such as the E. J. Pratt medal for *Double Persephone* (1961) and the Centennial Commission Poetry Competition for *The Animals in That Country* (1967), she has been awarded an extensive list of prizes and commendations. Many of the early awards, naturally, came from Canadian sources, and in 1987, she became a fellow of the Royal Society of Canada. Rapidly, however, Atwood's literary reputation took on international standing. There are many examples that one could choose to illustrate her reach and impact. She has twice won the regional award for the Commonwealth Writers' Best Book Prize (for *The Handmaid's Tale* in 1987 and *The Robber Bride* in 1994). She was awarded the Government of France's Chevalier dans l'Ordre des Arts et des Lettres in 1994 and the Norwegian Order of Literary Merit in 1996. In 2000, she won the prestigious Booker Prize for Fiction for *The Blind Assassin*, a prize for which she has been shortlisted a further four times (for *The Handmaid's Tale*, 1986; *Cat's Eye*, 1989; *Alias Grace*, 1996; and *Oryx and Crake*, 2003). In 2019, she won the Booker Prize again, for *The Testaments*, sharing the award jointly with British writer Bernadine Evaristo. She holds honorary doctorates from – among others – the University of Cambridge, Harvard University and the Université Sorbonne Nouvelle. In 2016, she won the PEN Pinter Prize, awarded annually to a writer of 'outstanding literary merit' who, in the words of Harold Pinter's

Nobel Prize in Literature speech, 'casts an "unflinching, unswerving" gaze upon the world and shows a "fierce intellectual determination . . . to define the real truth of our lives and our societies"',[10] and in 2017 she was given PEN's Lifetime Achievement Award. These latter honours, one imagines, are particularly prized, as Atwood is a longstanding supporter of and advocate for both PEN and Amnesty International, prominently championing liberty and freedom of expression. Each of these awards, in turn, speaks to the high standing in which Atwood is held as a literary figure of significant international stature.

While Atwood's biography is well rehearsed, and the echoes between her life and her work are often observed, she herself has been notably reluctant to engage in biographical readings of her texts and is typically resistant to questions that attempt to pursue such a mode of analysis. In 1998, two biographies of Atwood were published, and both were unauthorized. Nathalie Cooke's *Margaret Atwood: A Biography* is an intimate portrait, charting Atwood's progress through childhood, education, relationships, motherhood and an increasingly international career. Cooke explores the two halves of what she terms 'a doubled life': that of Margaret Atwood ('poet and novelist [. . .] known for her pointed pen') and Peggy Atwood ('family member, stalwart friend, keen listener').[11] In *The Red Shoes: Margaret Atwood Starting Out*, instead, Rosemary Sullivan examines Atwood's career in the context of a generation of Canadian women writers and artists who resisted the idea that 'women were meant to be muses, not maestros'.[12]

In a recent interview, Atwood notes: 'I was averse to biographical interpretation when I was twenty. I wanted only the work, not the context for it. But that was then. Context is more interesting to me now.'[13] And in 2002, she provided a brief autobiographical sketch in the first chapter of her non-fiction work, *Negotiating with the Dead: A Writer on Writing*, in which she reflects on her childhood and adolescence. The themes that recur are her parents' self-sufficiency, the manner in which they encouraged independence and curiosity in their children, the freedom and adventure of outdoor living, a general lack of gendered expectations for her and her brother, and the persistence of 'books and solitude'.[14] As she proceeds through the years of settling into post-war suburban life and attending school, her recollections are couched primarily in terms of her reading, which was 'wide but indiscriminate – everything from Jane Austen to True Romance magazines to pulp science fiction to *Moby-Dick*'.[15] *Negotiating with the Dead* began life as a collection of lectures on what it means to be a writer. By commencing with this autobiographical reflection, Atwood balances the book's encyclopaedic knowledge and sweeping reflections on writers and writing throughout time with a simple acknowledgement that she – like all writers – is the product of a very particular matrix of national, cultural and familial influences.

Organization of this guide

The aim of this book is to provide the student and interested reader with an overview of some of the most characteristic, influential and insightful critical responses to Atwood's work. Given the extraordinary amount of scholarship on Atwood that exists and continues to proliferate without pause, it is impossible to provide a comprehensive account of everything that has been written. Where works are briefly cited, readers are encouraged to make use of the extensive bibliography provided at the end of this volume to pursue in their entirety the many excellent critical responses to Atwood. For those seeking still further examples of Atwood criticism, and details of the most recent publications, the *Margaret Atwood Studies* journal publishes an invaluable annual bibliography of works by and about the author.

The Fiction of Margaret Atwood traces a broadly chronological path through Atwood's key publications, and each chapter highlights some significant themes that have come to predominate in the evolving reception of particular texts. Chapter 1 examines early responses to the first two published novels, *The Edible Woman* and *Surfacing*. Chapter 2 addresses the texts that established Atwood as a significant Canadian writer: *Lady Oracle*, *Life Before Man* and *Bodily Harm*. Given its continued status as her most acclaimed novel, Chapter 3 focuses solely on *The Handmaid's Tale*, while Chapter 4 considers critical readings of two of Atwood's most morally ambiguous female characters in *Cat's Eye* and *The Robber Bride*. Chapter 5 examines *Alias Grace*, *The Blind Assassin* and *The Penelopiad* as Atwood's most prominent forays into historical fiction, and Chapter 6 addresses responses to Atwood's dystopian trilogy, *Oryx and Crake*, *The Year of the Flood* and *MaddAddam*. And finally, in the conclusion, I briefly consider the short story collection *Stone Mattress*, and Atwood's later novels, *The Heart Goes Last*, *Hag-Seed* and *The Testaments*, before ending with a reflection on the nature and legacy of what has been termed 'the Atwood phenomenon'.

1

Early works and early reception
The Edible Woman and *Surfacing*

With the publication of her first two novels, Atwood's status as an award-winning young Canadian poet was rapidly supplemented by her newfound reputation as a writer of striking and uncompromising prose. Her first two published novels are in many ways very different texts. *The Edible Woman* commences as a satirical urban comedy about a young office worker juggling a conservative landlady, a progressive flatmate and the expectations of her handsome fiancé. *Surfacing* is an immediately more elliptical text, in which a nameless narrator searches for her missing father on a remote island. The setting, tone and style of the two novels are quite distinct. Nevertheless, these early works contain notable sympathies and continuities of concern, and together *The Edible Woman* and *Surfacing* established some of the elements that would come to be deemed characteristic of Atwood's work: not least, a female protagonist, a concern with gendered power relations and an interest in genre subversion.

The underlying similarities between the two novels are addressed in an early essay on Atwood by fellow novelist Marge Piercy, in which she observes a larger schematic pattern at work. Piercy acknowledges the two texts' differences; *The Edible Woman*, she notes, is a clever, comic novel with traces of terror (in particular, we might think of the nightmarish scene in the middle of the novel, in which Marian comes to perceive herself as quarry and tries to escape her hunter boyfriend), while *Surfacing* contains satirical elements but is fundamentally 'a grim, desperate novel'. She also, however, works to uncover continuities of theme in Atwood's developing canon. Piercy's essay was written in 1973, when Atwood had published just these two novels, alongside five books of poetry and the critical text, *Survival*. In her analysis, Piercy identifies the persistence of Atwood's poetic technique in her fiction and develops her discussion of the novels alongside a reading of key thematic concerns in Atwood's poetry. She also focuses in her essay on the theme of victimhood in Canadian fiction, which Atwood explored in *Survival*, and considers how it might be applied to a reading of Atwood's own novels. In both, Piercy points out, the protagonist is 'a woman who becomes aware she has lost her identity – her self – who comes to experience herself as a victim, and finally to reject that state'. For Piercy, this attempt to resolve the problem of identifying one's self as a victim is the thematic concern that underpins all Atwood's early work and which provides continuity between her poetry, her criticism and her fiction.[1]

The Edible Woman

Written in the mid-1960s, although not published until 1969, *The Edible Woman* appeared on the cusp of the rising second wave of feminism and was quickly and enthusiastically taken up by feminist critics. Marian's epiphany that her female body is a site of consumption, and her eventual rejection of the restrictions of heteronormative marriage, were identified as clearly feminist conclusions. Such readings did not sit comfortably with Atwood, however, who was reluctant to be retrospectively co-opted by a movement that, for various reasons, she deemed problematic. In 1979 she appended an introduction to the novel, in which she states: 'I myself see the book as protofeminist rather than feminist: there was no women's movement in sight when I was composing the book in 1965, and I'm not gifted with clairvoyance.'[2] For Atwood, simply put, a novel conceived before the rise of feminism cannot be the product of feminism.

In my 2007 monograph *Margaret Atwood: Feminism and Fiction*, I attempt to get to grips with this rather defensive position, and I argue that it is based in part on a falsely rigid chronology of the feminist movement. Second-wave feminism did not spontaneously erupt in 1970 but instead had its roots in myriad disparate reflections on the inequity of gender relations. Foundational feminist texts such as Simone de Beauvoir's *The Second Sex* (1949) and Betty Friedan's *The Feminine Mystique* (1963), which Atwood acknowledges in her introduction that she read 'like many at the time [. . .] behind locked doors',[3] preceded the 1970s surge in feminist theorizing. My argument in *Feminism and Fiction* is that, while Atwood's self-conscious defence of her own ideological autonomy certainly complicates any too-easy feminist reading of her work and its intentions, 'it cannot disengage her texts from a pervasive feminist discourse in which they are inarguably implicated'.[4] Atwood's themes, particularly around the packaging and consumption of the female body by a marketized society, anxieties around pregnancy and motherhood, the exposition of the limited options available to women in the labour market, and the manner in which men and women play out socially constructed roles of victim and aggressor, all place the novel squarely within the realm of feminist enquiry. And indeed, discussing something of the issue of the novel's contested feminism in 1977 with Linda Sandler, Atwood describes herself, in writing the novel, as 'plugging in to the popular sensibility' of the time.[5] This is perhaps a better way to describe the mood of a novel that is very much about a society on the cusp of seismic changes, whether or not the coming revolution is yet to be consciously acknowledged by the men and women within it.

Overview

In an early interview with Graeme Gibson from 1972, Atwood describes her first novel as an anti-comedy: a romance in which the expected comic resolution of marriage 'would be a tragic solution for Marian'.[6] Whereas in a standard eighteenth-century comedy, as Atwood explains, a young couple has to overcome some figure who represents the restrictive forces of society in order to eventually marry, in *The Edible Woman,* Marian instead must ultimately come to the realization that it is Peter, her fiancé, who represents the restrictive forces of society and therefore it is Peter whom she must escape. This underlying premise subsequently leads the novel along unexpected paths as it swerves to avoid the conclusion expected of what initially appears to be a fairly conventional contemporary romance.

The novel commences with Marian MacAlpine as a competent, financially independent young woman living in Toronto in the 1960s. She shares a flat with the somewhat erratic Ainsley, whose sexual exploits bemuse rather than shock her, and she works at an uninspiring job for a marketing firm at which she has no hope of progression. The company, as Marian explains, is 'layered like an ice-cream sandwich', with a factory-like all-male lower floor of computers and machines, an executive top floor, 'referred to as the men upstairs, since they are all men', and a 'gooey layer in the middle' of women market researchers (19). Marian accepts, without protest, that her opportunities are restricted to the dispiriting all-female middle floor, where her co-workers are either husband-hunting 'office virgins' or ageing matrons, toad-like and sluggish. Happily, she is saved from sharing the desperate state of the office virgins by her boyfriend and lover, Peter: a perfectly eligible, if rather uninspiring, young man, whom Marian imagines as 'ordinariness raised to perfection like the youngish, well-groomed faces in cigarette ads' (61). Indeed, normalcy is what Marian craves.

When her college friend Clara terms her 'almost abnormally normal', she finds the description comforting and is 'reassured' (206).

Discussing this insistence on the 'normal' in the text, Rowland Smith suggests that each of the characters are 'perfectly drawn examples of the hellishly commonplace'[7] and that idea of the horror within the ordinary persists in the novel. While Marian deems herself perfectly well adjusted and perfectly happy, elements of a more disturbing alternate reality increasingly intrude into the narrative as Atwood introduces what will become a familiar characteristic of much of her subsequent work: the manner in which the ordinary and the everyday can quickly turn sinister. For Marian, this turn towards the macabre is prompted by a seemingly irresistible push towards marriage and motherhood, suddenly accelerated when Peter unexpectedly proposes. From Clara, a seemingly perpetually pregnant housewife, to Ainsley, determined to seduce womanizer Len in order to conceive a child she plans to raise alone, Marian is surrounded by unappetizing images of fertility and maternity. Despite her increasing sense of unease, however, and a seemingly inexplicable incident in which Marian's body proceeds to act of its own accord and cause her to run from Peter, when Peter asks her to marry him, she agrees.

The proposal acts as a turning point in the novel and marks a change in Marian. Suddenly, she finds herself saying words that she does not recognize as her own: passive, conciliatory phrases such as 'I'd rather leave the big decisions up to you' (90). Shortly afterwards, the narrative voice shifts from the first to the third person, providing a clear signal to the reader, if not to Marian, that the protagonist has lost her autonomy. This loss of voice is accompanied and compounded by a loss of appetite. From initially finding herself uncharacteristically unable to finish a filet steak, Marian rapidly finds herself almost entirely unable to consume any food at all.

Against a growing sense of alienation, the narrative climaxes with Marian and Peter's engagement party, to which Marian invites all of the disparate figures in her life, including Duncan, an enigmatic graduate student she met when doing market research and has since had sporadic encounters with. Where Peter represents the social normalcy Marian consciously desires, Duncan functions as a kind of dark anti-hero and a fairy-tale guide to the underworld of her unconscious desires. As Jane Rule argues, 'It is his refusal of adult and masculine roles which attracts Marian.'[8] At the party, it is Duncan who voices derision at Marian's seeming capitulation to gendered social expectations, before abruptly leaving. Dressed, at Peter's request, in a tight red dress and full makeup, Marian looks in the mirror and sees a kind of doll, 'plastic, boneless, flexible'

(229). Overwhelmed with claustrophobic panic, she runs away from the party, and from Peter. After spending the night with Duncan, she follows him on a rambling journey through a ravine, until he tells her she must proceed alone. After this surreal and disorientating journey, Marian returns home and bakes a cake in the shape of a pink smiling woman. When Peter arrives, she accuses him of trying to destroy her and offers him the cake instead. Confused and angry, he leaves, and Marian, her appetite now returned, starts to eat the cake herself. The cake proffers itself in the novel as a deeply symbolic object, resonant with interpretative possibilities. The text, however, is highly ironically aware of this over-abundance of signification as Marian archly declaims it 'only a cake' (273).

Early reception

Atwood has on a number of occasions reflected on some of the early responses to her work, particularly the manner in which reviewers commonly focused on her appearance and her gender. She often recollects that interviewers were fascinated by her naturally curly hair. In *Negotiating with the Dead*, she recalls being asked at a poetry reading: 'Is your hair really like that or do you get it done?' (55–6). While she speaks now of these incidents with a dry humour, it is also clear that she often felt a real frustration at what she perceived to be an insistence on reading a women writer in terms of her relationships, her personality and her body. Asked in a 1979 interview to comment on one critic's assessment that there is 'a chill' in her poetry, Atwood correctly identifies the critic and dismissively responds: 'She spent much of the article analysing my cover photos, saying that I didn't smile in them.'[9]

While this assessment is an exasperated overstatement, the article in question, Linda Rogers's 1974 essay for *Canadian Literature*, 'Margaret the Magician', notably focuses on what Rogers terms 'the Atwood persona'. Describing the writer as a kind of haunting, magical figure, Rogers discusses Atwood in a manner that blurs the author's personality with her photographic image, her image with her writing, and the author with her characters, particularly the unnamed narrator of *Surfacing*. The analysis is oddly intimate – indeed Rogers describes reading Atwood's work as an intimate encounter – and it makes a connection between reading one of Atwood's books and then encountering the author's image on the back cover, where 'The eyes stare out hypnotic from the pale mask surrounded by her furry camouflage'. Atwood, for Rogers, functions as an illusionist, with the implication that her writing has no substance, that it 'dazzles without illuminating'.[10] This highly impressionistic account develops into a discussion that seems at times to merge its assessment of characters and author, so that when Rogers writes: 'The woman at the centre of her universe is numb' (84), the subject of the assertion is impossible to discern.

In the light of such criticism, it is not unreasonable to conclude that Atwood, as a woman writer in the 1960s and 1970s, was subject to the kind of intrusive, body-oriented, quasi-mystical readings that frequently overlooked the professionalism of the writer's craft in the search for intimate, biographical readings of her work. It is unsurprising, therefore, if Atwood sometimes felt frustrated by early critical responses to her work.

We can see certain assumptions around what Atwood, as a young female writer, was attempting to achieve with her first novel by examining some of the early reviews of *The Edible Woman*. While *The Edible Woman* and *Surfacing* soon secured Atwood's reputation as a novelist, some early reviewers of the first book focused primarily on the novel's comic tone and readily accepted Marian's final disavowal of deeper meaning. A brief but excoriating review by Jane Miller in the *Times Literary Supplement* identified in Atwood's work 'some kind of embarrassment about her own intentions', which has 'made her trim her novel with that self-deprecating humour lady columnists in Sunday newspapers use to protect themselves', and termed the cake-eating scene 'excruciating'.[11] With a less dismissive tone, Millicent Bell, writing in *The New York Times Review of Books*, read the novel as a simple zany comedy in which Marian wants a husband and Ainsley does not, until eventually Marian rejects Peter and Ainsley realizes her baby needs a father, 'and the comic turn-about is achieved'. Bell rather damns the novel with faint praise when she suggests that its 'comic distortion veers at times into surreal meaningfulness'. And while she recognizes the significance of Marian's inability to eat, describing it as 'a piece of truth-telling dementia that is a symbolic answer to lying sanity', she again disavows the text's weight when she suggests that Atwood only ever intends us to read it 'half-seriously'.[12]

T. D. MacLulich, discussing in 1978 the novel's fairy-tale strategies, notes that most early reviewers seem to have read *The Edible Woman* as 'primarily a novel of social commentary, an up-to-date comedy of manners',[13] and Jerome Rosenberg, writing in Linda Sandler's 1977 edition of *The Malahat Review*, reflects that, for many readers and critics, Atwood in her early career was considered 'a rather terrifying writer who creates black humour out of the trivial absurdities of day-to-day life'.[14] But while *The Edible Woman* may have been deemed as a light, sometimes farcical social comedy by some, a body of criticism soon developed around Atwood's work that was interested in more closely dissecting her unflinching exposition of contemporary gendered society.

Critical readings of Atwood's first novels, including *Lady Oracle*, most commonly saw a writer concerned with a localized Canadian setting in which contemporary characters navigate modern social relations. While this emphasis on the familiar and the everyday was sometimes accompanied by a suspicion of triviality, many critics recognized the potential for a deeply political reading of the quotidian. Jane Rule, for example, in her 1977 essay 'Life, Liberty and the Pursuit of Normalcy', examines Atwood's interrogation of society's expectations: in each of the first three novels, Rule suggests, 'While characters struggle to embrace normalcy, they are often being pursued by it, so that the searcher becomes the victim of her own hopes, projected into one man or another.'[15] In this manner, suggests Rule, Atwood questions and challenges social values, forcing her characters to reassess their investment in a social system that is often detrimental to their well-being.

In 'Margaret Atwood: The Stoic Comedian', another essay from *The Malahat Review*, Rowland Smith similarly sees both *The Edible Woman* and *Surfacing* as a ruthless exposition of a contemporary society in which Atwood's narrators often feel 'menaced and consumed'.[16] For Smith, the success of Atwood's first novel is that she manages to make us care about the survival of a character who is, ultimately, as 'hellishly commonplace' as the people that surround her. As readers, he argues, we desperately hope to see Marian emerge from the gaping void that threatens her, 'Yet she *is* a mindless creature. We react to her as a victim, and she moves in an aura of passivity.'[17] Smith notes that Marian wants to be normal: she *wants* to marry the up-and-coming young lawyer, Peter, and when that particular relationship encounters problems, she looks to Duncan to save her (although Duncan explicitly rejects the proposed role of saviour). For Smith, there is something about Marian's cool detachment that remains attractive to the reader, even in her frustrating passivity. And crucially, he argues, despite the novel's deliberate undermining of the genre, the pull of the romance remains strong, and the reader is left at the end of the novel to anticipate if Marian will end up with either Peter or Duncan. (This view, it must be noted however, has been countered quite decisively by many more critics who have instead read Atwood as thoroughly closing down the possibility of either relationship.)

The romance plot and fairy-tale gothic

If some critics read *The Edible Woman* in terms of its representation of the modern, urban, everyday life that Marian is ostensibly leading as she moves through the familiar spaces of home, office and contemporary Toronto cityscape, others instead identified in the novel an altogether more fantastical and non-realist subtext.

In 'The Dark Voyage: *The Edible Woman* as Romance', a perceptive and influential essay from 1981, Catherine McLay defines the novel as 'a disguised romance'. Using Northrop Frye's definition of the traditional mythic romance plot, McLay reads Atwood's novel as crucially concerned with the central theme of the loss and regaining of identity, which typically takes the form of some kind of quest. In the quest romance, the protagonist-hero (typically male) ventures into a nightmarish underworld, where he experiences trials of isolation, imprisonment and symbolic death, before eventually enacting a rebirth and return to the social world, which is reaffirmed 'through ritual, as represented by marriage and/or the feast' (125).[18]

For McLay, the tri-part structure of *The Edible Woman* supports this interpretation. The novel commences in the perfectly satisfactory, if not exactly idyllic, world of the everyday, in which Marian has all that a modern young woman might hope for: job, apartment, boyfriend and no real commitments. This pleasing state of irresponsibility is increasingly imperilled, however, by encroaching visions of pensions and old age, marriage and babies. As these entrapments press closer and the narrative becomes more claustrophobic, the novel's episodes become increasingly bizarre. In one episode, Marian instinctively hides under the bed, but like a rabbit run to ground and dug out by a hunter, she is dragged out by an exasperated Peter. Marian, however, wilfully ignores the signals of her unconscious mind, and 'accepts her bondage to Peter and to the conventions of society'.[19] Consequently, she must endure the further ordeals of Part Two, in which Marian enters into an enchanted, underground world, which is also a space of madness, where her body and mind are no longer unified. This alienation of mind and body climaxes in her inability to recognize herself in her reflection in the mirror, seeing only an uncanny doll. In this phase, Marian encounters Duncan, whom McLay identifies as the supernatural guide – 'dehumanized, even grotesque' – who helps her to uncover the truth: that only by rejecting the prospect of marriage to Peter can she find liberation. Finally, following the logic of the romance, once Duncan's function is complete, Marian must also reject him 'and return alone to the daylight world of freedom and true selfhood' represented by the novel's brief Part Three.[20]

Sherrill Grace also develops a mythic reading of Duncan in her 1980 monograph, *Violent Duality: A Study of Margaret Atwood*, in which she identifies in Atwood's work a preoccupation with images of doubled, duplicitous and divided selves, gothic and otherwise. Grace proposes that the protagonist in Atwood's works commonly oscillates between two unhealthy and destructive extremes: either 'withdrawal into the self' or, alternatively, submersion in 'the false perceptions of others or the natural world'. Only by accepting the duality within us all can the protagonist be freed from destructive attempts to deny 'the subject/object duality of life'.[21]

Starting from this premise, rather than reading Duncan as Marian's supernatural guide, Grace proffers another potential reading of him as 'another Atwood double, a kind of doppelgänger, an objectified part of Marion [sic] herself' (93).[22] Where Smith suggests that the novel contains a residual pull of the romantic plot, by which the reader is left to wonder if Marian will choose Peter or Duncan, Grace instead argues that while Duncan is an opposite of Peter, he is never a possible alternative. Recalling a scene in the text in which Duncan tells Marian, who is wearing his dressing gown at the time, that she looks like him, Grace concludes: 'Duncan is most successful as a symbol of Marion's inner life or subconscious; he represents her fantasies, her attempts to escape, as well as her sensible return to consumer reality'.[23]

Fairy-tale imagery

In addition to identifying the non-realist quest motif and gothic tropes of uncanny doubles, other critics have also noted elements of fairy tale in *The Edible Woman*. Indeed, there is a significant body of work concerned with examining the predominance of fairy-tale motifs in Atwood's writing: from the Little Red Riding Hood imagery of Offred in her red cloak and shopping basket in *The Handmaid's Tale*, to Iris's multi-layered self-identification as Little Red Riding Hood, grandma and the wolf in *The Blind Assassin*. The most influential critic of this theme is Sharon Rose Wilson, whose 1993 book, *Margaret Atwood's Fairy-Tale Sexual Politics* explores in detail Atwood's use of fairy-tale motifs throughout her earlier works. Examining *The Edible Woman*, Wilson provides a sustained analysis of the fairy-tale aspects of the plot. She commences her study by noting that the theme of eating has a longstanding identification with 'ancient images of witches, wizards, parents, and spouses, who, deliberately or not, eat the precious "food" – other human beings'. Specifically, Wilson points to the Grimm Brothers' story, 'The Robber Bridegroom', in which the monstrous husband eats each of his unsuspecting brides in turn. This particular tale, of course, is notably appropriated by Atwood in her 1993 novel, *The Robber Bride*, in which the voracious Zenia overturns gendered expectations, preying on and 'consuming' a succession of unwitting men. Wilson, however, demonstrates Atwood's much earlier interest in this fairy tale (and others), connecting it to her first novel and to Marian's 'mock-Gothic fears of eating, being eaten, suddenly changing into someone else, and being unable to transform at all'.[24]

Marian, for Wilson, is the reluctant bride who surreptitiously enters the Robber Bridegroom's house in the woods and discovers his secret: that he chops up and eats his many young brides. Like the plucky young heroine, Marian also uncovers her fiancé's secret just in time to avoid her scripted fate. In addition to this primary intertext, Wilson also identifies a host of familiar fairy-tale characters and tropes: from the witch who would keep young Rapunzel trapped in the tower (the landlady and the child), to the ugly sisters seeking a prince (the office virgins), and the three bears in their cottage (Duncan and his flatmates). For Wilson, these multiple fairy-tale tropes combine in the novel to establish 'a tone both comic and gothic'. *The Edible Woman* functions, she argues, as a parody of Cinderella's expectations of a happy-ever-after romance, exposing the fear and suspicion that Prince Charming might actually prove to be Bluebeard in disguise. By the end of Atwood's novel, we are by no means assured, suggests Wilson, 'that, for either male or female, it is possible to marry anyone but the Robber Bridegroom or death'. Set against such a deeply gloomy conclusion, however, Wilson notes that, in fairy tales, the heroine is rarely eaten, and eventually, '[l]ike Gretel, Marian tricks the trickster and escapes the oven'.[25]

While Wilson's fairy-tale analyses have been influential, she was not the first to examine *The Edible Woman* in this manner. In T. D. MacLulich's 1988 essay 'Atwood's Adult Fairy Tale: Lévi-Strauss, Bettelheim, and *The Edible Woman*', MacLulich adopts anthropologist Claude Lévi-Strauss's method of investigating, not so much the specific details of a particular story, but rather the mythic patterns or structures discernible within a work. For Lévi-Strauss, these deeper, recurring patterns tell us something crucial about the manner in which a culture devises meaning. Consequently, MacLulich identifies at work in *The Edible Woman* Lévi-Strauss's primary topic of mythic thought: the dichotomy of culture and nature. Using Lévi-Strauss's structural method, MacLulich plots out, in a chart, the narrative of *The Edible Woman* set against that of the fairy tale of the Gingerbread Man. Identifying the fairy tale's various elements (the Gingerbread Man is prepared, animated, runs away, meets the fox, is eaten), he then draws parallels with Atwood's novel. For example, he argues that, in *The Edible Woman*, 'the parallel to being eaten by the fox is being seduced by Duncan', who pretends to be a virgin.[26]

Like Wilson, MacLulich also identifies the influence of multiple overlapping fairy tales at work in Atwood's novel. He connects Marian in her tight red party dress to Little Red Riding Hood, and describes the engagement party as a scene in which 'Redness, sexuality, and fear of being eaten are vividly brought together'. In this fairy-tale scenario, there is a doubling of the wolf figure. Peter, with his camera and his gun, is a technology-wielding wolf, whereas Duncan is the wolf in sheep's clothing. Where Marian thinks she must make the correct choice between the two, she needs instead, argues MacLulich, to realize that Duncan is merely an equally unpalatable obverse of conformist Peter. For MacLulich, 'The unknown alternative, the middle way between aggression and submission, still eludes her at the novel's end.' As in a children's fairy tale, he concludes, the heroine survives, but the manner in which she does so is uncertain and unsettling. *The Edible Woman* does not, therefore, represent the kind of wish-fulfilment that the influential child psychologist Bruno Bettelheim describes as being the beneficial function for children of fairy tales, but is instead 'a problematic story, challenging to grown-up intellects – a sort of adult fairy tale'.[27]

Consumption and the body

The Edible Woman is replete with highly suggestive symbolism and one such element that has attracted much critical attention is Marian's refusal of food. Often described in fairly superficial terms as a mode of anorexic eating disorder, the sudden, seemingly irresistible refusal of Marian's body to consume does not comfortably fit this medicalized analysis. Instead, multiple critics have better pointed to symbolic readings of the protagonist's refusal of food. Most commonly, it has been connected to *Surfacing*, and the narrator of that novel's refusal to be a consumer/murderer/aggressor, or, instead, associated with a more general interiorized misogynistic disgust expressed in the novel at the female body and reproduction. For example, Rogers, in 'Margaret the Magician', suggests that Marian experiences a 'classic psychiatric phenomenon' prompted by repulsion at the feminine function of childbearing, and concludes that her refusal to eat 'is a rejection of the function of motherhood'.[28]

A particularly useful extended analysis of Marian's relationship to food and eating is offered by Sarah Sceats in *Food, Consumption and the Body in Contemporary Women's Writing* (2000). In a chapter that examines *The Edible Woman*, *Lady Oracle* and *Life Before Man*, Sceats argues that Atwood's first novel uses food and its related activities as a means of interrogating gender roles in mid-twentieth-century Canada. Marian's growing inability to eat, suggests Sceats, functions as a classic hysterical symptom, linking her to a psychoanalytic tradition of supposedly hysterical women, but it also provides a resonant pun on

Marian's newfound inability 'to swallow, or stomach, the facts and implications of her situation'. Marian's protest may appear stereotypically feminine and self-negating, but it is, for Sceats, a subversive, inscrutable act; rather than representing Marian's attempt to become something else, 'her not eating is simply a refusal'.[29]

Focusing on the motif of food, Sceats explores the idea that, for Atwood, 'women collude in their oppression (in being edible), through passivity and the assumption of innocence'.[30] (This idea, as we will see, also comes to the fore in *Surfacing*.) As Sceats rightly observes, Marian's refusal to eat is deeply problematic and leaves many questions unanswered. In her analysis, Sceats tries to draw out some of these ambiguities and uncertainties. Most crucially, there is the fact that Marian's experience of not eating is a peculiarly passive one: she wants to eat, but simply finds that she cannot. This passivity is hard to reconcile with a reading of her actions as an empowering mode of protest. Relatedly, when she returns to consumption, it seems that she becomes an empowered actor once again. But eating is also an ambiguous trope in the novel, associated with aggression and violence, but also with acquiescence to the status quo. If Marian's refusal to eat is a refusal to participate in the heteronormative script that Peter's proposal represents, what does her return to consumption signify? And finally, as Sceats notes, Marian's consumption of the cake-woman is entangled with notions of self-consumption: which, again can be read in contradictory ways, as either narcissistic or self-abnegating.

For Sceats, the deeply ambiguous symbolism of eating and not eating is not resolved in Atwood's text, but instead opens up a series of complex and uncomfortable questions for the reader to ponder, including: 'to what extent do victim and persecutor collude and what are the possibilities for action for a woman deeply implicated in a consumer culture that casts her as the (passive) filling in a sandwich?' (99).[31]

Surfacing

Overview

The elements of the romance quest narrative that critics such as McLay identified in *The Edible Woman* recur with more visibility in Atwood's second novel, *Surfacing*. The story commences with the familiar literary trope of a journey or quest, as the protagonists leave the socialized space of the city and head out into the wilderness. The unnamed narrator travels with her partner Joe and two casual friends, a married couple, Anna and David, up into Northern Quebec. The ostensible purpose of the journey is to look for the narrator's father, a botanist living alone in the family cabin on the edge of a remote lake, who has inexplicably gone missing. The novel functions, therefore – on the surface, at least – as a kind of mystery or detective story.

Once they arrive at the cabin, relations between the four protagonists, which initially seem amicable enough, quickly deteriorate. Anna and David's marriage appears to be founded on a dull mutual loathing that occasionally sparks into sadistic cruelty, while the narrator's feelings for Joe are muted and uncertain; at one point, she muses: 'I'm trying to decide whether or not I love him' (36). Cumulatively, human relations in the novel appear cold, exploitative and superficial: a summation that the narrator extends, at various points in the novel, to tourists, Americans and hunters.

As the city-dwellers explore the island, there follows a series of false clues for the reader, as the narrator recalls fragments of her marriage and child – providing disjointed snippets of information that do not quite seem to fit together. Eventually, the mystery of her father's disappearance is resolved. Having found images of strange markings that he was seemingly obsessed with, the narrator fears that her isolated father may have gone mad, but eventually realizes that they were 'Indian' (the now-outdated term for indigenous Canadians used in the novel) petroglyphs or rock markings found on the island, which her father had been plotting on a map. Seeking to reassure herself that his project was rational and real, she goes in search of the marks. Realizing that the one she is looking for must be underwater, she dives down into the lake and finds her father's floating body, weighed down by his camera. Confronted by the watery corpse, repressed memories resurface of her married lover and the abortion she felt coerced into. As she imagines the aborted foetus as an animal seeking sanctuary in her body, only to be killed by her hand, she is forced to acknowledge her own capacity for violence.

As it becomes apparent that the unreliable narrator is nursing a repressed trauma, it also becomes clear that her sense of traumatized, innocent victimhood has been externalized and projected onto an innocent nature brutalized by man's unthinking technology. Disgusted and dismayed by what she sees as the cruelty and destructive violence of society, she attempts to retreat into innocence by relinquishing all social responsibility. Having gained from her father the gift of knowledge with the return of her repressed memories, she receives from her dead mother another gift, in the form of a recovered childhood drawing of a pregnant woman. Suddenly knowing what she must do, she initiates sex with Joe in the certainty that she will conceive a child. Then, convinced that she must protect the growing foetus from the three friends and the social corruption they represent, she burns her books and clothes and flees into the bush, vowing to live like the animals: naked, innocent and free. Eventually, however, the narrator comes to the realization that she cannot live like an animal or a tree and must instead accept her social responsibility. The novel ends, therefore, with Joe calling her name and the narrator on the brink of stepping forward, out of the wilderness and back into society.

Early reception

By the time Atwood comes to publish *Surfacing*, the review in *The New York Times Book Review* is markedly longer than that previously afforded to *The Edible Woman*. The reviewer, Paul Delany, invites a comparison between Atwood's second novel and Sylvia Plath's *The Bell Jar*, published ten years earlier. Both, he notes, are tales of a young woman 'made desperate by a stifling social milieu and who can find relief only by abandoning what those around her have defined as sanity'. For Delany, where Plath's Esther Greenwood can, in the early 1960s, only rail against a world she has no hope of changing, Atwood's nameless narrator, a decade later, refuses to be resigned to victimhood and the novel ends on the hope of re-entering the world on new terms. Like many others, this review connects *Surfacing* to the thesis proposed in *Survival*, and argues that, taken together, the texts 'have brought into sharp focus for Canadian literary intellectuals the problem of their country's cultural identity in the seventies'.[32]

Picking up instead on the connected themes of artifice, appearance and surface that run through the narrative of *Surfacing*, novelist Margaret Laurence, in a laudatory review, sees the narrator's journey as concerned with the attempt to discover a sense of truth and a core reality to cling to in the face of social artifice. In a manner that recalls some readings of *The Edible Woman*, Laurence identifies in *Surfacing* the mythic trope of the quest, whereby the narrator must leave civilization and descend into the wilderness – which is also a descent into madness – before she can 'break through' into newfound knowledge and return to the social world. For Laurence, this hard-won knowledge involves the narrator's recognition of her own power, 'a power which had frightened her and which she had therefore denied', as well as a recognition that the desire to be a blameless victim is an abnegation of responsibility that can lead to becoming complicit in the victimization of others.[33]

This theme of victimization and, more contentiously, the question of who is victimized and by whom, exercised many early critics of the novel. In a short 'Reply' that Atwood wrote for a 1976 issue of the journal *Signs*, which appeared alongside two articles in the same issue that examined her second novel in terms of feminist theology (discussed below), Atwood noted: '*Surfacing* was reviewed in the United States almost exclusively as a feminist or ecological treatise; in Canada, it was reviewed almost exclusively as a nationalist one.'[34] Canadian reviewers, she explains, tended to successfully draw from the text a series of corresponding binary oppositions of man/woman, culture/nature, America/Canada, in which the first element of the binary was invariably dominant and aggressive. American reviewers, instead, generally failed to identify the final pairing or chose instead to read 'America' as a purely metaphorical concept, standing in for society as a whole rather than literally for the American state. (And of course, the novel itself disrupts any too-easy identifications of aggressor and victim when the noisy, thoughtless 'Americans' that the narrator abhors are revealed to be Canadians after all.)

Delany's review offers the Canadian perspective on these matters as he picks up on the question of victimization in a national context. In it, he draws a distinction between Atwood's work, with its 'acute responsiveness to the Canadian landscape' and that of 'established Canadian writers of more cosmopolitan outlook' such as Mordecai Richler, Leonard Cohen and Irving Layton. In her novel, he notes, Atwood creates an opposition between a corrupt 'American' society associated with violence, technology, and the ruthless pillaging of natural resources, and the primitivism of the Canadian wilderness. Reflecting on the manner in which moral values are associated with nations, Delany looks back to a nineteenth-century common comparison between the European novel (concerned with man as he is shaped by social institutions) and the new American romance ('man in relation to moral absolutes and to nature'). In the twentieth century instead, suggests Delany, as America's claim to untainted innocence is long gone, it is Canadian literature that now conceives of itself as powerless but virtuous. And so, as in Atwood's second novel, for the Canadian protagonist, the wilderness continues to provide a space of retreat in which one can recover one's true, untainted self.[35]

While *Surfacing*, with its wilderness setting and its narrator's erroneous fury at the 'Americans', certainly invites nation-focused readings, these were inevitably further encouraged by the novel's proximity to *Survival*, which was published in the same year (and is discussed in more detail in the introduction). Poet and critic Eli Mandel, for example, notes that the victim/aggressor pattern, which recurs throughout the novel, is repeated from *Survival*, which, he suggests, 'reads like a gloss on *Surfacing*'.[36] In *Survival*, Atwood set out four basic victim positions and proposed that the theme provided a useful way in which to examine and understand the preoccupations of Canadian literature. The dynamics of victimhood, she declares, are the same, 'whether you are a victimised country, a victimised minority group or a victimised individual'.[37]

Subsequently, this has remained a significant theme in readings of *Surfacing*, from the earliest newspaper reviews to more recent analyses. For example, Marion Wynne-Davies, in her 2009 monograph *Margaret Atwood*, argues that Atwood's early works explore her theories of victimization and survival and connect these ideas particularly to her representations of women and Canada. For Wynne-Davies, 'Atwood neither ignores nor accepts national and gendered victimization' but instead – in the manner set out in *Surfacing* – looks to move beyond negative, passive victimhood positions in order to attain the desired state of what Atwood terms, in *Survival*, a 'creative non- or ex-victim'.[38] In such readings – and there are plenty – we see how certain key understandings of Atwood's early works have maintained their influence and credibility across decades of critical analysis.

Feminist readings

In addition to her reading of *Surfacing* as a quest narrative, Laurence's review concludes by pointing to a number of other key themes that occur in the novel – themes that she identifies as some of the most urgent of contemporary issues: 'the role of women, the facts of urban life, and most of all, the wounding and perhaps killing of our only home, Earth'.[39] With this summation, Laurence points to two of the key approaches that, alongside the kind of Canadianist readings noted above, would later come to characterize much Atwood criticism, specifically: ecological readings and feminist readings.

As with analyses of *The Edible Woman* that sometimes struggled to square the passivity and self-negation of Marian's refusal to eat with an active and articulate feminist protest, so feminist responses to *Surfacing*, and particularly to its troublesome concluding scenes, have been mixed. While the unnamed narrator undergoes an epiphany in which she recognizes that she can no longer continue to passively collude in the casual sexist violence of others, her response to this realization is deeply ambiguous. Shucking off the limits of a corrupt patriarchal society, the narrator temporarily attains a natural wildness, conceiving a child beneath the light of the moon, before returning to a society full of a vital, maternal life force. The imagery here is towards some kind of timeless female power that exists outside of the social. This resolution is problematic, however; as feminist critic Carol P. Christ observes, 'Atwood does not show how her protagonist will integrate motherhood with work, relations with other adults, or politics.'[40]

In an influential 1976 article 'Margaret Atwood: The Surfacing of Women's Quest and Spiritual Vision' – which she later went on to develop into a book, *Diving Deep and Surfacing* (1980) – Christ provided a potent reading of Atwood's novel as a tale of spiritual quest in which a woman seeks redemption. For Christ, the novel requires a critical reading that sits at the juncture of theology and literary studies. Where the social quest describes an alienated protagonist seeking integration into a human community, the protagonist on a spiritual quest instead seeks a kind of self-knowledge that does not necessarily translate into a new social role. In her article, Christ notes some of the reservations some feminist critics had about Atwood's novel, and she cites Piercy's questioning of whether the narrator can really choose to refuse victimhood: 'I don't believe one woman can single-handedly leave off being a victim; power exists and some have it.'[41] Piercy's concern here is that the symbolism of the narrator's individual refusal to be a victim neglects to acknowledge or address the structures that deprive certain groups of power. Christ's argument, however, is that feminism's task is to challenge not just social and political structures, but also 'the perception of reality which underlies and legitimates them': which is an altogether more intimate and individual task.[42]

The key transformational element in *Surfacing*, for Christ, occurs at the moment in which the narrator recovers her repressed memories. At this point, faced with the resurfacing fact of her abortion, she refuses the masculine, logical, hierarchical distinctions between creatures that are deemed fit to live and those that can instead be destroyed: between "good" (legitimate) foetuses which grow up to have birthday parties, and "bad" (illegitimate) foetuses which must be killed'. The narrator asserts instead a more feminine, intuitive sense of reality. At this same moment, the narrator also experiences a revelation of her newfound feminine power. Communing with the gods of nature, having visions: she becomes cognizant of herself as powerful. Discussing this sense of feminine power that she identifies in Atwood's novel, and responding to Piercy's objections, Christ argues that the female quest involves an awakening to the violence and the limits of the 'male-defined world'.[43] This awakening may involve the recovery of feelings that have been suppressed in order to acquiesce to the male logic of the social, which can be painful, but also results in the potential for healing and joy. This transformation, she argues, represents a move from victimhood to power.

In Judith Plaskow's response to Christ's article, and in other readings of the novel elsewhere, the feminist debate around *Surfacing* largely hinges on interrogations of what Plaskow terms 'the old idea that there exists a special sympathy or a special connection between women and nature'. Whereas, for Christ, there is revolutionary power to be unlocked in exploiting women's connection with nature, Plaskow notes that this supposed connection has historically been co-opted as an ideological basis for the subordination of women. The question, then, is whether the problems of associating women with nature 'render its theological use inadvisable'.[44]

Plaskow cautions against Christ's celebration of the narrator's seeking of 'self in cosmos' – her internalized, spiritual quest for selfhood – rather than 'self in society'. She argues, much like Piercy, that an internalized quest for power within will only leave social power in the hands of others. In theological terms, Plaskow argues, a preoccupation with the spiritual to the neglect of the social may pretend to be politically neutral, or even progressive, 'but actually supports the status quo'.[45] That is to say, the narrator running naked in the woods will change nothing.

In a further notable element of this essay, Plaskow touches on what has always been a controversial element of the novel: the narrator's response to her unwanted abortion. While recognizing that it would be too crass to simply describe the novel as an anti-abortion text, Plaskow suggests that in only giving voice to the narrator's traumatized view that all modes of killing are inherently evil – in refusing to acknowledge that there may be justified killings – the novel retreats from the difficult but necessary engagement with the human dimension of our relationship to nature and the decisions and responsibilities that it necessarily entails. Atwood, she states, 'does not allow us to say when an abortion might be appropriate or allowed'. For Plaskow, the novel poses complex questions around our connection to nature and the extent to which women can safely explore this connection without being corralled into longstanding and limiting beliefs that women are more 'natural' and therefore less fully human and less rational than men. The novel, for Plaskow, fails to offer a workable middle ground between exploitative culture and victimized nature; and what is needed, but absent, is 'a conception of identification with nature as the basis for responsible action'.[46]

For Atwood, writing in her Reply to the two essays, 'The crux of the Christ-Plaskow debate seems to be a disagreement over whether stories should be about what is or what should be.' Refusing to be drawn on whether she advocates a view of women as closer to nature or not, she notes that as a writer, her responsibility is to the text – 'to the thing being made'.[47] Her story unfurls as it does, she declares, because it follows the logic of the narrator and what she has experienced. It does not seek to make either a statement of how things are or a prescription for how things ought to be.

A gothic novel

In an early interview, Atwood describes *Surfacing* as a ghost story, and in an essay on what he calls 'Atwood Gothic' (an increasingly prevalent term), Mandel notes that this comment inspired much subsequent analysis of the novel. More significant for Mandel, however, is the wider element of the gothic that runs through much of Atwood's writing. Reading the novel alongside repeated instances of ghosts, haunting, doubling and the uncanny in works such as *You Are Happy*, *The Journals of Susanna Moodie* and *Survival*, Mandel returns to the novel, and asks: 'Who are the ghosts of *Surfacing*?' It is, as he observes, a text filled with the dead: the narrator's parents, her unborn child, the indigenous peoples, the animals. For Mandel, these 'ghosts' all function as 'symbols of vitality, life, our real humanity, that has disappeared and must be brought back'.[48]

Like Grace in *Violent Duality*, Mandel notes the persistence of the trope of doubleness in Atwood's work. Patterns, he observes, repeat, as she recycles images across her poetry and prose. He points, for example, to the poem, 'This is a Photograph of Me' from *The Circle Game*, which commences with the image of a body submerged in a lake. In *Surfacing*, as elsewhere in Atwood's work, images of birth and death repeat, overlap and blur, creating uncanny continuities between 'the baby not born, the baby aborted, the baby about to be born'.[49] As the narrator comes to imagine that the ghosts of her parents are becoming human again, there is, proposes Mandel, a promise that the text's gothic horrors might be vanquished. But, he argues, nothing is ultimately resolved in this doubling and reduplicating text in which there is potential for recovery, but also the threat of repetition.

For Cynthia Sugars, instead, *Surfacing* is haunted – as has famously been said about Canada – by its lack of ghosts. In her essay she points to the similarity between the death of the narrator's father and that of the real-life Canadian artist and naturist, Tom Thomson, who drowned in an Ontario lake in 1917. Sugars identifies in Atwood's novel a desire for native ghosts – for a *genius loci*, or spirit of the place – which, she suggests, Thomson fulfils in the Canadian national psyche. But the desire for 'native' ghosts is complicated by Canada's colonial history, which troubles any call to a 'native' culture. For Sugars, crucially, the figure of Thomson's ghost emerges in a novel in which indigenous people 'constitute a prominent absence'. In recalling Thomson as the prototypical Canadian pioneer, the novel, argues Sugars, only 'skirts around this guilty absence'.[50]

Language and form

While acknowledging the pull of both nationalist and feminist readings of the novel, in her reflections on *Surfacing* in *Violent Duality*, Grace calls on the reader to also consider the text's formal aspects, particularly the unreliable narrative voice of the unnamed protagonist. Noting that we learn few concrete details about this woman with whom we share such intense experiences, Grace draws attention to the 'cool distance' created by this voice, which is so seemingly in control and competent, yet proves in the end to have been 'a trap', as we discover that we have been deceived.[51] With the deferred realization of this deception, the reader is forced to reconsider the novel and its events and to question all of the narrator's judgements and assertions. Just as the references to a husband and child prove false, along with allusions to the disapproved-of divorce that prompted her estrangement from her parents, so we must question each of the suspicions and intuitions we have been subject to. As Grace asks, 'How accurately has she ever seen Joe?'[52]

This deceptive mode of narrative address is crucial to the novel and the way it works. As Grace observes, the reader, alongside the narrator, effectively experiences a false perception of the world, followed by a revelatory revision of everything he or she has held to be true. While this strategy is potent, however, it also creates problems. Language, as Grace points out, is crucial to the text of *Surfacing*. Through her impersonal, economical use of language, the narrator strives to maintain control over her resurfacing memories and her rising hysteria. In the allusive brevity of her writing, Atwood conveys the narrator's 'cerebral approach to life, her inability to feel', while the frequently brief, fragmented sentence structure resonantly conveys the narrator's disjointed alienation from the world.[53] But caught within this cool, authoritative narrative perspective, we can struggle to be convinced that the narrator has achieved the sense of development and reintegration that she eventually claims for herself. Once we realize that we have been lied to throughout the body of her narrative, how can we bring ourselves to trust her at the end?

For many critics, *Surfacing* concludes on a problematic irresolution. Atwood, however, proposes an alternative reading. In an interview with Sandler, she suggests that, if the plot of *The Edible Woman* is circular, with Marian concluding in more or less the same situation in which we find her at the start of the novel, the plot of *Surfacing*, instead, might be better described as a spiral: circuitous and winding, but ultimately progressing; 'the heroine of *Surfacing*', declares Atwood, 'does not end up where she began'.[54]

Following the success of *The Edible Woman* and *Surfacing* and the growing critical acclaim they garnered, Atwood's next three novels work to develop the concerns she displays in her early fiction. Over the next decade of writing, her preoccupation with genre, particularly fairy tale, myth and romance, continues to develop, as does her deep concern with gender and power.

2

A developing canon and developing themes
Lady Oracle, Life Before Man and Bodily Harm

From the mid-1970s to the early 1980s, as Atwood was steadily building her reputation as a significant contemporary writer and attracting an increasingly international readership, critics looked to conceptualize her developing canon and identify the characteristically 'Atwoodian'. In *Margaret Atwood* (2009), Marion Wynne-Davies divides Atwood's writing into four distinct periods. She encompasses the first three novels within the theme of 'Refusing to be a Victim: 1966-1978' and observes that in the second period, 1979–87, *Life Before Man* and *The Handmaid's Tale* see the established theme of survival 'drawn further back into prehistory and pushed forwards into science fiction'. Terming this second period: 'It's Time to Like Men Again', Wynne-Davies argues that male characters at this point in Atwood's work become more complex, more finely drawn figures.[1]

Focusing on recurring concerns, in the introduction to the 1988 collection *Margaret Atwood: Vision and Forms*, Kathryn VanSpanckeren highlights the author's preoccupation with genre, feminism and nature, and pays particular attention to her critical engagement with the United States, specifically its 'ecological carelessness, excessive materialism, and violence'.[2] Other commonly noted Atwoodian tropes at this time include a notable interest in gender, power and the body, as well as, typically, a focus on a female protagonist within a contemporary setting. As Atwood's writing progresses into the 1980s, she establishes herself as a writer concerned with exposing the manner in which society constructs potent narratives from familiar tropes and forms.

Lady Oracle

After *Surfacing*, with its elliptical plot and traumatized narrator, Atwood's third novel revived something of the comic aspects of her first. Like both of the earlier novels, *Lady Oracle* foregrounds the disruptive potential of genre subversion. Where *The Edible Woman* is an urban romance that unexpectedly turns into a mythical quest romance and *Surfacing* combines the quest with elements of detective fiction, *Lady Oracle* instead provides a riotous, increasingly irrepressible engagement with gothic romance in all its most pleasurably melodramatic aspects.

Overview

The novel opens with Joan Foster, a celebrated poet and pseudonymous writer of historical romance novels, living in hiding in Italy, having recently faked her own death in a desperate attempt to escape an increasingly complicated series of events. Commencing in the present-day frame narrative, Joan proceeds to give an account of her life, from an unhappy childhood up to the recent entanglements that necessitated her dramatic escape. Joan, it becomes clear, has undergone many transformations in her life. She describes a troubled relationship with her overbearing mother and an adolescent retreat into obesity in defiance of her mother's attempts to control and improve her. Joan is, by her own admission, 'hooked on plots' (342) and a 'compulsive and romantic liar' (165), and much of the novel involves her various attempts to rewrite herself. In her study of Atwood's reworking of the female *Bildungsroman*, Ellen McWilliams makes connections between Joan's various appetites that see her 'voraciously consuming' textual narratives as she constructs a life story that seems to 'relish, even gorge on' multiple pillaged literary sources.[3] As Barbara Hill Rigney observes in her 1987 monograph *Margaret Atwood*, Joan conceives of her life story 'as a series of recognisable patterns'.[4] From the fairy-tale plots of childhood, which cast her mother as the evil queen to Joan's Snow White, to the various tragic romantic heroines gleaned from film, poetry and art, Joan constructs her identity from a bricolage of familiar plots, from highbrow to low.

Trapped, like Rapunzel, in the imprisoning tower of her mother's house, the young Joan is equally trapped in the sexless anonymity of her obesity: a 'magic cloak of blubber and invisibility' (157). For Sofia Sanchez-Grant, examining embodiment in *The Edible Woman* and *Lady Oracle*, Joan's size, and that of the hallucinatory figure of the Fat Lady by which she is haunted, 'symbolizes the patriarchal fear of unchecked femininity and the need to cut the female body down to size'.[5] Even when she loses weight and becomes conventionally attractive, Joan will continue to battle against this cultural prohibition against women who take up too much space.

As an adolescent, however, Joan's only friend is her beloved Aunt Lou, equally overweight and equally unsatisfactory to Joan's exasperated mother. Together, they enjoy companionable trips to the cinema and attend services at Jordan Chapel, an eccentric Spiritualist church: both of which provide Joan's imagination with yet more romantic and gothic plots. When Aunt Lou dies, leaving her an inheritance on the condition that she lose 100 lbs, Joan is hurt by the perceived implication that her Aunt secretly wished her to change, but nevertheless accepts the challenge, claims the money and runs away to London: one of many escapes that occur in the novel. In London, she meets Paul, a melancholy émigré Polish Count, and becomes his lover. Upon discovering that he supplements his income by writing nurse romances, Joan attempts her own romance novel. Finding that she has a talent for constructing page-turning plots, she commences a successful career as a romance writer, publishing under her Aunt's name as Louisa K. Delacourt.

In *Margaret Atwood: A Critical Companion*, Nathalie Cooke makes a connection between the figure of the female artist in *Lady Oracle* (in this instance, a writer), and the narrator of *Surfacing*, who works as an illustrator. She notes that later novels, such as *Cat's Eye* and *The Blind Assassin*, also have artist-writer protagonists, and for Cooke, Atwood's choice to make Joan a writer enables Atwood to illuminate the difficulties of being a woman in a male-dominated field and also to display 'her strategies for resolving her concerns'.[6] In part, Cooke suggests, these strategies include a purposeful disruption of male-dominated narrative codes and forms. And so, in *Lady Oracle*, we see Atwood setting out to 'trouble' the reader's expectations of genre and form.

Eventually, Joan leaves the increasingly possessive Count for Arthur, a young Canadian political activist. When her mother's unexpected death obliges her return to Toronto, Arthur unexpectedly follows her home, and Joan commences another role within another familiar plot, agreeing to marry him. While she plays at being a ramshackle housewife, supporting Arthur's various short-lived radical campaigns, she hides her (economically productive) writing from him, both afraid of his condescension but also secretly glad to have a second, hidden identity. Joan's life, as always, is comprised of increasingly disjointed elements that she struggles to hold together. This sense of precariousness (which manifests in the novel in the recurring image of the Fat Lady tightrope-walking) is rapidly heightened when an experiment with automatic writing – a trick learnt at Jordan Chapel – unexpectedly produces reams of enigmatic verse. Impulsively, Joan sends the writing to a publisher under her own name and the ensuing epic poem, 'Lady Oracle', becomes a literary sensation and Joan becomes a 'real' writer.

The novel's plot becomes rapidly more complicated and its various subplots increasingly entwined. When Joan begins an affair with a performance artist, a bitter literary critic threatens to tell Arthur. Simultaneously, another unknown party starts to blackmail her, promising to reveal her true identity. Surrounded by menace and threat, Joan plots yet another escape, faking her own death in Lake Ontario. In Italy, however, she finds herself once again the target of multiple sinister men. Reality and the plot of her incomplete novel, *Stalked by Love*, become increasingly entangled. When she discovers that the friends who assisted her escape have been arrested on suspicion of her murder, the novel is finally revealed as an account she gives to a journalist in Italy in an attempt to set the complicated record straight. As Molly Hite observes, however, Joan's attempt to tell her side of the story and wrestle back her narrative authority is inevitably an exercise in telling 'the story of her construction by others'.[7]

Gothic romance

For Annette Kolodny, Joan's increasingly melodramatic life 'is a catalog of the gothic conventions she employs in her writing'. Examining the shift in Atwood's work from romance to realism, Kolodny identifies in *Lady Oracle* the continuation of key elements of gothic romance: the magical transformation of Joan from an obese unattractive child to a beautiful slender young woman; the element of the supernatural provided by Joan's automatic writing; and the recurrence of ambiguous and potentially dangerously attractive men. As the novel progresses, Joan's multiple selves start to collide, and threats – both real and imagined – begin to coalesce, as her real life becomes increasingly indistinguishable from the plot of her gothic romance fiction. Just as she threatens to lose her grip on reality entirely, Joan finally comes to realize that 'her belief in miraculous rescues and timely escapes is the real danger'. Forcing herself to confront the man at the door, Joan realizes that she has been pursued by a reporter, not a murderer, and the necessary process of disentangling fact from fiction can begin. For Kolodny, *Lady Oracle* is 'a romance about the dangers of romance'.[8]

In *Reading the Gothic in Margaret Atwood's Novels* (2003), Colette Tennant extends the discussion of Atwood's use of the gothic in *Lady Oracle* to her other works. In a chapter that examines 'Shadow Males' in Atwood's gothic fictions, she argues that Atwood's heroines are commonly forced to confront the danger posed to them by the men in their lives. Crucially, however, by placing her protagonists in a gothic world in which men are ambiguous figures, neither heroes nor villains, Atwood removes the traditional gothic role of a passive female victim and 'forces her heroines to accept responsibility for their own survival'.[9]

Tennant borrows the term 'Shadow Males' from Joanna Russ's 1983 essay 'Somebody's Trying to Kill Me and I Think It's My Husband', in which Russ argues that the emotional centre of the gothic novel is typically the 'handsome, magnetic suitor or husband who may or may not be a lunatic or murderer'.[10] For Tennant, all of Atwood's male characters are Shadow Males of one kind or another. In *Lady Oracle*, the various unsuitable men in Joan's life, from Paul to Arthur to The Royal Porcupine, all combine elements of the ridiculous and the mundane with glimpses of potential gothic violence. Tennant suggests that Joan's attraction to such men is explained by the psychological impact of her emotionally absent father, whose role as a doctor in the war and later as an anaesthetist with the power to put people to sleep and return them to life, encapsulates a gothic duplicity. When Joan's mother dies in uncertain circumstances, Joan starts to suspect that her inscrutable father may have been responsible. It is only when she starts to recognize her father's call to her complicity as an act of violence against his wife that Joan, for the first time, experiences sympathy for her unhappy mother. As Tennant notes, Joan finally realizes that 'Joan's home was a prison for her mother and her father was the jail keeper'.[11]

While critical readings of Atwood's gothic aesthetic have always been popular, *Lady Oracle*, with its metafictional techniques, inevitably invites particular attention. In *The Fat Lady Dances: Margaret Atwood's Lady Oracle*, a 1993 critical companion to the novel, Marjorie Fee devotes the larger part of her short monograph to discussing the novel's gothic themes. Like Tennant, Fee focuses on the heroine's unconscious desires and points to Joan's active role in imagining and exaggerating the threat posed by the various men in her life. Reflecting on the improbability that any of the variously inept or mild-mannered men in her life are actually gothic murderers, Fee argues that Atwood has to make the male characters innocuous, because if any were to prove to be true gothic villains, the textual resolution would require a gothic hero. 'But, as Joan discovers, all men are complex mixtures of both, which complicates life enormously.'[12] For Fee, this lesson is one that Joan has been taught since childhood, but which she refuses to learn. She points, for example, to 'the daffodil man': a stranger who comes to Joan's rescue when she is abandoned by bullying girls in a ravine, and who may or may not be the same man who, on another occasion, had exposed himself to her in the same ravine. As Joan muses to herself: 'Was the man who untied me a rescuer or a villain? Or, an even more baffling thought: was it possible for a man to be both at once?' (61). Repeatedly, Joan is faced with the evidence that men, like women, can be ambiguous and contradictory, but she nevertheless persists in her gothic romance-inspired pursuit of their 'true' identity as hero or villain.

While Atwood may satirize the gothic romance genre and its tendency to see male villainy and threat around every corner, the possibility of violence remains real in this comic novel, as it does in all of Atwood's work. Fee makes the same point: Atwood, she notes, gently mocks Joan's melodramatic fears that the various men in her life might be conspiring to kill her, but nevertheless, collectively, they represent a genuine threat to her safety in a patriarchal society that disempowers women. Developing this argument, Fee reflects that the original nineteenth-century reader of gothic romances was typically a middle-class young woman facing probable marriage to 'a relative stranger . . . with sexual rights and absolute authority' over her. The terror at the heart of the female gothic tradition, therefore, is a terror of violence, of impotence and, crucially for Fee, of 'the loss of identity, a loss that can lead to madness'.[13]

This same anxiety around the loss of identity motivates Atwood's novel, in which Joan has many selves and many names. She is Joan Delacourt, named by her mother after Joan Crawford whose real name was Lucille LeSueur; she is also Louisa K. Delacourt and Joan Foster and the Lady Oracle. Each name is taken in turn from someone else; none of them are truly hers. If a name signifies an identity, Joan's troubling excess of names signifies, paradoxically, the absence of identity, or at least, the absence of a secure, unified selfhood. This instability – in itself a gothic trope – echoes throughout *Lady Oracle*. In a novel full of mirrors, reflections and doubles, Fee argues that the gothic transformations of the various men in Joan's life into strangers, monsters and murderers are best understood as a projection of Joan's anxieties about her own lack of identity: they represent the fear that a person's identity is inherently unstable – that they could, eventually, prove to be anyone at all. For Fee, crucially, this fear tells us less about the men in Joan's life than it does about Joan herself.

Princesses and goddesses

Many of the features that mark *Lady Oracle*'s gothic aspect – elements of the fantastical, themes of entrapment, transformation, rescue and so on – are also common fairy-tale tropes. Picking up this thread, critics such as Sharon Rose Wilson, Shuli Barzilai and Marilyn Patton have identified in the novel a significant preoccupation with images taken from fairy tale and myth, all of which are productively used by Atwood to explore cultural constructions of femininity.

In a 1991 article 'The Politics of the Body', Patton makes good use of archival research to trace Atwood's interest in the mythic figure of the White Goddess. Patton explains that the Goddess, which Atwood encountered via Robert Graves's book *The White Goddess*, is a multifaceted myth: she is the earth mother, a cannibal, the (silent) muse, 'both lovely and cruel, ugly and kind'. She is a Triple Goddess: 'seen in three phases: virginity, fecundity and hag'.[14] As a mythic trope, she embodies and condenses many fears and desires. Patton's article excavates earlier drafts of Atwood's third novel, identifying later-excised sections that contained more instances of Goddess imagery and also points to research that Atwood undertook on the White Goddess while preparing her manuscript. The image, suggests Patton, interests Atwood because it makes connections between powerful female bodies and powerful female imaginations as she 'condenses fears of being large and fat, fears of being powerful, fears of devouring or overpowering lovers and children, and the fear of being a writer'.[15]

In *Lady Oracle*, Joan experiences – like many Atwood protagonists – a deeply rooted ambivalence towards femininity, and particularly towards the female body. For Hite, the figure of the Fat Lady in the novel embodies the cultural repulsion at excessive, unchecked femininity that threatens to 'overflow boundaries, obliterating distinctions and violating proprieties'.[16] If Marian in *The Edible Woman* unexpectedly found herself unable to eat, getting thinner and hungrier, then Joan in *Lady Oracle* represents her counterpart: she is the fat woman, all body and excess. Where Marian denies herself, refusing to consume, Patton observes that *Lady Oracle*, instead, 'is about the eating woman'.[17] The disgust and fear that this figure inspires are evident in various scenes in the novel. For example, Patton points to the grotesque, gothic scene in which Joan dreams that the clothes that she buried after making her escape become inhabited by the animated flesh she 'lost' when dieting. Joan imagines this monstrous creation digging its way to the surface and coming to look for her: 'it would look like a big thigh, it would have a face like a breast minus the nipple' (353). For Patton, such passages signify women's fear 'that their own female bodies will overpower their minds'.[18]

The significance of 'the Triple Goddess' is also noted in Sharon Rose Wilson's discussion of *Lady Oracle* in *Margaret Atwood's Fairy-Tale Sexual Politics*, where it is placed alongside a number of other mythic and fairy-tale themes that shape the novel.[19] For Wilson, the most significant intertext in *Lady Oracle* is Hans Christian Anderson's 'The Red Shoes', in which a woman is forced to dance to exhaustion by a pair of enchanted shoes. The story inspired the 1948 film of the same name, starring Moira Shearer and directed by Michael Powell and

Emeric Pressburger, which Atwood has often cited as an early influence and which Joan watches at the cinema with Aunt Lou. Wilson argues that Atwood's female characters commonly recognize that they can either 'dance' '(be artists, be "themselves," be "free")' or marry, but that they cannot do both. As a comic novel, however, *Lady Oracle*, she suggests, resists this imperative and instead parodies the moralizing of 'The Red Shoes', in which dancing is a symbol of uncontrolled sexuality and female vanity. In Atwood's novel, instead, dancing becomes 'a means of self-expression, communion with other women, magic, transformation, and art'. Eventually released from the compulsion to keep 'dancing' in her increasingly manic plot, Joan nevertheless refuses to repent, and chooses instead to tell another story, or as Wilson puts it, to simply become 'a different kind of dancer'.[20]

Fairy-tale imagery is also explored by Barzilai in a 2000 article in which she examines *Lady Oracle*'s playful replication of 'the Rapunzel Syndrome', a phenomenon that Atwood first described in *Survival*. In that critical work, Atwood argues that the narrative pattern of the Rapunzel fairy tale is commonly adopted in '"realistic" novels about "normal" women'. Defining the Rapunzel Syndrome, she identifies four key elements: the main character (Rapunzel); the wicked witch ('usually her mother'); the imprisoning tower ('the attitudes of society, symbolized usually by her house and children'); and the rescuing prince, whom Atwood notes is usually 'not much help'. In some instances, Rapunzel is her own tower; having thoroughly internalized society's restrictions, she carries her prison within her. Typically, argues Atwood, such novels fail to enact a rescue and conclude with Rapunzel still trapped in her tower, only better able 'to cope with it'.[21]

Lady Oracle is full of images of imprisonment and would-be rescuers. The novel's self-conscious engagement with Rapunzel, however (refigured as Tennyson's Lady of Shalott: another princess trapped in a tower), remains vigilant to the traps afforded by the fairy tale and works to disrupt and reroute narrative expectations. And so Joan eventually comes to recognize that her mother was both the wicked witch and, in Barzilai's phrase, 'a self-as-prison figure, an unhappy Rapunzel with no prince in sight'. The novel is full of such contradictory reversals of fairy-tale expectations. Familiar tropes occur, but are inverted or revised, so that they take on multiple, often contradictory meanings; Joan's obesity is both a prison and a 'fortress-defense', an act of resistance and a rebellion.[22] In such ways, the novel works against the simple moralizing of mythic and fairy-tale narratives that would police female behaviour. Consequently, Joan must come to realize that, like her mother, she is both the princess trapped in the tower and the imprisoning witch who holds the keys that might release her.

For Barzilai, Atwood's novel is a tale of *two* Rapunzels: where Joan eventually escapes her tower and learns how to survive outside of its limits, her mother, instead, remains trapped. As Joan comes to realize, like the Lady of Shalott, her mother 'couldn't stand the view from her window, life was her curse', and death is her only release.[23] Her mother's fate acts as a warning to Joan of the danger of the various romantic, gothic, fairy tale and mythic narratives to which she is compulsively drawn. And yet, as Barzilai notes, the novel's ending is ambiguous: Joan's apparent relinquishing of stories is enacted by a telling of her story, and the reporter she visits in the hospital every day becomes yet another potential prince. Joan, it seems, is not entirely free of the pull of romance, and Barzilai suggests that her dry, ironic tone does not, in itself, indicate her readiness to abandon old habits. Reflecting on this imperfect resolution, Barzilai cites Atwood's observation: 'You cannot create a character who is fully liberated in every sense of the word in a society which is not.'[24]

Life Before Man

Atwood's fourth novel remains in many ways a distinctive text within her canon. The shift in tone from the comic excess of *Lady Oracle* is striking, as is the novel's structure, in which the third-person narrative is divided into brief sections, each one focalized through one of three central characters: Elizabeth, Lesje and Nate. The tone of the novel is determinedly realist, and the labelling and dating of each narrative section, with its connotations of data or evidence collection, add to the attempt to achieve a scientific, rational perspective on the quotidian lives of the three protagonists. Coral Ann Howells notes that Atwood has described the novel as a homage to George Eliot's classic Victorian realist novel, *Middlemarch*. Howells points out, however, a crucial difference between *Middlemarch* and *Life Before Man*: Atwood's novel omits the authoritative voice of an omniscient narrator, directing the reader's judgement and understanding, and relies instead on three competing, partial narrative voices. Consequently, *Life Before Man* is revealed to be 'a very slippery text indeed, composed of multiple discourses, some of which conform to realism but many of which do not'.[25]

For Wynne-Davies, the novel's inclusion of Nate's perspective ensures that *Life Before Man* is Atwood's first novel to really consider 'how men might also be trapped within social conventions'.[26] While a number of critics, as she notes, found Nate to be childish and weak, Wynne-Davies argues that he is a more complex and nuanced character than such assessments allow. Where the two other significant male characters in the novel, 'animal-like Chris' and 'career-orientated William', draw on 'one dimensional stereotypes of the 1960s' (something she suggests also occurs in Atwood's previous novels), the decision to divide the narrative between three equally finely drawn perspectives ensures that Nate's character and view of the world are taken seriously. Just like Atwood's many female protagonists, Nate, argues Wynne-Davis, is depicted as 'a self-acknowledged victim who might just survive'.[27]

In addition to representing the fullest examination to date of a male character's interior life, *Life Before Man* also presents a more self-conscious depiction of multi-ethnic contemporary Canada. While characters of different nationalities and ethnicities have appeared in Atwood's work before, in *Life Before Man* she foregrounds Lesje's experience as a Lithuanian-Canadian. Lesje's relationship with 'William Wasp' founders, in part, on her realization that, while he finds her 'impossibly exotic', he could not imagine having children with someone who was not of 'his own kind' (20–1). In *Living Over the Abyss: Margaret Atwood's Life Before Man*, a short critical companion volume to the novel, Carol Beran notes that some early reviewers were unconvinced by this aspect of the text, finding it 'underdeveloped' and 'superficial'. Barbara Amiel's review in *Maclean's*, for example, dismisses it as 'Atwood's nod to multiculturalism'.[28] Beran, however, points to archival evidence that Atwood researched Lesje's ethnic background with some care. And certainly, by describing part of the novel from Lesje's perspective, Atwood throws Canadian 'WASP' identity into relief as never before. Canada's perception of itself as an open and tolerant society is viewed with some scepticism. As Wynne-Davies notes, while Toronto's developing multiculturalism emerges in *Life Before Man*, Atwood also 'makes it clear that the racial codes that govern the city's hierarchy are still firmly in place'.[29]

Despite these innovations, *Life Before Man* remains under-represented in criticism on Atwood. While critics writing today do sometimes return to *The Edible Woman*, *Surfacing* and *Lady Oracle*, few seem motivated to re-examine *Life Before Man*. Even in companion texts, it is the novel that is most readily overlooked. It is, for example, one of the novels Nathalie Cooke's 2004 work, *Margaret Atwood: A Critical Companion* skips over, as she proceeds from chapters on the first three novels straight to *Cat's Eye*. This relative neglect is consistent with responses at the time of the novel's publication. Reviewing the critical reception of *Life Before Man*, Beran notes that many readers found the book problematic, with common complaints being that it was bleak, inconclusive and despairing. In an interview from 1985, Atwood acknowledges that critics struggled with the novel, stating: 'they didn't quite know what to do with that one because it didn't have the things in it that they were looking for'.[30] For Beran, this absence was the desired happy ending. She argues, however, that the novel's conclusion, 'although not a joyous affirmation', does contain the germs of the traditional comic resolution of reintegration and new life and offers the hope, at least, 'that life before man – that is, a life yet to come – will not be totally bleak'.[31]

Overview

Life Before Man is set in the present-day Toronto of the late 1970s, and the city's landmarks – particularly, the Royal Ontario Museum where two of the central characters work – are closely drawn from life. The novel is comprised of the interiorized reflections of Elizabeth, director of the museum, her husband Nate, formerly a lawyer and now a maker of artisanal children's toys, and Lesje, a palaeontologist and colleague of Elizabeth's. Elizabeth and Nate are unhappily married but attempting to stay together for the good of the children. As the novel opens, Elizabeth is mourning the death of her former lover, Chris, who has committed suicide, and Nate is recovering from the end of an affair. As the novel progresses, Lesje begins an affair with Nate, which Elizabeth reveals to Lesje's boyfriend, William, who then attempts to rape Lesje. Elizabeth and Nate eventually separate, and Nate moves in with Lesje, but he and his wife remain closely entangled in their shared parenting. Frustrated at the continuing influence of Elizabeth on their lives, and by the comparative precarity of her own role in Nate's life, Lesje secretly endeavours to become pregnant: 'if having [children] was the only way she could stop being invisible, then she would goddam well have some herself' (293). It is, in the spirit of the novel, a Darwinian strategy for survival.

In its account of failed and damaged relationships, the action of the novel – which takes place across approximately two years – is grounded in reflection, recrimination and regret. At the same time, the characters must start to conceive of a future that might potentially relinquish the past and evolve. As Elizabeth slowly comes to terms with Chris's death, which throws up long-repressed memories of her unhappy childhood and her sister's perhaps self-inflicted drowning, Nate and Lesje work towards a relationship that might, in defiance of all the pain and suffering, be life-giving and forward-looking.

The novel's plot is relatively light, especially when compared to the excess of plot in *Lady Oracle*. Where Atwood's previous novels had all, in different ways, relied on the twists and revelations of external details, in *Life Before Man*, the focus instead is largely on the interiority of the three characters. Marilyn French, in a very positive 1980 review for *The New York Times*, suggests that 'the life of the novel really lies in its texture, in the densely interwoven feelings, memories and insights of the characters'.[32] In a 1988 essay, Gayle Greene describes the 'powerful and haunting' novel as more closely affiliated with modernism than realism, and compares it to Virginia Woolf's experiments with time, reality, perspective and interpretation. With *Life Before Man*, she suggests, Atwood accomplishes what the modernists were striving for: 'she has freed the narrative from plot so that she can focus on the inner events that are the real adventures.'[33] Karen Stein similarly describes *Life Before Man* as a minimalist novel: one with few characters and little action, set in a limited space and time, where all the major events happen off-stage, either before the novel commences or taking place elsewhere.[34]

Between romance and realism

Although sometimes overlooked as an anomaly in Atwood's canon, many critics have usefully reflected instead on how *Life Before Man* connects to the author's ongoing concerns and preoccupations. For Stein, the novel is the first of a sequence of three in which 'the observer's gaze is powerful and destructive'. In *Bodily Harm*, she suggests, violence against women rapidly escalates from pornography to physical violence and rape, while images of violent observation proliferate in *The Handmaid's Tale* in which the secret police are called 'Eyes' and women are covered to protect them from the male gaze. In *Life Before Man*, instead, 'the violence of observation is psychological rather than political' and characters constantly feel under scrutiny and inadequate.[35]

Kolodny, instead, offers a persuasive reading of *Life Before Man* as Atwood's 'first true novel'. She observes that each of the first three novels invent 'worlds in which the marvellous and the mundane easily intermingle'. In each, at certain points in the narrative, 'monsters . . . invade the stage' and the protagonists must subsequently work at 'untangling the real from the unreal'.[36] For Kolodny, these discernible elements of the fantastic underscore Atwood's involvement in the major conventions of the romance form: where *The Edible Woman* is a comic romance, *Surfacing* represents a serious romance quest, and eventually, with *Lady Oracle*, Atwood ends up parodying the form. Indeed, Kolodny discerns an impatience, by the end of the third novel, with the idea of romance, and particularly with the romance motifs of rescue and magical transformation. Noting that *Lady Oracle* concludes with Joan deciding to forgo her usual escapist fantasies and instead to tell the full and unembellished truth for once, Kolodny proposes that, in Joan's resolution, 'Atwood was announcing her own intention to take up a different narrative design'.[37] What follows, of course, is the determinedly realist *Life Before Man*, which Sherrill Grace terms 'Atwood's first attempt at social and domestic realism'. Like Kolodny, Grace discerns a move away from the 'romance conventions' of the previous novels – fantasy, satire, myth and the gothic – and an attempt instead to 'capture the empty inconclusiveness of modern marriage and urban existence'.[38] And unlike the earlier texts, *Life Before Man* offers no promises of fantastical transformation or escape, no matter how much the protagonists may wish for them.

In sympathy with this new commitment to realism, the long-extinct creatures on display in the Royal Ontario Museum where Elizabeth and Lesje work do not come alive, but function instead only as a suggestive backdrop, commenting on the lives of the present-day characters and the novel's themes of threat and survival. When Nate jogs through the city, Kolodny observes that he passes between the Parliament Buildings, representing 'political statecraft', and the Museum, representing prehistory. For Kolodny, crucially, neither politics nor the past 'provide alternate realities for healing or escape'.[39] In this transitional novel, in which the elements of romance that shaped Atwood's previous three works are still discernible, romance is always ultimately exposed and rejected. Although they may yearn for a magical transformation or a mythical guide, each of the three central characters eventually discovers that transformation is still possible within the realms of the real. While these resolutions might lack the kind of mysterious metamorphoses that the protagonists of *The Edible Woman*, *Surfacing* and *Lady Oracle* undergo, each character survives, recovers and abandons fantasies and daydreams of the past in order to make a necessary commitment to the present and the future. For Kolodny, with the publication of *Life Before Man*, 'Atwood the romancer had turned realist'.[40]

Kolodny's reading of the novel as a transitional text, marking Atwood's progress from romance to realism, is taken up and examined by Stein in her essay, 'It's About Time: Temporal Dimensions in Margaret Atwood's *Life Before Man*'. Stein argues that the novel is better read as a text that contains and juxtaposes two contrasting narratives: a surface realist narrative and a mythic subtext. In the surface narrative, 'time drags on and the characters are bored and disillusioned', but in the mythic subtext, instead, the characters trace a more natural, cyclical pattern of birth, death and rebirth. In these two different layers of narrative, the novel opposes a 'gray world of contemporary urban culture' to 'a green world of nature'.[41] Consequently, there is a tension, argues Stein, between the realist narrative (linear, chronological and full of precise, verifiable detail) and the more mythic counter-narrative (multiple, contradictory and circular). While surface readers of *Life Before Man* most readily observe a cruel and pessimistic plot functioning in the realist tradition, a deeper reading reveals the novel's 'covert subtext' which offers a more optimistic promise of revival and rebirth.[42]

Where critics such as Kolodny and Howells point to the dating of the various sections in *Life Before Man* as indicative of the novel's commitment to realism, Stein instead suggests that the dates draw the reader's attention to the passing of the seasons, foregrounding the ritualistic holidays of an earlier, agrarian concept of natural time before mechanization. Time, for Atwood's characters, seems to represent the inevitability of death – just as the dinosaurs died out, so will man – and the novel is, as Stein notes, filled with memories of the dead and the rituals of mourning and memorializing. But set against this bleak, deadening aspect is the pressure on the characters to look forwards: to enact the pagan rituals of renewal and new life. Atwood's novel repeatedly intertwines the realist and the mythic in its imagery and symbolism. Stein, for example, points to the symbolic function of Lesje in the novel: as a palaeontologist, she is associated with the dead world of fossils and the fixed, unitary world of the past, but her forename (a Ukrainian version of Alice) connects her to Alice in Wonderland, and thus a multiplicity of dimensions of space and time, while her surname – 'Green' – affiliates her with the natural, fertile world. Eventually, she becomes 'A pregnant paleontologist [...] a contradiction in terms' (308). Ultimately, for Stein, in its juxtaposition of linear/realist time and cyclical/mythic time, the novel, rather than being bleak and pessimistic, suggests instead 'possibilities of healing and transformation through connection to nature'.[43]

Consumption and survival

Life Before Man develops a number of Atwood's characteristic concerns, specifically around gendered power relations, violence and threat, and the consumption of the female body. In 'The Politics of Eating', Emma Parker places *Life Before Man* at the heart of an extended thematic analysis of eating as a metaphor for gendered power in Atwood's work. While *The Edible Woman* and *Lady Oracle* readily lend themselves to such readings, Parker notably extends the theme to *Life Before Man* and identifies the relationship between eating and power as central to the text. From Elizabeth's determination to maintain tight control over everything, including her own appetites, to Lesje's powerlessness, 'conveyed by the fact that she eats very little and frequently refuses food', Parker traces the various power plays in the novel. Meetings, she observes, commonly take place over meals, and the novel contains persistent images of rotting food. The smell of decay, she argues, evokes 'the unhealthiness of relationships based on the pursuit of power'.[44]

Sarah Sceats identifies a '*quid pro quo* in the food relations of lovers and potential partners' across Atwood's work, and although her study does not focus on *Life Before Man*, she does note that when Nate first takes Lesje out for a cheap sandwich lunch, 'the highly charged atmosphere indicates that this food has a higher tariff'.[45] Parker's essay makes a similar connection between eating, power, and sex. She notes the frequency with which mouths, stomachs, throats and teeth recur in Atwood's imagery, and how often male protagonists are described in terms of their teeth, particularly during sexual encounters – at various times gritting, clenching, prominent and bared. In this way, as Parker observes, 'Consummation slides easily into consumption; sexual and physical appetites converge'. The erotic chain of significance between food, sex and violence is particularly prominent in *Bodily Harm* and *Life Before Man*, in which Jake almost kills Rennie and William almost kills Lesje, both through near-strangulation during sex. In Atwood's fiction, concludes Parker, 'the powerful not only eat, they eat the powerless'.[46]

This cannibalistic motif provides a potent undercurrent in *Life Before Man*. During a tense dinner party, the characters play 'the Lifeboat game', in which each participant must justify his or her place in the lifeboat. Elizabeth proves her determination to survive, arguing that the losers should be eaten rather than thrown overboard: an example, notes Parker, of how the 'strongest sustain themselves by eating the weakest'.[47] Discussing this same scene, Patton suggests that the game 'serves as a miniature of the human interactions throughout the novel'. Where Elizabeth is the ruthless consumer-survivor, Nate's distaste for aggression, she argues, marks him as a potential victim. Representing both the figure of the artist in the text and the role of Canada on the world stage, he is 'forced to choose between action and silence'.[48] This game of death and survival is put into relief in the novel by Lesje's recurring fantasies of walking among dinosaurs; the extinction of creatures of such large appetites seems to forebode man's future demise, 'when men and women treat each other as meat in a fight for survival'.[49] Atwood's foregrounding of consumption exposes the myriad ways in which the strong consume the weak: a theme that once again comes to the fore in her next novel, *Bodily Harm*.

Bodily Harm

Life Before Man exposes the threat of violence lurking beneath the veneer of civility and demonstrates Atwood's preoccupation with survival 'in a world characterised by hostility and violence that is both latent and overt'.[50] With *Bodily Harm*, these concerns are further expanded in what Rigney terms Atwood's 'profoundly political' fifth novel, which significantly extends the geographical reach of her work, making looping connections between violence and coercion on an intimate, local, national and international scale.[51] A similar point is made by Patton in an article that examines early drafts of the novel. She suggests that *Bodily Harm* is more profoundly political than *The Handmaid's Tale*; where the latter novel focuses primarily on the rise of the evangelical right, *Bodily Harm* uses cancer as a metaphor by which to connect seemingly disparate systems of power and misogyny, from the police to the CIA to authoritarian governments, to drug cartels, healthcare, pornography and advertising, 'thus making visible the relationship between sexual and political oppression'.[52] In this manner, as Diana Brydon argues, the novel's title conflates the 'body politic, female body, and colonized space/tropical island', pointing to the ubiquity of violence and harm.[53]

Overview

Bodily Harm proceeds in the present day, with the protagonist's past revealed in episodic flashbacks. The narrator, speaking to an unknown interlocutor in an unknown location, commences: 'This is how I got here' (11). Once a politicized student journalist, now a 'lifestyles' features writer producing determinedly non-political feel-good pieces, Rennie's life is thrown off track by a breast cancer diagnosis. The consequent stress throws up complicated feelings about her body and disturbs memories about her unhappy childhood in conservative Grimswold, where she learned to be quiet and no trouble. The disruption to her usual equilibrium precipitates the breakdown of her relationship with her boyfriend Jake, who moves out of their shared apartment. All of these events precede the start of the novel, which opens instead on a disturbing scene in which an unknown intruder has entered Rennie's empty apartment, leaving behind a suggestive coil of rope on her bed. Feeling uneasy, and with no particular responsibilities to keep her in Toronto, Rennie offers to do a travel piece on a little-known Caribbean island and sets off in pursuit of a relaxing escape from reality.

Like *Lady Oracle*, *Bodily Harm* adopts a pastiche of styles and genres. It begins in the mode of a crime novel when Rennie comes home to find the police in her apartment, although Rennie imagines it more like a Golden Age detective puzzle: 'Miss Wilford, in the bedroom, with a rope' (14). When she falls in love with her oncologist, she chides herself for betraying the clichéd behaviour of 'women in nurse novels and sex-and-scalpel epics with titles like *Surgery*' (33) – indeed, the kind of novels that Paul in *Lady Oracle* writes. And when her 'Fun in the Sun' (16) travel piece leads her into unanticipated dangers, the holiday romance novel unexpectedly swerves into a dark political spy thriller. As each of these genres is alluded to and rejected, Rennie progressively learns that there are no 'sidesteps', no 'small absences from real life' (16). By the end of the novel, she will instead accept that she is a reporter, with a duty to observe and report.

Rennie's development fits with the trajectory of Kolodny's thesis, which reads *Life Before Man* as a transitional text in Atwood's progression from romance to realism. As Kolodny notes, when Atwood discussed *Bodily Harm* (as she would also discuss *The Handmaid's Tale*), she was at pains to point out that she had 'anchored even the most bizarre elements [. . .] to demonstrable realities'. For Kolodny, this new emphasis on the real is a crucial element in Atwood's fictions at this time. From *Bodily Harm* onwards, Atwood moves away from her previous preoccupation with 'the power politics of intimate relations' and begins to concentrate instead on 'the abuse of power in the public arena'.[54] If *Life Before Man* was a transitional text, marking a rejection of romance, *Bodily Harm* represents Atwood's realism come to fruition.

When Rennie finally reaches St Antoine, the relaxed holiday escape she was seeking proves elusive. Even before she arrives, there are intimations – which Rennie seems determined to ignore – that she is entering a complex, highly fraught political situation. Dr Minnow, a former government minister she meets on the small local plane, gestures towards the island's poverty, government corruption, poor infrastructure and fragile stability in the wake of the very recent departure of the British colonial administration, but Rennie misreads him as an overly familiar bore and potential pest. Rennie's subsequent experiences are similarly shaped by her fundamental miscomprehension of the political realities that surround her. As a single white Canadian woman on islands that are not common tourist destinations, she finds herself standing out and feeling watched. Local tensions, she discovers, are running high in the run-up to the first independent elections in the region. Rennie's sudden appearance as a travel writer is generally deemed unlikely, and she is assumed to be a political journalist and probably a spy.

Simone Drichel notes that, in the scene with Minnow and others, Rennie– an avid reader of thrillers and murder mysteries – wishes she had a book to insulate herself from unwanted attention. For Rennie, fiction is a mode of escapism. Drichel extends this equation, making connections between the kinds of texts that Rennie consumes and produces. She argues that travel writing (like pornography – a key theme in the novel) provides the reader/viewer with a safe, controlled image that protects him or her from 'an unsettling (or even threatening) encounter with the real'.[55]

Throughout the novel, Rennie is subject to various advances that she rarely fully understands. At her hotel, she runs into Paul, an American who lives and works on the island. With a history of involvement in geopolitical hotspots, 'always advising' (46), Paul, it appears, is either a mercenary or a spy, or perhaps both. Once again, however, Rennie seems oblivious to what is before her and conceives of their developing relationship as a holiday romance. It is Paul who explains the turbulent local politics to her and assures her 'you won't get hurt. You're a tourist, you're exempt' (78). Later, Rennie is picked up by Lora, another white Canadian woman, whom Rennie instinctively dislikes but is unable to shake off. Lora, it turns out, is the girlfriend of Prince, one of the opposition candidates in the forthcoming elections. Like Minnow, and like the various locals, waiters, vendors and beggars she encounters, Lora seems to want something from Rennie that she feels unable and unwilling to give.

As the novel proceeds, events on the islands rapidly gather pace. Minnow, also standing as opposition candidate, appears to have won the elections, but is shot by a CIA agent. A brief insurrection is brutally put down and, unwittingly caught up in the turmoil on the streets, Rennie is imprisoned and finds herself sharing a cell with Lora. In prison, Lora exchanges sexual favours with the guards for the promise of being allowed to see Prince. When they eventually reveal that he was killed in the uprising, her howls of protest are met with a brutal, possibly lethal beating. Shortly afterwards, Rennie is released and interviewed by a Canadian official, who tacitly requests her silence about what she has witnessed. Wanting only her passport and passage home, Rennie concurs, but secretly, she knows everything has now changed: 'she is a subversive. She was not one once but now she is. A reporter. She will pick her time; then she will report' (301).

A postcolonial novel?

In an article entitled 'Tourists and Terrorists', Patton describes *Surfacing, Life Before Man*, the 1975 short story 'A Travel Piece' and *Bodily Harm* as 'tourist stories'. In each, the protagonist believes herself to be a neutral observer – a tourist – but must eventually accept 'the impossibility of real "neutrality" in an increasingly interdependent "global village".⁵⁶ A similar point, as Patton notes, is made by Ildiko de Papp Carrington, who also discusses the connections between 'A Travel Piece' and *Bodily Harm*. For the protagonists of both texts, suggests Carrington, tourism equates to being an onlooker, to refusing 'the vulnerability of active participation', but both are ultimately forced to take responsibility and participate.⁵⁷ Patton builds on Carrington's reading, connecting the figure of the tourist to Atwood's concern with the politics of writing; in *Bodily Harm*, she suggests, Atwood's 'political and aesthetic principles are finally combined' as she expounds on the political implications of writing.⁵⁸ Noting that Atwood's first working title for *Bodily Harm* was '*The Robber Bridegroom*', Patton reflects on the fairy tale, in which a young girl secretly visits her fiancé's house and witnesses atrocities, before returning home and telling her tale. Patton takes from this intertext the message that 'telling tales may be a way of saving lives'.⁵⁹

Patton and Carrington's essays both gesture towards the postcolonial politics implicit in *Bodily Harm*. With its Caribbean setting and departing colonial administration, *Bodily Harm*'s postcolonial concerns make it anomalous in Atwood's canon. For Drichel (writing in 2008), this explains why, apart from some critical work done in the 1980s and 1990s, the novel has rather fallen out of favour with Atwood critics. At the same time, however, as she observes, it was never taken up by postcolonial critics, and instead has a contested and problematic status in the field. For Helen Tiffin, the novel's paralleling of sexual and political violence 'glosses over' material differences: 'the metaphorical connection is made at the expense of real engagement with the "other" culture'.⁶⁰ Brydon, instead, while acknowledging this limitation, argues that the novel both exposes Canada's complicity in colonizing practices and refuses Rennie's dearly held belief in her own innocence. For Brydon, Atwood's novel 'locates some gaps in the apparently seamless web of white cultural discourse' and 'challenges postcolonial critics to refine their terminologies and rethink their methods'.⁶¹ Drichel takes up this debate between Tiffin and Brydon and suggests that *Bodily Harm* has been overlooked by postcolonial critics because it does not do what they expect it to do. But like Brydon, she argues that, because it 'sits uncomfortably' in the field, it works to 'reveal postcolonialism's blind spots' (26).

Drichel's essay focuses on Atwood's exposition of the manner in which the tourist's gaze unwittingly replicates the colonizing gaze. Atwood once again complicates claims to victimhood by showing how 'a male gaze of which Rennie is the object in Canada is replicated in the neo-colonial gaze of the tourists that Rennie brings to the islands'.⁶² After the break-in, Rennie feels watched, 'as if she was a moving target in someone else's binoculars' (40). Caught in a maze of 'violating gazes' that transform her from a self-determining subject into the object of someone else's predatory desire, Rennie's instinct is to flee, to make herself invisible. But for Drichel, the ethical conclusion of the novel only occurs when she learns to exchange the violent gaze for 'the immediacy of touch'.[63]

Working against the ready equation of sexual-violence-done-to-women and colonial-violence-done-to-nations that critics such as Rigney, Patton and Drydon all identify in *Bodily Harm*, Kate Marantz offers a more sceptical reading in her focus on gaps and absences in the text. Pointing to the opening scenes in which the objects of fear are the absent intruder, the rope coiled around nothing, and the removed breast, she suggests that these 'absences in space, text, and meaning often "speak" or signify the most complex and troubling messages' of the novel.[64] While the narrative traces Rennie's 'political and emotional awakening', Atwood, argues Marantz, disbars her readers from the empathetic resolution they desire. Instead, she employs gaps to expose the limits of seeing, comprehension and telling, and to point to the difficulties and problems of equating different modes of violence and oppression (even as she admits connections and parallels). She suggests that Atwood cautions her predominantly North American feminist readership against 'totalitizing political narratives' that erase context and difference. This critique, she suggests, is directed at a second-wave feminism that proved too ready to erase material differences between women while still prioritizing the perspectives of white women. For Marantz, Atwood's exposition of the gaps in experience and understanding is not a refusal of the importance of trying to make connections – and of exposing the ubiquity of violence – but is instead a determination to acknowledge that such gaps exist. This results in a novel that is 'more nuanced and self-reflexive' than it might initially appear to be.[65]

Touch and responsibility

Just as Drichel's essay finds resolution in the power of touch, so the importance of touch in Atwood's novel is examined by Jerome Rosenberg in his 1984 monograph *Margaret Atwood*, in which he traces the significance of hand imagery in *Bodily Harm*. Rennie has a recurrent disturbing memory of her grandmother, suffering from dementia, wandering into the kitchen looking for her hands. When the young Rennie tells her they are still on the ends of her arms, her grandmother impatiently replies: 'Not those . . . the ones I had before, the ones I touch things with' (57). Rennie's cold and unyielding grandmother lost her capacity to touch others – her capacity for care and compassion – long before her mind gave way. At one point, Rennie recalls herself as a small and frightened child, desperately clinging to her grandmother's legs: 'but she's prying my hands away, finger by finger' (53). It is apparent that Rennie has been damaged by the coldness and distance imposed by her grandmother. As Frank Davey puts it, 'Later as an adult, she will look at the world without touching it', writing superficial articles and conducting superficial relationships that touch no one.[66]

For Rosenberg, this recurring hand motif is primarily about connection: about the manner in which our lives touch others. Rennie, so invested in her independence and her lack of responsibility, must eventually accept 'the cancerous emblem of involvement in human imperfection and mortality', but also, in a more positive sense, look towards 'joining in communion with her fellow human beings'.[67] At the novel's conclusion, the moral urgency of connecting with others comes to the fore, again through the imagery of hands and touching. Sharing a prison cell with Lora, Rennie finds the other woman's tears embarrassing and distasteful. She 'looks down at her hands, which ought to contain comfort. Compassion', but cannot bring herself to touch her (286). Later, when Lora is beaten almost beyond recognition, Rennie undergoes, in Rosenberg's words, a 'spiritual transformation'.[68] Where previously she had maintained her distance, not wanting to feel obliged or entangled, her experiences in prison teach her that 'she is not exempt' (301).

Rosenberg argues that 'Rennie's newly formed moral landscape' is revealed in the novel when she finally remembers the conclusion of the scene with her grandmother, in which her mother soothes the confused old woman by clasping her dangling hands in her own. Knowing now what she must do, Rennie approaches the bloodied body of a possibly dead Lora and holds her hands, willing life back into Lora's cold frame. Rosenberg notes that some reviewers were sceptical of this scene, arguing that Rennie is 'an unlikely healer', too 'self-absorbed' to provide the healing touch of God. But he argues that this is not the point: as the novel closes, 'we do not know whether Rennie has accomplished a miracle, only that she has tried'.[69] As with many of Atwood's inconclusive endings, the novel does not offer a resolution so much as a proposition that something has changed.

A healing comedy?

Contemplating the conclusion of *Bodily Harm*, Kolodny contends: '[e]ssentially, the plot is about recovery.' Commencing in a state of damage and emotional frigidity, Rennie recovers her sexuality, her compassion and the 'outrage at injustice that had once fuelled her journalism'.[70] A similar assessment is proposed by Davey in *Margaret Atwood: A Feminist Poetics* (1984). In a chapter titled 'Four Female Comedies', Davey connects *Bodily Harm* to Atwood's first three novels (once again, skipping over *Life Before Man*). While his reading of *Bodily Harm* as a comedy contradicts Kolodny's assessment of the novel's political realism, Davey argues that it follows the familiar comic romance narrative pattern in which a protagonist commences in social disruption, enters a healing green world and then returns to society 'capable of restoring it to wholeness'.[71]

Crucially, for Davey, the familiar comic romance pattern represents another form of entrapment within 'patriarchal second-order constructions' that the protagonists must escape.[72] He argues that critics such as Catherine McLay (whose essay on the quest motif in *The Edible Woman* is discussed in the previous chapter) have failed to recognize this and continue to read the novels as though the protagonists can achieve liberation through established patterns. These archetypal patterns that recur in Atwood's novel, Davey argues instead, 'are circle games which trap characters into fruitless repetitive action'. Like Joan in *Lady Oracle*, imprisoned in the maze of her formulaic plots, Atwood's protagonists do not need to complete the comic formula of descent and renewal, rather they need to escape prescriptive narrative patterns altogether. In *Bodily Harm*, Rennie eventually succeeds in doing this. Through touch, which circumvents language, and through a new understanding of 'language's inadequacies and ambiguities', she envisions a way to subvert patriarchal plots. By the end of the novel, suggests Davey, 'the action of her hands becomes infinitely more powerful than spoken words'.[73]

Read together, *Lady Oracle*, *Life Before Man* and *Bodily Harm* securely establish Atwood's reputation as a writer of female-centred, present-day narratives that work to expose the gendered nature of power structures. We see, over this period, the expansion of her interest in themes of power, violence and victimhood. With her next novel, the phenomenally successful *The Handmaid's Tale*, Atwood further explores these themes, while also taking her most notable early foray into an alternate world from her own contemporary Canadian setting and constructs what will go on to become a foundational work of feminist dystopian fiction.

3

'Are there any questions?'
A focus on *The Handmaid's Tale*

The Handmaid's Tale, Atwood's sixth novel, is her most well known and critically acclaimed to date. This remains true, despite the fact that any new novel by Atwood is now an assured publishing 'event'. A dystopian fiction set in the United States of the near future in which a brutal theocratic regime has come to power, it was immediately successful, and its striking imagery of silent Handmaids dressed in red is now embedded in the popular cultural imagination. *The Handmaid's Tale* has become something of a contemporary literary phenomenon. Writing in an article for *The Guardian* in 2012, Atwood notes that it 'has sold millions of copies worldwide and has appeared in a bewildering number of translations and editions'.[1] In 1990, it was adapted into a film starring Natasha Richardson, Faye Dunaway and Robert Duvall, with a screenplay by Harold Pinter. In 2000, an opera based on the novel was commissioned by the Royal Danish Opera and in 2003 Poul Ruders's work was transferred to London by the English National Opera. This was followed by the hugely successful 2017 Hulu television production, starring Elisabeth Moss and Joseph Fiennes. With a ten-part first series based on the plot of Atwood's novel, a subsequent second, third and fourth series take the story of Offred in new directions, extending the world of Gilead beyond the ending of the text.

Renewed interest in Atwood's 1985 novel was also generated by the inauguration of President Trump in January 2017. Atwood responded directly to the connections being made by many commentators between the current political climate and her then thirty-two-year-old novel. In an article for *The New York Times* entitled 'What *The Handmaid's Tale* Means in the Age of Trump', she observes: 'In the wake of the recent American election, fears and anxieties proliferate. Basic civil liberties are seen as endangered, along with many of the rights for women won over the past decades.'[2] For Atwood, the novel's call to bear witness remains current whenever human rights are in danger of erosion.

Trump's presidency prompted a spike of interest in classic dystopian fictions such as George Orwell's *Nineteen Eighty-Four* (1949) and Philip K. Dick's *The Man in the High Castle* (1962) and motivated a spate of newspaper articles with titles such as 'Prescient About the President: Which Writers Can Help Us Read Trump?'.[3] While most of the typically discussed writers were male, Atwood's novel clearly spoke to a particular set of concerns. As I observed in 2017, 'renewed battles in the US over women's access to affordable health care and abortion providers means that Atwood's novel, which imagines a fundamentalist Christian regime predicated on the absolute control of female sexuality and reproduction, has taken on a new resonance'.[4] Indeed, *The New York Times* reported at the time that Atwood's publisher had reprinted 100,000 copies of *The Handmaid's Tale* to meet renewed demand.[5] As Atwood reflects, 'Some books haunt the reader. Others haunt the writer. *The Handmaid's Tale* has done both.'[6]

As if prompted by the novel's concluding line – 'Are there any questions?'[7] – analysis of *The Handmaid's Tale* continues unabated to this day. Given the continuing relevance and popularity of Atwood's sixth novel, this chapter provides an extended close examination of critical responses to *The Handmaid's Tale*.

Overview

The Handmaid's Tale is set around Cambridge, Massachusetts, in the United States: a region settled by the Puritans in the early 1600s. The date of the novel's present day is around the early twenty-first century. Through scraps of information gleaned from Offred's disjointed narrative, we learn that America in the late twentieth century was facing a crisis of falling birth rates, cumulatively caused by pollution, sexually transmitted diseases and a conscientious refusal of many women to reproduce at a time of significant nuclear threat. This imagined America of the 1990s, while familiar, also appears to be characterized by a heightened threat of violence against women, a rampant unregulated market for sex and pornography, and, consequently, a more militant feminist block. In an article that draws out the influence of George Orwell's *Nineteen Eighty-Four* on *The Handmaid's Tale*, Earl Ingersoll notes that Atwood and Orwell both depict a totalitarian future that offers a grim choice between 'either freedom and anarchy or repression and security'.[8] Accordingly, in response to perceived social decay and disorder, the Christian New Right have consolidated their forces and staged a coup, gunning down Congress and the President, and establishing Gilead, a totalitarian state organized around Old Testament principles combined with the seventeenth-century values of American Puritanism.

In Gilead, individualism is something to be stamped out and everyone has a state-appointed role. The architects and authorities of the regime are Commanders, who wield total patriarchal power. Households are led by Commanders' Wives, dressed in maternal blue, servants are Marthas, dressed in functional dark green, while Handmaids, dressed in red, are fertile women whose function it is to conceive and deliver a child to be raised by the Commander and his Wife. State authority is enforced by a combination of Aunts, who take charge of the indoctrination and discipline of the Handmaids, by a security force of Guardians and by a shadowy web of spies and informers known as Eyes. Everyone must act in service to the state, and as a Handmaid, Offred – her name a patronymic of her Commander, Fred – is little more than a vessel of reproduction: a useful body, forbidden to read or write, and with strictly delimited speech. Because the narrative is delivered by Offred, women such as her are the most visible victims of this regime. We also learn, however, that all non-conformist or transgressive groups are deemed enemies of the state, whether homosexuals, Roman Catholics, Quakers or Baptists, while the 'Children of Ham' – all black citizens – are 'relocated' outside of Gilead's borders. As Coral Ann Howells notes, 'Atwood's feminist concerns are plain here but so too are her concerns for basic human rights.'[9]

Offred's narrative is filled with the minutiae of everyday domestic life, as she walks and shops with Ofglen, and describes the boredom of marking time in her room between the monthly 'ceremonies' in which the Commander attempts to impregnate her in the presence of his wife, Serena Joy. In his essay, Ingersoll picks up on this depiction of Offred's room and connects it to Orwell's Winston Smith seeking refuge in his room from the surveillance of the state. Atwood, he suggests, draws on the image of Winston as a 'writer in his room', producing his illicit diary, to encourage us to see Offred as a writer, 'or at least as the generator of a "text"'.[10] For both Offred and Winston, 'writing' is simultaneously an attempt to recover privacy and to overcome crippling isolation. Where Winston, however, eventually faces the devastating revelation that everything he thought was private and hidden was always known, the absence of a key to her room leaves Offred under no illusion that she has any control over this space that is nominally hers. For Ingersoll, 'Winston and Offred are quite different "writers" in large part because their relations to their rooms are radically different.'[11] Where Winston has a misplaced sense of privacy and autonomy that drives his written account, Offred is always conscious of the fragility and permeability of her tale.

Offred's life in Gilead, while punctuated by brutal violence and characterized by persistent threat, is also highly ordered and oddly mundane. Her narrative is a survival narrative; she manages trauma by keeping quiet, staying still and repressing her emotions. Her accounts of attending the regime's various ritualized practices, including group executions, are factual and often impassive. In an article that examines Atwood's use of 'fascist style' in the novel, Angela Laflen looks at how fascist regimes edit and censor imagery to manipulate their citizens.[12] Disparate visual exhibits in *The Handmaid's Tale*, from public hangings to Puritan artwork, all act as 'spectacular displays' that publicly enforce the regime's ideological agenda. Throughout the novel, Gilead's success in 're-educating' Offred is evident in the struggle she often has to identify and reject the regime's influence on her thoughts. For example, in her memories of 'the time before' (16), her very ordinary life now appears to her as extraordinarily free. In this manner, suggests Laflen, we understand that she now views the world 'at least initially, through Gilead's lens'.[13]

Offred's disjointed memories of the past are peopled by her mother, her best friend Moira, her partner Luke and their daughter. We learn that during a foiled escape from Gilead in its chaotic early days, Luke was probably killed, and the child was taken by the regime. As a fertile woman, Offred was offered a choice between forced labour and becoming a Handmaid. As she dryly notes, while enduring the ritualized rape of the monthly ceremony: 'Nothing is going on here that I haven't signed up for' (105). Commencing in relative stasis, events rapidly develop. Firstly, the Commander initiates a clandestine relationship, inviting Offred to his study to play scrabble and talk: both strictly prohibited activities. Around the same time, Ofglen reveals herself to be part of Mayday, an underground resistance network, and Serena Joy, desperate for a child, pushes Offred into a sexual liaison with Nick, the Commander's driver. Offred and Nick commence a secret relationship that consumes Offred's attention, and she relinquishes her interest in the resistance. Later, the Ofglen she knew is replaced by a new Ofglen and she learns that her subversive former companion killed herself when she saw the secret police coming. The novel concludes with a similarly ominous black van arriving for Offred. As she is led away, Nick reveals himself as a Mayday rescuer, rather than an Eye, and Offred, with no way of knowing the truth, relinquishes herself to an uncertain fate.

Early responses

Contemporary reviews typically identify *The Handmaid's Tale* as a significant work from an important writer, although some find cause for criticism. Mary

McCarthy in *The New York Times* terms it an accomplished and engaging work – 'a poet's novel' – but ultimately unimaginative and 'powerless to scare'. She laments Atwood's failure to imagine a new form of future language in the mode of *Nineteen Eighty-Four* or *A Clockwork Orange*, arguing that 'a future that has no language invented for it lacks a personality'. This complaint seemingly overlooks the fact that Gilead is a near-future dystopia, set just twenty years ahead, and also neglects the various neologisms that Atwood does introduce. Nevertheless, for McCarthy, the novel lacks the necessary shock of surprised recognition: 'the book just does not tell me what there is in our present mores that I ought to look out for'.[14]

Lorna Sage's review for *The Times Literary Supplement* is largely descriptive and non-committal but declares that Atwood synthesizes a fictionalized future 'with aplomb'. Her significant observation is that Offred seems to struggle to inhabit the imagination of the male characters. Sage argues that, on the one hand, Offred/Atwood (Sage assumes some overlap between character and author on this matter) is rather too sympathetic to the Commander, who is presented to the reader as 'a puzzled, mildly perverse ex-market researcher' who seems to require our understanding. On the other hand, however, Offred's alienated attempt to imagine sexual intercourse from a male perspective – 'To have them putting him on, trying him on, trying him out, while he himself puts them on, like a sock over a foot'[15] – is akin to someone trying to describe the behaviours of a different species; 'Surely', asks Sage, 'even patriarchal male sexuality can't feel *this* strange?'[16]

Like McCarthy, novelist John Updike, writing in *The New Yorker*, has some reservations around the likelihood of Atwood's imagined scenario and suggests that few Americans could take seriously the idea of an armed uprising of the New Right. Overall, however, Updike's review is very appreciative. Noting that futuristic novels are often in danger of rapidly dating, he suggests that *The Handmaid's Tale* is protected from this fate because, among its many critiques and warnings, Atwood has 'threaded a curious poem to the female condition'. Noting the manner in which Offred's life is lived amid the details of shopping and waiting, 'timorous strategizing and sudden bursts of daring', he observes that it provides 'an intensified and darkened version of woman's customary existence'.[17] Crucially, for Updike, Atwood's novel is ultimately far less pessimistic and claustrophobic than *Nineteen Eighty-Four*. Where Orwell's novel shuts down all opposition and is suffused with the author's knowledge of his impending death, Atwood's novel, Updike argues, is instead suffused 'by life – the heroine's irrepressible vitality and the author's lovely subversive hymn to our ordinary life, as lived, amid perils and pollution, now'.[18]

What genre *is* it?

In a 1996 chapter titled 'Science Fiction in the Feminine', Howells suggests that much as Offred's narrative voice evades Gilead's imposed silence, so Atwood's novel 'eludes classification'.[19] Indeed, there have been many attempts to define the novel's genre. If some early reviewers struggled to find the novel's dystopian premise persuasive, Atwood, on the contrary, insists on its rootedness in reality. Howells cites her in an unpublished essay explaining: 'there's nothing in it that we as a species have not done, aren't doing now, or don't have the technological capability to do'[20] – a variation of which formula Atwood has gone on to repeat many times. With such declarations, Atwood deliberately pushes against attempts to locate her dystopian novel within the correlate genre of science fiction. When asked if her novel might be termed science fiction, Atwood responds, quite directly:

> No, it certainly isn't science fiction. Science fiction is filled with Martians and space travel to other planets, and things like that. That isn't this book at all. *The Handmaid's Tale* is speculative fiction in the genre of *Brave New World* and *Nineteen Eighty-Four*. *Nineteen Eighty-Four* was written not as science fiction but as an extrapolation of life in 1948. So, too, *The Handmaid's Tale* is a slight twist on the society we have now.[21]

Commenting on this same early interview, Gina Wisker observes that Atwood's definition of science fiction is deemed by many to be too narrow and prescriptive. (Indeed, Atwood got into a very public debate with science fiction writer Ursula Le Guin about this very matter.[22]) For Wisker, 'the transfer into the future or elsewhere of issues common today is precisely what much science fiction does'.[23]

In a later 2006 essay on *The Handmaid's Tale*, Howells attempts to breach the gap between opposing definitions of science fiction, speculative fiction and dystopia. Reading the 1985 novel in conjunction with the 2003 work, *Oryx and Crake*, Howells examines them both as 'an imaginative writer's response to contemporary situations of cultural crisis' (161). Both texts are evidently working within the realm of dystopia, but in notably different ways: *The Handmaid's Tale*, with its totalitarian state, belongs to a tradition of political dystopias, while *Oryx and Crake* is part of another distinct tradition of post-apocalyptic narratives. For Howells, *Oryx and Crake*, with its overreaching scientist and irresponsible genetic experiments, is firmly embedded in a lineage of science fiction by writers such as Mary Shelley and H. G. Wells, whereas *The Handmaid's Tale* is determinedly of this world. Indeed, its practices are wilfully archaic, harking back as they do to the seventeenth-century Puritans. The distance between the two texts, therefore, seems wide. Howells, however, makes the striking suggestion that *Oryx and Crake* can be read as a kind of sequel to *The Handmaid's Tale*, where elements in the earlier text are accelerated in the later work. And so, the 'pollution and environmental destruction which threatened one region of North America in the earlier novel' have escalated in *Oryx and Crake* 'into worldwide climate change through global warming'. Similarly, the kind of liberal-market mass-consumerism that the morally conservative architects of Gilead violently rejected has metamorphosed, in the future world of *Oryx and Crake*, into the high-tech 'consumerist decadence' that characterizes the later novel.[24]

Atwood uses a dystopian framework to explore contemporary political concerns. While her spectacular vision draws attention to the imagery and the ritual of the regime's extraordinary practices, Barbara Hill Rigney, in her 1987 book, *Margaret Atwood*, focuses on the novel's political realism. Rigney reads *The Handmaid's Tale* in conjunction with *Bodily Harm* and the 1981 poetry collection, *True Stories*, categorizing them as a trio of works concerned with oppression 'in all its manifestations, both physical and psychological'.[25] Like Annette Kolodny's thesis that *Life Before Man* represents a transition in Atwood's work from romance to realism (discussed in the previous chapter), Rigney focuses less on the memorable idiosyncrasies of Atwood's dystopian vision in *The Handmaid's Tale* – the uniforms and the rituals – and more on the manner in which the novel continues the author's developing preoccupation with real-world power and its (all too commonplace) 'universal forms: dictatorship, tyranny, torture and the reality of violence'. For Rigney, there is a clear correlation between Rennie's decision at the end of *Bodily Harm* to report the truth of what she has witnessed and Offred's subversive eye-witness account of the Gilead regime's atrocities. In this manner, Rigney's work exemplifies a strand of critical readings of *The Handmaid's Tale* that locate it within the realms of political witness, testimonial or survival narratives.

While *The Handmaid's Tale* is Atwood's first extended foray into dystopian fiction – a form that will become increasingly prevalent in her work over the coming decades – it nevertheless betrays a familiar interest in genre subversion. In its speculations around Ofglen and Nick's shadowy affiliations, it functions as a spy thriller, while Offred's red cape and basket mark her as a fairy-tale Little Red Riding Hood surrounded by wolves. It is also a romance of sorts, charting Offred and Nick's developing relationship. Examining Atwood's use of the romance plot in *The Handmaid's Tale*, Madonne Miner notes that, for many critics, love in the novel is a subversive force, providing an intimate site of resistance against the regime's authority. While acknowledging that such readings are persuasive, Miner argues instead that the novel exposes 'love's tendency to follow decidedly conservative narrative forms'.[26]

Miner observes that Offred strives to separate and distinguish between the three significant men in her life: Luke, the Commander and Nick. At one point, she declares: 'They cannot be exchanged, one for the other' (198). However, argues Miner, despite her best efforts, the three men increasingly merge and blur in the text. In particular, Atwood draws attention to similarities between Luke and the Commander: both men are interested in language; both say that women are incapable of abstract thought (Luke in a light-hearted manner, the Commander in all seriousness); Offred suspects that Luke rather enjoys her new dependence on him, much as the Commander later does; and both men take Offred to the same hotel to cheat on their wives with her. When the regime starts to strip women of their rights, Offred suddenly realizes that her relationship with Luke has fundamentally changed: 'We are not each other's, anymore. Instead, I am his' (188). This inequality stifles honesty and trust within their once equitable relationship in a manner that is echoed and intensified in her later relationship with the Commander, in which she is entirely supplicant to his whims. *The Handmaid's Tale*, argues Miner, 'provides us with two male characters who mirror one another; structurally, these two are twins'.[27]

The similarities between Luke and the Commander, argues Miner, cast doubt on Offred's love story with Luke, 'but also upon love stories more generally'.[28] Consequently, while Luke and Nick appear very different, the reader must be alert to potential connections. Notably, just as Luke discourages Offred from attending a women's protest march, so Offred's affair with Nick lessens her interest in Ofglen and the resistance. Romance, it seems, diminishes Offred's political commitment. As Miner observes, when Offred first describes her sexual encounter with Nick, she instinctively reaches for the language of romance novels of the kind that Joan Foster writes in *Lady Oracle*: 'I can hardly breathe [. . .] his mouth is on me [. . .] I'm alive in my skin, again, arms around him, falling' (269). For Tae Yamamoto, discussing the difficulties of reading *The Handmaid's Tale* as a feminist, such scenes are indicative of the manner in which Offred seems frustratingly willing to 'niche herself so meekly into a banal romance plot'.[29] Offred remains, argues Miner, trapped within 'a limited number of scripts'.[30] Unable to conceive of a scenario that exists outside of the traditional romance plot, Offred ignores the alternative script potentially being offered by Ofglen and Mayday – one of resistance and self-determination – and remains instead a passive princess awaiting her rescuing prince.

Writing about feminism in the 1980s

Atwood's fictions commonly engage with feminist debates, particularly in their depiction of women's entrapment within conservative narrative structures. *The Handmaid's Tale* goes further than her previous novels, however, in its explicit commentary on the contemporary feminist movement. Consequently, the nature of the novel's feminist intent has been the object of much critical scrutiny. When asked in an early interview for *The New York Times* if the novel is 'a feminist tract', Atwood was unsurprisingly dismissive of the idea, responding promptly: 'Novels are not slogans [. . .] If I wanted to say just one thing I would hire a billboard.' *The Handmaid's Tale*, suggests Atwood, is concerned with questions of 'power, and how it operates and how it deforms or shapes the people who are living within that kind of regime'. Repeatedly, in such discussions, she looks to redirect focus away from the text as a feminist work and towards a broader conception of the novel's concern with human rights, and the degradation of individual freedoms within the apparatus of a totalitarian state.[31]

This somewhat defensive response chimes with Atwood's longstanding reluctance to be claimed as an advocate for the second-wave feminist movement. Shirley Neuman makes this same point in her article, '"Just a Backlash": Margaret Atwood, Feminism and *The Handmaid's Tale*', in which she traces the lineage of the author's relationship with feminism. While Atwood was, from the start of her novel-writing career, enthusiastically taken up by feminist critics, she often felt that the label was too easily used to mischaracterize her work. She frequently attempted to qualify her understanding of what feminism entails or to reiterate that it does not preclude her advocacy of other interests. Neuman, for example, cites an interview from 1985 in which Atwood defines her feminism along the lines of universal human rights and cautions: 'if practical, hardline, anti-male feminists took over and became the government, I would resist them.'[32]

To understand such seemingly melodramatic concerns, it is necessary to have a sense of the contemporary moment in which Atwood was writing. As Wisker notes, the novel was published at the height of second-wave feminism, and Atwood's preoccupations are with some of the foremost issues of her day: 'women's lives, freedoms, procreation and rights over their own bodies'. Wisker also notes that the 1980s was 'a period of the rise of fundamentalist religious regimes, especially in Iran, which Atwood visited just prior to writing the novel'.[33] So Atwood's sense of what can happen when women's rights are eroded is very real. Similarly, Theodore Sheckels in *The Political in Margaret Atwood's Fiction* (2012) suggests that the 1990s setting of Offred's pre-Gilead life depicts some of the nascent elements of Atwood's own 1980s society come to fruition. Heightened casual violence against women is met by a rising fanatical feminism, and the government and the police 'seem powerless to stop either the violence directed against women or the increasingly angry reactions by women'. (Indeed, moving beyond the timeframe of the novel, Sheckels observes that Atwood's vision of the ubiquitous 'PornoMarts' industry has in fact come to pass in our own time, albeit in then unimagined digital form: 'not on street corners but on the Internet'.) Sheckels proposes that, in Atwood's very-near-future world of the imagined 1990s, fear of a rising militant women's movement is a large part of what prompts the misogynistic founders of Gilead to enact their patriarchal revolution.[34]

The mid-1980s was a period of transition and reflection for feminism, as a second generation inherited the women's movement of the 1970s and took it in new directions. The 1980s also saw a concerted attack on feminist gains orchestrated by the conservative New Right in America, as closely documented by Susan Faludi in her 1991 polemic, *Backlash: The Undeclared War against American Women*.[35] For Neuman, this cultural context is crucial to understanding *The Handmaid's Tale*, which she describes as 'a fictional realization of the backlash against women's rights that gathered force during the early 1980s'.[36] This was a period in which the 'Moral Majority', galvanized by the Televangelists and the increasingly militant anti-abortion movement, mounted a sustained attack on feminism and attempted to row back on hard-won equality legislation. Offred, as Neuman notes, belongs to a generation that, 'in the confidence born of their mothers' success [. . .] asserted that they didn't need feminism'.[37] A similar observation is made by Greene, who notes that Offred 'grew up as a postfeminist'. For both critics, a key lesson that Offred learns as a Handmaid involves reassessing her mother and their often difficult relationship. For Greene, the revelation, however, is left to 'the thoughtful reader', who 'takes the mother's feminism more seriously than the condescending daughter'.[38] Neuman instead notes that, in her interior life, Offred engages in 'a rich dialogue' with her mother in which she is finally able 'to acknowledge some of the ways in which her mother was right'.[39]

In 'Feminist Utopias and Questions of Liberty: Margaret Atwood's *The Handmaid's Tale* as Critique of Second-Wave Feminism', I also examine the manner in which Atwood reflects on contemporary feminism in her novel. Key to understanding the often-anxious feminist politics of *The Handmaid's Tale*, I argue, is a recognition of the high regard in which Atwood holds the correlate notions of liberty and free will. At times, these principles run up against the collectivist spirit of second-wave feminism, which famously called women to 'sisterhood'. In Atwood's novel, pressures towards conformity and group identity (made most visible in the colour-coded uniforms of the various social groups) are totalitarian in nature and to be resisted. Atwood also remains sceptical of the utopian impulse inherent in second-wave feminism which was, ultimately, an attempt to reimagine the world as a better place. Atwood, however, cautions that utopian aims can unintentionally lead to dystopian consequences, and *The Handmaid's Tale* 'depicts a society that has unconsciously and paradoxically met certain feminist demands'.[40]

Unexpected sympathies between the principles of the feminist movement and the actions of the Gilead regime recur throughout the novel. When Aunt Lydia shows the Handmaids old video clips of sadistic pornography, she asks them: 'You see what things used to be like? That was what they thought of women, then' (124). As I point out in my article, in eradicating pornography, Gilead 'has realized a feminist goal'.[41] This deliberate, sardonic echo of feminist ideology is further reinforced in what Greene terms the 'spooky resemblance' between the feminists' bonfire of pornography, which Offred recalls attending as a child with her mother, and the regime's fascist policy of book-burnings, 'house-to-house searches, bonfires' (162). Similarly, Aunt Lydia's vision of 'Women united for a common end! Helping one another in their daily chores as they walk the path of life together' (167) apes the language of the feminist project. For Greene, Atwood demonstrates that the 'feminist sentimentalization of women's bodies and "women's work" produces new forms of old stereotypes'.[42] Atwood's novel is not anti-feminist, but it advises readers to 'defend liberty before ideology'.[43] For Neuman, a women's utopia is not to be found in *The Handmaid's Tale*, either in Gilead, or in the time before: 'It exists outside of the "either/or" thinking so beloved of Aunt Lydia, and outside the world of the novel.'[44] Atwood, suggests Neuman, does not offer us a utopia, but she does caution the reader to stay vigilant and prepare to bear witness.

Offred's storytelling: Language and narrative

While Atwood's novel is sceptical of some of the developments in the feminist movement of the 1980s, the narrative structure of her novel, in which a disenfranchised woman speaks her story in defiance of the patriarchal state, naturally lends itself to a mode of feminist-engaged critical analysis. Gender typically plays a large part in critical analyses of Offred's storytelling, although the complexities and nuances of Atwood's narrative form have inspired multiple and various close readings. As Marta Dvorak notes, the novel's structure is complex, 'involving multiple producers and receivers', and frequently blurs the distinction between fact and fiction.[45] Forced into silence and isolation, Offred resorts to constructing a fictive listener: '*Dear You*, I'll say. Just *you*, without a name. [. . .] *You* can mean thousands. [. . .] I'll pretend you can hear me' (46). Offred's narrative also contains the stories of many other women within her own. In this manner, argues Howells, she creates 'the impression of a multi-voiced narrative which undermines Gilead's myth of women's silence and submissiveness'.[46] In addition to this multiplicity, Offred's tale contains many self-conscious reflections on the veracity of her narrative, on the nature of her interlocuter and on the reliability of her memory. At different times, she variously admits: 'I made that up. It didn't happen that way. Here is what happened' (269). For Dvorak, such interjections serve to highlight the fact that 'history too is an invention, a collage, a subjectively pieced-together text'.[47] In these instances and more, *The Handmaid's Tale* invites and rewards close careful analysis of its uses of language and narrative form.

In an analysis that focuses on the gender politics of Offred's narrative, Mario Klarer examines the oral nature of her tale. Noting that the banning of books is a common trope in dystopian fiction, he suggests that *The Handmaid's Tale* adapts this 'dichotomy of literacy and orality' in a notably gendered way. In Atwood's novel, the imposition of an oral culture on women becomes another means of asserting power. Orality is used by the regime to cement its authority and as a way of 'eliminating the destabilizing potential inherent in literature'.[48] Klarer notes the importance of literacy in Offred's pre-Gileadean life in which she worked as a librarian and her friend Moira worked for a feminist publishing house. When the regime seizes power, this close female engagement with language comes under sustained attack as it systematically dismantles the structures of literacy, abolishing journalism, publishing presses and libraries, and forbidding women to read or write. Reflecting on the specifically gendered significance of this push to orality, Klarer observes some significant distinctions between oral and literate cultures, specifically the manner in which orality necessitates a close proximity between speaker and listener, while written communication allows spatial distance between author and reader. Orality traps Offred in a kind of present tense, denying her the time and space to develop a wider perspective. While the 'archaeological character' of a literate culture enables a documented history to accrue, the immediacy of oral culture is fleeting, preventing historical thinking. For Klarer, these various elements of orality combine with the intention 'to make female criticism of a system impossible'. Atwood, he suggests, champions literacy as a means to resist tyranny.[49]

Examining the nature of Offred's 'pieced-together text', Wisker concentrates on Atwood's playful exploration of language and its power. She observes that ironies and subtexts proliferate in the text. For example, the regime's chosen term for servants overlooks the fact that the dutiful Martha of the Bible was admonished by Christ for failing to recognize what is truly important (while her sister Mary, who neglected to serve, was praised). Wisker also reflects on the unintended allusions conjured by 'the Red Centre': a term intended to indicate a site of submission and indoctrination, but which also suggests 'blood, power, violence, fertility'.[50] As Laflen noted when discussing fascist imagery, the regime uses and abuses language to impose its ideology. Through its many euphemisms and neologisms, it works to corrupt language so that words reverse and obscure rather than reveal meaning. For example, as Wisker observes, '[s]alvagings are also a form of control; they are not strictly about salvaging which is a form of rescue and rehabilitation, but instead about destroying'.[51] But language, as Wisker demonstrates, is slippery and elusive and often works against official intentions to become unexpectedly subversive. By using and musing on language, Offred's story resists the limits and manipulations of the regime; it offers an alternative perspective and utilizes a richly allusive, nuanced discourse that exists beyond the limits of the totalitarian vision. Echoing Dvorak's point, Wisker argues that Offred's habit of self-consciously foregrounding the processes of her storytelling exposes the manner in which histories are simply 'versions of events that are legitimated'.[52]

The elements of irony in Offred's narrative, which Wisker reads as disruptive and subversive, are taken up by Jennifer Wagner-Lawlor, who proposes that, on first sight, 'Offred's narrative is simply too ironic'. For readers looking for a sincere feminist politics, Offred's discourse is too self-consciously artful, non-committal and unremitting. Irony is employed in the text through black humour and wordplay, through incongruities and discrepancies between surface meaning and reality. Verbal irony pervades the text as Offred becomes increasingly alert to both 'the satisfactions and the risks of using it'.[53] When Offred tests the new Ofglen's allegiances with an oblique reference to 'May Day', her sudden intuition that Ofglen recognizes the codeword but is not a sympathizer leaves her horribly shaken at the danger to which she has exposed herself: 'I walk the last blocks in terror. I've been stupid' (297). At the same time, despite such risks, what Wagner-Lawlor terms 'ironic double talk' enables those trapped within the regime to communicate illicitly: to use sanctioned phrases to transmit submerged coded meanings. When messages are successfully exchanged in this manner, it opens up 'a small space of freedom' in Offred's world. Like Wisker, Wagner-Lawson suggests that the multiplicity and mobility of irony resist the kind of monologic fixity of totalitarian discourse. Irony opens up 'gaps' in Gilead's defences, providing 'spaces for negotiation'.[54]

Dvorak also focuses on narrative as a mode of resistance. In her essay, she examines *The Handmaid's Tale* as a postmodern text. She identifies a number of postmodern narrative strategies at work: for example, the way in which Offred's self-conscious narrative repeatedly draws attention to its own constructedness with lines such as 'There wasn't any thunder though, I added that in' (269). Dvorak further points to the novel's 'fractured time sequence, its embedding and doubling back, its gaps and blanks, its hesitations and multiple variants of the same event' as postmodern techniques. Through its frequent, complex use of analepsis and prolepsis (flashback and flashforward), the novel exposes and problematizes the way that we see the world. This, explains Dvorak, is part of the larger postmodern challenge to traditional constraints on perspective, 'such as linearity, causality or textual closure'. Removing the comforting security of verisimilitude exposes the ideological constructedness of the systems we inhabit, which we otherwise assume are natural and inevitable. For example, by providing multiple contradictory versions of the same scene – the three versions of what really happened to Luke, or the three versions of her first sexual encounter with Nick – Offred's narrative works to 'question the authenticity of any one image, of any one "truth"'. Within a totalitarian state, which insists on there being only one, unopposable way of being, multiplicity, ambiguity and contradiction become powerfully subversive narrative techniques.[55]

In Gilead, Offred's narrative – feminine, intimate, unauthorized – is relegated to the margins and to the private, domestic spaces that persist within the patriarchal, dystopian society of Gilead. As Greene observes, Offred's marginalized status impacts on the reader's comprehension of events. Because of her low status in the social hierarchy, 'she does not see the total picture', and consequently we, who can only know what she knows, 'share her bewilderment and disorientation'.[56] Nevertheless, as Howells notes, 'Offred asserts her right to tell her story'. For Howells, the novel is a 'survival narrative'. Like Rennie in *Bodily Harm*, Offred provides an eye-witness account of the atrocities committed by power. In defiance of the many limitations placed on her voice, Offred constructs a female-centred 'herstory' that successfully overshadows the dominant patriarchal history of the regime and thereby 'relegates the grand narratives to the margins as mere framework for her story'.[57] Offred's narrative is a rebellion against the state, but it is also a reclamation of her own existence as a thinking, feeling subject. To the state, Handmaids are merely 'two-legged wombs' (142). In telling her own story, Offred insists instead 'on chronicling her subjective life from within her own skin'.[58]

In her examination of Offred's narrative, Yamamoto picks up on a number of the concerns just discussed and reflects on the extent to which Offred seems able to resist the totalizing narrative of the Gilead regime. For Yamamoto, there are moments in the text when Offred's perceptions seem closely assimilated with the regime, for example when she succumbs to the hypnotic ritual of the birthing ceremony. At other points, instead, Offred works hard to maintain a critical distance on Gilead's doctrine. When Offred is at her most critical and circumspect, the distance between her and the implied author, suggests Yamamoto, is very narrow. When instead she is 'unaware that she is under the sway of predominant cultural discourses', that distance becomes much greater. For Yamamoto, one of the frustrations for feminist readers of *The Handmaid's Tale* is the absence of a feminist alternative to either the repressive Gilead regime or the highly sexualized consumer culture of Offred's past. Tying this frustration to Offred's narrative, she suggests that the author points us towards recognizing that when Offred is able to maintain a critical distance from the persuasive rhetoric of the oppressive regime, while she may still be prisoner of the regime in those moments, she is nevertheless freer than when she simply succumbs to its will. As Yamamoto puts it, the novel tells us: 'we cannot go out of our language system, but we can know what kind of system we are in'. This then, for Yamamoto, provides the reply to the feminist's dilemma: like Offred, with whom we are encouraged to empathize, we must recognize that even when our capacity for action is limited, we must remain critical and aware if we are to have any chance of effecting change.[59]

Complicity, victimhood and responsibility

As Allan Weiss observes in an article that examines Offred's complicity with the state, there are three dominant critical readings regarding the nature of her engagement with the Gilead regime: she is either 'a valiant rebel', a 'powerless victim', or a 'willing or unwitting participant'. For those that would term her a rebel fighting against the regime's oppressive tyranny, most, working in the mould of those discussed in the previous section, cite her storytelling as an act of subversive resistance. For Weiss, however, such readings, which commonly assert the capacity of language to effect change, generally ignore the fact that Offred's narrative changes nothing. After her departure, the regime continues to operate, and indeed, according to the Historical Notes at the end, it gets worse.⁶⁰ Addressing the second reading, Weiss cites critics such as J. Brooks Bouson, for whom Offred is 'the victim of circumstances, not an active agent capable of directing the plot of her own life'.⁶¹ These readings, he suggests, fail to account for the ambiguities of power in the novel and the limited forms of resistance that Offred does engage in. Weiss instead places Offred within a lineage of 'heroes' of twentieth-century dystopian fiction, few of whom are heroic. In much the same way as many of these predecessors, Offred is exposed as a participant in the processes of her own oppression. Reflecting on her life before Gilead, she admits: 'We lived, as usual, by ignoring. Ignoring isn't the same as ignorance, you have to work at it' (66). For Weiss, this failure to act underpins Atwood's main point: totalitarian regimes arise when the population is too complacent or scared to resist. Consequently, Offred's 'cowardice and complicity convict us all'.⁶²

Where Weiss suggests that Offred's guilt is collectively shared, other critics more directly interrogate and condemn her role and choices in the text. In an interesting instance of careful close reading, Patricia Stapleton, in an essay entitled 'Suicide as Apocalypse in *The Handmaid's Tale*', searches the novel for clues as to what may have happened to Offred after her story has been recorded and concludes that she most probably kills herself. As supporting evidence, Stapleton points to an elliptical, embedded vignette in Offred's narrative in which she recalls, as a young child, watching a documentary about the Second World War. While most of Offred's memories are hazy, she remembers in some detail an interview with the mistress of a Nazi concentration camp supervisor. Photographed lounging by the pool, just a short distance from the camp, the woman 'denied knowing about the ovens'; asked about her lover, she replies 'He was not a monster' (151). Later, when Offred is having sex with the Commander at Jezebel's nightclub, she will think to herself: 'He is not a monster' (263). For Stapleton, this echo purposely draws a parallel between Offred and the Nazi mistress. In Gilead, musing on the other woman's proximity to such unthinkable atrocities, Offred wonders what she could have been thinking, and then answers her own question: 'She was thinking about how not to think. The times were abnormal.' The documentary, Offred recalls, included the final notice: 'Several days after this interview with her was filmed, she killed herself' (152). Stapleton argues that this suicide, in conjunction with the mirroring of Offred and the previous Offred, who also kills herself, provides a coded indication in the novel of Offred's probable fate. Just as the Nazi mistress, once she has told her tale and accounted for her complicity through inaction, realizes that 'there is nothing left', so, suggests Stapleton, after recounting her tale of being a 'Gileadean mistress', in order to 'reclaim her autonomy and to atone for her complicity, Offred takes her own life'.[63]

Stapleton charges Offred with complicity, which is a complicated notion in the novel. As Offred concedes, 'There wasn't a lot of choice but there was some, and this is what I chose' (105). For Neuman, examining the ethics of Offred's engagement with the regime, there is a qualitative difference between Offred's acquiescence to the role of Handmaid, given the severely limited 'choices' available to her, and her subsequent account of playing Scrabble with the Commander, which 'renders him both human and comic'.[64] Other instances in the novel are still more problematic. Attending a 'particicution' of an alleged rapist, Offred admits that she succumbs to group hysteria and is overwhelmed by 'bloodlust; I want to tear, gouge, rend' (287). For Neuman, the novel involves Offred coming to terms with her own complicity within the structures of the regime. Her political awakening, however, stumbles when it meets the burgeoning relationship with Nick. Like Miner, who examines the romance plot in the novel with some scepticism, Neuman reads the relationship, and the 'rescue' at the end, as an act of self-preservation rather than romance. Like Miner, she also notes that Nick distracts Offred from Ofglen and Mayday, and that Offred chooses romance over resistance. For Neuman, by the end of the novel, Offred finally recognizes that she has relapsed into 'willed ignorance', and this realization 'partly motivates the shame that so strongly marks her narrative' towards the end.[65] When the dreaded black van suddenly appears, Offred understands, too late, that she 'should have paid attention' (301).

The question of collaboration and guilt is also addressed by Rigney, who extends the charge of complicity beyond the actors within the Gilead regime to the members of Offred's former, pre-Gilead society. Like Rennie in *Bodily Harm*, Offred and her pre-Gilead contemporaries prefer not to look too closely at what is happening around them. When the President is shot and Congress is massacred, a stunned Offred can only ineffectually ask, 'How did they get in, how did it happen?' (179). For Rigney, Offred's entire society is guilty of complacent inattention, and it pays a deadly cost. Offred, like Rennie, believes herself to be innocent and powerless and retreats in the face of growing oppression and both characters reflect Atwood's longstanding concern that 'victimisation, in a real sense, is at least partly a matter of choice'. While Offred is inarguably a victim of a violent and oppressive misogynistic regime, Atwood contests that male aggression does not absolve women of their own actions or inactions.

This assertion is most visible in the strata of female control that the state inserts within the edifice of its security systems. Both Aunts and Wives display their capacity for cruelty; both factions participate with enthusiasm in the brutalizing and dehumanizing of other women. For Atwood, clearly, no group – whether defined by gender, race, religion or any other characteristic – can be deemed exempt from complicity or blame. Rigney argues that, ultimately, like all of Atwood's previous heroines, 'Offred values her own physical survival above sisterhood, and in so doing sacrifices her own integrity'. Unlike Moira, whom Rigney identifies as the sole heroic woman in the novel, Offred retreats into self-preservation and thus sacrifices her liberty. For Rigney, Offred's eventual decision to defy the regime, to record her testimony and perform as a witness to atrocity is, finally, a recognition that political engagement is not a choice but 'a human responsibility'. With the act of bearing witness, Offred finally makes a commitment to her society, and to her own humanity.[66]

Reading the conclusion

The Handmaid's Tale is a deeply claustrophobic novel. Offred's liberty and agency are circumscribed at every turn. It is, therefore, suggests Howells, particularly pleasing to discover in the 'Historical Notes' on which the novel concludes that 'it is Offred the silenced Handmaid who becomes Gilead's principal historian'.[67] At the same time, there remains an unresolved tension in *The Handmaid's Tale* between the immediacy and power of Offred's present-tense narrative, and the distance and limitation imposed on her 'tale' when it becomes the past-tense history of the novel's eventually-revealed frame narrative. Having concluded on the deep ambiguity of Offred's final line – 'And so I step up, into the darkness within; or else the light.' (303) – the reader is abruptly wrenched from Offred's dystopian world into the civilized rituals of an academic conference being held in the Arctic region almost 200 years later. The implications of this shift are myriad and have prompted much critical reflection.

Through the keynote paper being delivered by Professor Pieixoto, a historian and expert in Gileadean Studies, Atwood fills in some of the missing details regarding the delivery and reproduction of Offred's story. We learn that the narrative that comprises the text of 'The Handmaid's Tale' was discovered in fragmented recordings in a box of approximately thirty jumbled cassette tapes. Pieixoto and his colleague transcribed the recordings and determined their correct sequence 'based on some guesswork [. . .] pending further research'

(310). Nothing more is discovered about Offred herself, including her name or her eventual fate, although the fact of the tapes' existence suggests that she at the very least managed to reach some kind of safe house where she was able to record her testimony. Discussing this frame narrative, Stapleton concludes of Offred: 'history will not be kind to her, and her narrative will not be understood'. Just as in the Gilead regime women are interchangeable – 'Offred for Offred, Ofglen for Ofglen' – so in the Historical Notes it is apparent that the scholars of the future have failed to identify the speaker and that she will remain forever the anonymous 'Handmaid'.[68]

In a 1988 essay, 'Future Tense: Making History in *The Handmaid's Tale*', Arnold Davidson focuses closely on the novel's epilogue and presents an alternative reading to Stapleton's. *The Handmaid's Tale*, he notes, offers 'two different projected futures': the future regime of Gilead and the second, later future depicted in the Historical Notes.[69] The purpose of the epilogue, he suggests, is manifold: it gives 'the history of Offred's history' (an explanation of how her private account became a public document); it provides some external scrutiny of Offred's intimate, insular version of events; it supplies theoretical context to the Gilead regime (observing, for example, that the Aunts were a 'cost-effective' security measure); and it also, crucially, signifies hope: the conference is evidence that Gilead eventually fell.[70] This latter point is endorsed by Atwood, who states that the existence of Offred's narrative means that 'The possibility of escape exists. [. . .] Her little message in a bottle has gotten through to someone – which is about all we can hope, isn't it?'[71]

In addition to such productive functions, however, Davidson also suggests that there is 'something ominous' in the authoritative, masculine, academic tone of the final section. Pieixoto's lecture implicitly assumes that a 'Retrospective analysis by a Cambridge don – male, of course – is ostensibly more authoritative than a participant woman's eyewitness account' (114). Also discussing the epilogue, Hilde Staels notes that, although Offred repeatedly insists that neither the objective truth nor her full experience can be related, the historians persist in trying to reconstruct a complete factual account of her time in Gilead. Despite Offred's characterization of her tale as a reconstruction, prone to misrememberings and ambiguity, the historians are in pursuit of 'closed interpretations'.[72] Pieixoto's academic voice valorizes 'objectivity' in assessing an account in which women and all minorities have been brutally objectified by the state, with real consequences. For Staels, the conference paper represents an 'ironic repetition of Gileadean discourse' – a kind of 'supreme rationalism' that precludes empathy.[73] Furthermore, Howells also suggests that the epilogue works to shock us into realizing that we are implicated in this final scene: the fact that we have access to Pieixoto's 2195 lecture suggests that we are of his time, rather than Offred's. The narrative's temporal shift, she suggests, 'challenges the reader on questions of interpretation', forcing us to reflect on what assumptions we bring to Offred's story.[74]

Like the rest of the novel, the Historical Notes repay close attention. The conference in the Arctic circle offers a new vision of a further future. Unlike the rest of America in Offred's time, the northern region, it seems, is not massively polluted (as Howells notes, the participants are invited on a nature walk and a fishing trip), and many of the participants are Native Peoples (Professor Crescent Moon and Professor Running Dog). Davidson, however, observes that, while the unpolluted far north 'has apparently become the seat of power in North America', gendered power hierarchies clearly persist. Discussing the perpetuation of patriarchal systems, he points to the sexual innuendo and mildly sexist jokes that litter Pieixoto's presentation. Pieixoto assumes that Offred's passive domestic role within the regime is of less significance than the active role of the masculine resistance movement and regrets that it is her story that has survived, rather than that of someone more important. The Professor trivializes Offred's account, argues Davidson, because he assumes that women's lives are inherently trivial. Misogyny, it appears, persists far into the foreseeable future. In some ways, suggests Davidson, the Historical Notes provide a kind of 'comic relief' after the claustrophobia of Offred's traumatized narrative, but in crucial ways – specifically, in how it diminishes, re-objectifies and marginalizes Offred's voice – 'the epilogue is the most pessimistic part of the book'.[75]

Tellingly, Offred appears to have foreseen this erasure. Reflecting on the absence of Handmaids in family photo albums, she thinks 'From the point of view of future history [. . .] we'll be invisible' (236). Howells, however, argues against this pessimistic conclusion. Although she observes that Pieixoto 'is abusing Offred as Gilead abused her', she points out that Offred's voice survives. Even when delivered to us through the frame of Pieixoto's masculine academic presentation, which always threatens to drown out Offred's voice, the interest of the tale is sustained by Offred's ability to capture our attention: 'This is history written in the feminine gender'. For Howells, just as Offred's resistive story shows up the limits of Gilead's authority, 'so it defies Pieixoto's appropriation 200 years later'. If Pieixoto's account gives us pause – if we are dissatisfied by his framing of Offred's experience – it is her voice that calls us to reflect on his method. Howells also points to a resonant pun in the location of the conference in 'Denay, Nunavit'; to 'deny none of it' is, she suggests, 'a piece of authorial advice to the reader to believe Offred's story, no matter what interpretations or misinterpretations might be offered in the Historical Notes'.[76]

With the later expansion of her interest in dystopian writing, most notably in the *MaddAddam* trilogy, as well as the publication of *The Testaments*, her unexpected return to Gilead, *The Handmaid's Tale* will later go on to garner new connections and parallels in Atwood's canon. Immediately after its publication, however, Atwood seems to return to something closer to the kind of fiction she was writing previously. Unlike *The Handmaid's Tale*, with its near-future setting and far-future frame narrative, she situates her next two novels in the more familiar present-day Toronto that features in so many of her early works.

4

Spotty-handed villainesses
Cat's Eye and *The Robber Bride*

Following the publication of *The Handmaid's Tale*, Atwood produced a number of substantial novels that extend and develop her characteristic themes and concerns, and which cumulatively signal the work of a mature and ambitious writer at the height of her powers. In this chapter, I examine some of the critical responses to two of those works. *Cat's Eye* and *The Robber Bride* both return Atwood firmly to the Toronto settings that she knows so well; both are set in the contemporary moment but are predominantly comprised of retrospective narratives that take their protagonists variously back through the 1950s, 1960s, 1970s and 1980s. These analepses unfold in a manner that allows Atwood to ventriloquize the quotidian past in all its sensual and ephemeral details: a process at which she excels. They are also, notably, novels of female bad behaviour. In this, they can be readily connected to Atwood's subsequent novel, *Alias Grace*, although for the organizational purposes of this volume, I examine that 1996 work alongside Atwood's historical fictions.

Atwood's fictions of the late 1980s and 1990s are commonly read together. For Marion Wynne-Davies, this period is characterized by a return to the themes of the author's earlier works. In novels such as *Cat's Eye*, *The Robber Bride* and *Alias Grace* there is, she suggests, evidence of 'a dramatic revisionist reframing of gender, politics, time, space and the role of the author'. For Wynne-Davies, this phase in Atwood's writing is notably introspective, as the author retreats from her earlier concerns with large questions of national identity and gender identity, and instead focuses more closely on 'the inner, concealed discourses of individual and collective memory'.[1] Karen Stein similarly observes that the texts from this period revisit familiar Atwoodian themes, of which she particularly identifies a preoccupation with 'Gothic quests, female friendship, victims, doubles and doubling, memory, myth, and storytelling'.[2] Alice Palumbo, in an essay for Reingard Nischik's collection *Margaret Atwood: Works and*

Impact (2000), sees these same works as being connected by dominant themes of memory and the past. Like Wynne-Davis, Palumbo also identifies a turn away from the kind of examination of 'macro power relations' that occurs in *Bodily Harm* and *The Handmaid's Tale* towards a more intimate focus in the following three novels on 'an analysis of power in women's relationships, and the conflict between the conscious and unconscious, and memory and the present'.[3]

Alongside such notable recurring examinations of memory, friendship and similar topics, *Cat's Eye* and *The Robber Bride*, like *Alias Grace*, most strikingly foreground the trope of what Atwood has termed 'spotty-handed villainesses': a concept that informs a significant amount of criticism on her mid-career fictions. Barbara Hill Rigney, for example, writing in 2000, observes: 'Mostly men do terrible things to women in Atwood's fictions, but increasingly and particularly in the most recent novels, women do them to each other.'[4] The term itself is taken from an essay Atwood wrote, entitled 'Spotty-Handed Villainesses: Problems of Female Bad Behaviour in the Creation of Literature'. Originally delivered as a lecture in 1993 – the same year she published *The Robber Bride* – it was later collected in *Curious Pursuits* (2005), an anthology of Atwood's occasional writings. In the essay, Atwood discusses what it means to write female villains and asks: 'is it not, today – well, somehow *unfeminist* – to depict a woman behaving badly?'[5] The question, of course, is rhetorical, and Atwood decidedly rejects the proposition. Arguing against what she identifies as a kind of misguided second-wave feminist compulsion to depict women as inherently morally superior to men, Atwood suggests that the beatification of women is merely another form of misogyny, confining women to a pedestal of Victorian virtue – or in Atwood's words, to the 'salt-mines of goodness' – while granting men free reign to be 'gleefully and enjoyably worse than women'.[6] On the contrary, for Atwood, the depiction of evil women in literature is a vital acknowledgement that women too 'are fully dimensional human beings' that justify and require nuanced literary expression.[7]

Accordingly, Atwood's novels at this time closely explore manifestations of female treachery, aggression and malevolence. From Aunt Lydia in *The Handmaid's Tale* to Penelope in *The Penelopiad*, Atwood's female protagonists frequently commit acts of breathtaking cruelty against other women, but the two novels under discussion here arguably represent the pinnacle of the theme. As Wynne-Davies observes, the 'villainesses' of this period challenge feminist ideals of sisterhood and solidarity. Connecting Cordelia in *Cat's Eye* to Grace in *Alias Grace*, both of whom are incarcerated in a lunatic asylum, she cites Atwood's 1993 essay in observing that each of these characters, rather than being termed 'mad', might be better described, much like Zenia in *The Robber Bride*, as 'a woman behaving badly'. In these novels, suggests Wynne-Davies, Atwood draws on literary archetypes taken from myth and fairy tale (wicked witches, evil twins, ugly sisters), but rewrites these figures as 'attractive, sympathetic and realistic characters'.[8] Questions of realism and sympathy prompt different critical responses in analyses of *Cat's Eye* and *The Robber Bride*, but it is certainly true that both Cordelia and Zenia are able to enact their treachery in large part because of their ability to attract and charm their victims.

Cat's Eye

If *The Handmaid's Tale* performed a peculiar feat in depicting Offred's experience of an authoritarian patriarchal regime as a deeply woman-centred and domestic affair, Atwood's next novel does something similar. Growing up in the conservative, patriarchal 1950s era of working fathers and stay-at-home mothers, Elaine's world, while putatively ruled and ordered by men, is, in its lived experience, almost entirely shaped by women and girls. And as in *The Handmaid's Tale*, Atwood proposes that, afforded a little power within a structure that largely renders women powerless, there can be no assurance that women will behave better than men; indeed, given psychological pressures and the perverse incentives of an unequal system, they may well behave even worse.

In an interview, Atwood reflects on the risks of writing *Cat's Eye*, which depicts the claustrophobic world of pre-adolescent female friendships: 'wouldn't I be trashed', she recalls worrying, 'for writing about little *girls*, how trivial?'[9] The novel, however, works against the dismissal of female experience. As Molly Hite observes, *Cat's Eye* – like *Bodily Harm* and *The Handmaid's Tale* – 'is set in an environment of extremity, where the central concern is not merely well-being but survival'.[10] The visceral violence that Hite detects in the novel is in knowing discordance with its middle-class suburban setting. In the same interview, Atwood remarks that writing *Cat's Eye* provided her with an opportunity to indulge in a rich reconstruction of the materiality of her own 1950s childhood: the paper dolls, the Eaton's catalogues and the comic books. Writing this largely forgotten ephemera back into evocative being provides for a text that she terms 'elegiac'.[11] The comforting nostalgia of childhood, however, is brutally undercut in a novel in which little girls, innocent in their white socks and Mary Janes, also sport 'assessing eyes' and 'slippery deceitful smiles' like little Lady Macbeths (113).

Overview

Cat's Eye commences with Elaine Risley, a successful artist, happily married with two grown-up daughters and living in British Columbia, returning for the first time in many years to her hometown of Toronto to attend a retrospective of her work being held by a Toronto art gallery. The present-day narrative takes place over the few days of Elaine's trip, but the retrospective narrative that it contains spins back over the years of her childhood and adolescence. In an article that examines the fantastic in the novel, Julie Brown refers to this as the 'dream time' of the narrative, when Elaine 'wander[s] through a retrospective showing of her life'.[12] Each section of the novel is named after one of Elaine's deeply symbolic paintings, and unlocking the significance of the enigmatic imagery proves part of the puzzle of a text in which the traumatized narrator gradually comes to recognize the truth of her opening observation that time is liquid: '[s]ometimes this comes to the surface, sometime that, sometimes nothing. Nothing goes away' (3).

As Chinmoy Banerjee observes, the novel 'offers a coherent surface in the realistic mode',[13] but as with many Atwood fictions, the surface is soon revealed as concealing dark, gothic depths. Walking around the hated city of her youth, Elaine is confronted by memories of her complex relationship with the enigmatic, bullying Cordelia. In fragmented sections, Elaine recalls her early childhood, which is strikingly similar to Atwood's own and is spent in the backwoods of northern Ontario. After the war, the family settle in suburban Toronto, where Elaine and her older brother Stephen enter full-time formal education and Elaine first encounters the highly gendered, socialized world of girls and women. In the freedom of the wilderness, little distinguished Elaine from her brother in their manner of dress and play. In Toronto, however, Elaine is rapidly indoctrinated into an alien system of feminine codes of dress, behaviour, speech and manner. She reflects: 'at first I feel strange as I do it, self-conscious, as if I'm only doing an imitation of a girl. But I soon get more used to it' (52). As she learns to play at scrapbooking images of feminine domesticity cut from catalogues, these 'artifacts of desire', as Laura Martocci terms them, inscribe in Elaine 'feminine virtues' of 'self-effacement, conformity, and submission to authority'.[14] For Hite, focusing on the novel's function as a *Künstlerroman* – a narrative about an artist's progress and maturation – *Cat's Eye* is about 'the process of socialization'.[15] Art, suggests Hite, is used by Elaine as a means to escape the general fate of women to be socialized into womanhood. By becoming an artist, Elaine evades the world of suburban domestic femininity.

Elaine's immersion into school life is disorientating and anxious. As she acclimatizes to what Hite terms the 'gender-segregated urban landscape of the novel's Fifties', she is guided by two newly acquired friends, Carol Campbell and Grace Smeath.[16] The girls initiate Elaine into an unfamiliar world of social etiquette, popular culture and mass consumerism. The Smeaths also take on the religious education of Elaine, inviting her to their church, where she learns of sin and guilt under the disapproving, censorious eye of Mrs Smeath. With the arrival of Cordelia, the friendship dynamic shifts and Elaine is subject to a sustained campaign of bullying and psychological torment. Alternating derision and humiliation with approval and charm, Cordelia steadily breaks down Elaine's sense of self-confidence and self-worth. Bemused and defenceless, Elaine resorts to self-harm, stripping skin from her fingers and toes, and experiencing fantasies of suicide. While a pervasive sense of shame prevents her from seeking help, her realization that Mrs Smeath sees and tacitly condones the girls' behaviour adds to the illogical guilt of victimhood. In a chapter that examines the construction of shame in the novel, Martocci suggests that the moment when Elaine is able to turn her shaming by Mrs Smeath into hatred towards the woman is pivotal in the text, as her newfound rage shakes her from 'passive acceptance' and provides the 'means of resisting the further degradation and dissolution of self'.[17] Rage and shame, Martocci proposes, become inextricably entwined for Elaine; for many years, the experience of one triggers the other, until she is eventually able to disentangle the emotional knot.

Cordelia's reign of terror climaxes when Elaine is abandoned in a freezing ravine. Tempted to surrender to the obliterating cold, she is saved by an apparition of the Virgin Mary. Bolstered by this supernatural vision of maternal love and protection, a half-frozen Elaine is able to rouse herself and find her way home. The incident marks a shift in Elaine's relationship with Cordelia. Suddenly, she is able to defy her tormentor, and the whole edifice of coercive control crumbles. The girls drift apart, and Elaine sustains a kind of self-protective amnesia that persists into adulthood, shielding her from trauma but also shaping her relationships and limiting her self-knowledge. Over the years, repressed anger and fear resurface in her art, although she struggles to read its meaning. Examining one of her grotesque images of Mrs Smeath, Elaine thinks: 'It's still a mystery to me, why I hate her so much' (352).

Discussing language and representation in the novel, Kiriaki Massoura suggests that Elaine's 'insufficient cultural and linguistic knowledge' is part of what makes her an ideal victim for Cordelia.[18] Uncertain of cultural codes, Elaine's naivety is easily manipulated by a ruthless predator. Banerjee, however, offers a quite different reading of the compulsive attraction/repulsion between the two girls. Elaine and Cordelia, she suggests, are drawn together by their mutual 'wildness' – a concept developed by the young Elaine, who divides people into 'wild' and 'tame'. The wild ones, like Elaine's family, and like Cordelia, 'are elusive and wily and look out for themselves' (130). Elaine and Cordelia's shared wildness is in opposition to the middle-class tameness represented by Carol and Grace. 'Dirt and imagination', suggests Banerjee, 'unite the two girls in a subversive intimacy against the repressive codes of middle-class propriety and femininity'.[19] By this reading, Cordelia is attracted to a wild element in Elaine that she also recognizes within herself. Her persecution of Elaine, therefore, can be read as a kind of externalized masochistic self-punishment.

In adolescence, Elaine reconnects with Cordelia. As teenagers, they are a fearsome pair, sharp-mouthed and disdainful of everything, but the power dynamic has shifted, as Elaine recognizes: 'energy has passed between us, and I am stronger' (233). In another Atwoodian gothic doubling, Elaine becomes a dark shadow of Cordelia: best friend and tormentor. Banerjee explains this reversal in terms of Hegel's master–slave dialectic, whereby both sides of the power relation require the complicity of the other. While Cordelia's early power over Elaine is based on her understanding of Elaine's deep need for social acceptance, once Elaine is able to break this reliance on Cordelia's approval – when her near-death experience frees her of her dependence – the relationship then reverses. 'Elaine's mastery, on the other hand', argues Banerjee, 'is the mastery of a liberated Slave that does not need a Slave to maintain its position'.[20] In this manner, Elaine is actually stronger than Cordelia because she can live without her. Consequently, Elaine eventually leaves an increasingly erratic and troubled Cordelia behind, escaping into a masculine world of art.

At art school, Elaine commences an affair with her tutor, who embodies the clichés of a chauvinistic art world, and then another with Jon, a fellow student, by whom she gets pregnant. As the relationship breaks down, Elaine is overcome by a depressive impulse that she experiences as an externalized 'voice of a nine-year-old child' (374) inciting her to self-harm, and she slashes her wrist. Recognizing that something must change, Elaine leaves Jon, moves to Vancouver, meets Ben and settles into a happy, uncomplicated marriage and has a second child. Over this period, there are sporadic glimpses of an unravelling Cordelia. Their last encounter takes place in a mental asylum, where Elaine refuses a heavily sedated Cordelia's pleas to help her to escape. When she next attempts to contact her, Elaine is informed that Cordelia's whereabouts are unknown. In her essay, Banerjee makes a connection between the escapism of the two women, suggesting that through, respectively, art and madness, Elaine and Cordelia both reject the 'core of "normalcy" embodied in Grace and Carol'.[21] Both women remain bound together by their past, and by their damaged, disintegrated sense of self. As Wynne-Davies notes, much as Elaine's sense of self is always partial, so the character of Cordelia is constructed in the text from disparate scraps, split between 'what the child sees; what the adult remembers; what the artist constructs; and how others interpret that construction'.[22] This fragmentary depiction, she suggests, is a key aspect of Atwood's reflection on how the past is constructed in memory. It is only in middle age, helping her ailing mother to clear out the family basement, that Elaine discovers an old purse and within it the cat's eye marble she used to carry as a child. Gazing into the totemic object, Elaine experiences a sudden access to the past: 'I look into it, and see my life entire' (398). With her memory restored, she is able to reintegrate her past, her art, and her feelings towards Cordelia, and rather than a tale of bullying and victimhood, the novel becomes, as Banerjee notes, 'an account of survival'.[23]

A fictional autobiography?

In its detailed rendition of Elaine's childhood, adolescence and maturation into an established artist, *Cat's Eye* is both *Künstlerroman* and fictional autobiography. Examining the latter, a number of critics address the novel's narrative structure and the manner in which Atwood balances the voice of the older and younger Elaine. As Marta Dvorak observes, the novel distinguishes between the narrative voice of 'the older, wiser, narrat*ing* "I" which crosses and overlaps the limited point of view of the narrat*ed* "I," Elaine as child, adolescent, and young adult'.[24] For Earl Ingersoll, who suggests that, in its playfully self-referential use of fictional autobiography, *Cat's Eye* is Atwood's 'first full-fledged "postmodern" work', Elaine's recollections are self-consciously constructed. While the artist may seem, on the surface, to be recovering the truth of the past, in a truer sense, he suggests, she is 'creating, or writing, a past as she chooses now to see it'.[25]

For Hite, similarly, *Cat's Eye* is self-consciously concerned with autobiography, continually 'advancing and withdrawing it as a mode of authorization'. The novel, she suggests, simultaneously proposes a direct access to Elaine's past self and raises questions about our reliance on and belief in the notion of '*true*' and '*real*'.[26] Consequently, Hite points out, Elaine is fundamentally an unreliable narrator, 'inasmuch as she cannot *see* enough – either of her own motivations and desires and the forces conditioning them, or of the consequences of certain of her choices'. Her development in the novel, argues Hite, is marked by her growing awareness of her past, her feelings and the perspectives of others – although, like other Atwood narrators, her comprehension always remains more limited than that made available to the attentive reader.[27]

In addition to the structural complexities of narrating the past, *Cat's Eye* garners attention for its inclusion of elements from Atwood's own life story. Wynne-Davies catalogues the many points of congruence, gleaning her evidence from the short pieces of autobiographical writing Atwood has published in *Morning in the Burned House* (1995) and in *On Writers and Writing* (2002), in which Atwood recalls, like Elaine, moving to the city and being confronted by 'little girls – their prudery and snobbery, their Byzantine social life based on whispering and vicious gossip'.[28] While Atwood asserts that her own experience of school was largely happy, if disorientating, Wynne-Davies identifies further autobiographical echoes in Elaine's desire, like Atwood's, to escape respectable convention by embracing the bohemian art and poetry scene of 1960s Canada. For Wynne-Davies, the coincidences are too great, and there can be no doubt that Atwood has made use of autobiographical material to animate her fiction. Pondering why she might undermine her own anti-biographical position with such clearly traceable details, Wynne-Davies proposes that these autobiographical ambiguities enable Atwood to explore a key theme in her writing. By introducing elements of autobiography while simultaneously resisting the label, she is able to 'explore authorial identity, to question the veracity of narrative, and to explore the inner-self as a means of fragmenting and undermining any fixed interpretation of the past'.[29] In a similar vein, Ingersoll suggests that, given how frequently Atwood has expressed frustration at biographical readings of her work, her inclusion in *Cat's Eye* of recognizable details from her own past can only be read as a self-conscious and 'highly sophisticated expression of play with her audience's expectations'.[30]

Stein also observes the similarities between Elaine and Atwood's biographies, and like Wynne-Davies and Ingersoll, suggests that the decision is purposeful. She proposes that Atwood uses the conventions of autobiography 'to explore the possibilities and limits of autobiography, and of women's autobiography in particular'. Expanding on this idea, Stein notes that *Cat's Eye* was published when Atwood was approaching fifty (the same age as Elaine) and had just published her *Selected Poems II* (1987): 'a poet's equivalent of the artist's retrospective exhibit'.[31] These similarities, she suggests, heighten the sense of what is at stake in the novel. In her discussion, Stein draws on the work of Jill Ker Conway, who distinguishes between the common male autobiography plot structure of life as 'an odyssey, a journey through many trials and tests', and the more common female autobiography plot, taken from the romance, in which the heroine's life story ends with marriage.[32] Starting with this premise, Stein argues that *Cat's Eye* works to disrupt this 'odyssey/romance dichotomy' and resist traditional patterns of autobiography. Elaine's narrative, as she observes, is much less concerned with her love affairs and marriages – although these are depicted in the latter half of the novel – than it is with 'her girlhood and her career'.[33] In this manner, Atwood provides an alternative plot for charting the life story of a female artist.

Women beware women

In a review of *The Robber Bride*, Salman Rushdie suggests that the novel might better have been called *Women Beware Women*, 'if the title hadn't already been used', and the same might be said of *Cat's Eye*.[34] Indeed, the fact that the 'villainesses' in this earlier novel are not grown women but little girls arguably makes their malevolence even more sinister. As Dvorak points out in a discussion of Atwood's rendition of Elaine's childhood perspective, the device works to 'defamiliarize and to recontextualize, to question preconceptions or conventions and transmit a fresh vision'. Consequently, when as readers we are within the retrospective scenes of the novel, we largely stay within the limited, naïve perspective of the young Elaine. This limited perspective, as Dvorak argues, makes the account of bullying and torment all the more powerful because it is communicated in the context of Elaine's bewilderment and powerlessness.[35]

Just as Atwood pondered whether the lives of little girls would be deemed too inconsequential to sustain a novel, so she also worried: 'wouldn't I be trashed for saying that they weren't all sugar and spice?'[36] The question is perhaps disingenuous, however, for Atwood has never been afraid to depict the cruelty of little girls. Indeed, the climactic scene in *Cat's Eye* in which Elaine nearly dies in the ravine is strikingly similar to an earlier scene from *Lady Oracle* in which Joan is tied up and abandoned in a freezing ravine by some malevolent Girl Guides, leaving her in real material danger. For Atwood, the games of little girls are never inconsequential. More than merely exposing the capacity of women and girls to commit acts of cruelty, however, Atwood's novel is an examination of what motivates such destructive behaviour. This idea is proposed by Hite, who suggests that the restrictions and prohibitions of a conservative 1950s patriarchal society that limit and shape the girls are, for Atwood, central to understanding their behaviour. Elaine, she argues, is persecuted by the girls 'as a scapegoat in order to displace their own suffering as members of a patriarchy'.[37]

Throughout the novel, the young girls can be seen to enact a form of self-socialization. As Ingersoll observes, by cutting out pictures of household appliances, 'they study to be future housewives'.[38] But while the girls mimic the social mores of their mothers, they are always cognizant that real power resides with their fathers: distant and forbidding figures of authority and punishment. When they torture Elaine, they enact a regime of discipline and control in which they thrillingly adopt the patriarchal role. When she berates Elaine, Cordelia ventriloquizes her father with phrases such as 'What do you have to say for yourself?' (117). The real anger in the text, however, as Hite observes, is directed not at fathers but mothers – at the women who acquiesce to the patriarchy and educate young girls to do the same.

If fathers are distant figures of unassailable authority, mothers are much more ambiguous figures in *Cat's Eye*. Motherhood, argues Hite, is held up in the novel as an ideal, a 'force that can reverse the partitioning, blaming structure of the whole society'.[39] But real-life mothers inevitably fail to live up to such idealization. As Ingersoll observes, Elaine loves her mother, yet resents her failure to prepare Elaine for the treacherous world of girls and women. Her inexpressible resentment is internalized as guilt, which is then, he suggests, projected onto Mrs Smeath, who becomes the embodiment of the monstrous 'Bad Mother' in the text.[40] Elaine desperately desires a maternal figure who will protect her as her own well-meaning but insufficient mother does not. Hite notes that, in defiance of the Smeaths' Protestantism, Elaine chooses to worship the Catholic figure of the Virgin Mary. An icon of maternal love, the Virgin mother contrasts with the Smeaths' watchful, paternal God and functions, in Ingersoll's words, as 'the ultimate Good Mother'.[41] She also represents, as Hite suggests, a return to a pre-verbal, all-encompassing, life-giving nurturance, providing the 'succor and concern impossible for actual subjects of a disciplinary society'.[42] Massoura similarly identifies Elaine's attachment to the Virgin Mary as an attempt to return to the pre-oedipal moment of infancy, when the child does not distinguish itself as separate from the maternal body. Using Julia Kristeva's psychoanalytic definition of this 'semiotic' phase, Massoura concludes that, for Elaine, the figure of the Virgin Mary represents a healing return to the 'universal substitute mother'.[43]

When mothers fail to protect, when they actively sustain the violence of patriarchy, the anger they elicit is deep-rooted and visceral. At the same time, mothers maintain an adult authority that makes them untouchable, and the hatred expressed towards the femininity that they represent is instead manifest in bullying and self-harm. For Elaine, unable to voice her suffering or to direct it outwards, self-harm becomes a mode of inarticulate expression and release, as she punishes her unsatisfactory female flesh. As Massoura observes, Elaine uses self-directed pain to provide a sense of order and to control the chaotic violence inflicted on her by Cordelia. Her attempts to diminish her own body through pain – almost to the point of suicide – are, suggests Massoura, 'an attempt to save it from its own vulnerability': to transcend the body's pain by attaining 'complete disembodiment'.[44]

Eventually, Elaine is able to forgive her mother, and to acknowledge and relinquish her long-repressed feelings of anger and betrayal at her mother's failure to protect her. Much more difficult, however, is the forgiveness of Mrs Smeath. Discussing the visceral hatred of Mrs Smeath that finds expression in Elaine's painting, *White Gift*, Wynne-Davies notes how, with time, the painting's meaning changes and evolves, both for Elaine and for the various audiences that encounter it over the years. It eventually comes to represent Elaine's ability to find some measure of empathy, if not exactly forgiveness, for Mrs Smeath, as she starts to acknowledge the restrictions and pressures on the older woman: her worries and disappointments. Mrs Smeath, suggests Wynne-Davies, becomes a metaphor for changing social structures. The angry, grotesque image of her that Elaine creates is simultaneously 'the retaliation of a child against bigotry, a comment upon class, a challenge to morality; a feminist statement and an awareness of demographic changes in Canada'.[45] By painting both Mrs Smeath and the Virgin Mary, Elaine works towards a unified image of maternity and femininity that does not divide women into monsters and saints, but rather embodies complexity and ambiguity, strengths and weaknesses. It is an attempt, through art, to reconstruct the pivotal scene in the ravine, which Brown argues acts as a juncture of 'female cruelty, female suffering, and female comfort'.[46] For Massoura, this acceptance of the multifaceted nature of femininity is crucial, for while *Cat's Eye* is a novel 'about female cruelty, about women being their own worst enemies', it is also, eventually, a novel about 'surviving, aging and forgiving'.[47]

Art and representation

Although primarily known as a novelist, poet and short story writer, Atwood is also a visual artist. As Dvorak notes, she 'works in media not frequently exhibited in museums: sketches, watercolours, collages, linocuts'.[48] Also observing the manner in which Atwood's artworks are commonly deemed peripheral and incidental, Sharon Rose Wilson was one of the first critics to pay close attention to their significance. In a 1993 essay, Wilson argues that, while the parallels between her visual and literary images are typically ignored, since the publication of *Cat's Eye*, which positions a female visual artist at the centre of Atwood's written work, exploring such connections has 'become imperative'.[49] In a later and rare sustained study of one branch of these peripheral productions, read alongside Atwood's more canonical work, Reingard Nischik devotes a chapter of her 2009 book *Engendering Genre: The Works of Margaret Atwood* to Atwood's work as a cartoonist. Noting that Atwood often describes her earliest reading and writing experiences as being shaped by the American comics she grew up with, Nischik suggests that Atwood's youthful experiments in this 'hybrid genre' provided good training in 'pointed, minimalist, and often humorous language use'.[50] Of all her prose works, *Cat's Eye*, with its artist protagonist and closely imagined artworks, is the one that best draws together these different elements of Atwood's literary and visual production.

Art is crucial to the novel's exploration of memory. As Brown observes, just as the Toronto gallery director 'chronologizes, labels, and hangs' Elaine's artwork, so Elaine is similarly engaged in curating her own memories of the past.[51] Brown suggests that Elaine uses art to explore different modes of femininity, with witches representing female cruelty, the Virgin Mary representing comfort and female suffering being depicted in images of decapitation. Just as these images recur in the literary text of the novel, so they populate Elaine's visual art. For example, in what Brown identifies as one of Elaine's earliest artworks, created when the stress of Cordelia's bullying makes her retreat to her bed, Elaine creates a collage by cutting out ladies from the catalogue (as she was taught to do by Grace), and then chopping off their heads. By reading this imagery, we see that Elaine has 'internalised the cruel criticism of other women' and 'divided herself into fragments'.[52] Brown suggests that, in reconstituting the stereotypical images of women as witches and virgins through Elaine's art, Atwood proposes that if these stereotypes cannot be erased, we should at least learn to examine them anew.

Dvorak also focuses on the different visual and linguistic modes of representation and perception that Atwood uses in the 'doubled narrative' of her novel. She suggests that the two perspectives of the young and old Elaine create an 'anamorphosis' – a distorted projection that assumes its proper shape when seen from a specific angle – by 'telescoping past and present, ignorance and knowledge, seeing and telling'.[53] Art provides Elaine with a way to express her deepest feelings without being trapped by language, which, under Cordelia's authoritarian discipline, Elaine has come to fear. Similarly, Massoura also suggests that Elaine's art is a flight from language. Through the 'vision' of her art, she is able to 'come to terms with her past and reacquire her identity'.[54] Dvorak's analysis broadly concords with this reading but suggests that the novel also acknowledges the limitations of visual art.

Dvorak reflects on Atwood's use of ekphrasis – the detailed description of a visual artwork within a work of poetry or prose – and the manner in which Elaine's paintings are experienced by the reader and made to 'exist' in the text. Atwood describes Elaine's paintings in close, careful detail. She also sets up an ironic distance, whereby the reader often understands the significance of the painting's imagery, even where Elaine (consciously, at least) does not. In this manner, argues Dvorak, we both do *not* see the paintings as the fictional viewers in the gallery literally see them, but we also 'see' them more clearly, as we better understand what they represent. 'This would suggest', concludes Dvorak, 'a powerlessness of both text and painting to produce what could be called a "full" representation'. And she argues instead that it is somewhere in the space between these 'two imperfect media, linguistic and iconographic' – in the dynamic dialectic that is set up between them – that Atwood eventually arrives at something close to the wholeness that, with *Cat's Eye*, she is struggling to attain.[55]

Examining the use of art in the novel, Hite focuses on the theme of gendered 'looking'. She identifies an inherent tension for the woman artist because women are expected to be the object of the gaze rather than the observer. Paraphrasing the kind of analysis that John Berger outlined in his influential 1972 book, *Ways of Seeing*, Hite states: 'Women look like, while in general men only look.' This idea, Hite demonstrates, is self-consciously explored by Atwood in *Cat's Eye*. In a novel full of mirrors and full of shame, girls and women are repeatedly cautioned against 'making a spectacle'.[56] Using the work of French philosopher Michel Foucault and his famous analysis of Jeremy Bentham's model prison, the Panopticon, Hite suggests that, just as Bentham's prisoners are taught to internalize the watching gaze of the warden and to effectively police themselves, so Atwood's little girls police one another. And the consequences of a failure to comply are severe; when a young girl is found molested and murdered, Elaine thinks: 'it's as if this girl has done something shameful' (241). In becoming an artist, Elaine succeeds in evading and reversing the direction of the gaze, refusing to be its object. But this escape comes at a cost; in choosing to be an artist, she rejects the world of girls and women and allies herself with boys and men.

If Elaine's art is a mode of survival that requires a rejection of femininity, it also eventually provides a route back to her repressed selfhood. Wynne-Davies suggests that Atwood uses art to explore ideas about memory and the past, which are inherently unstable in the novel. This instability haunts Elaine, who often imagines that she glimpses Cordelia on the street. Cordelia is impossible to pin down, however, because she exists as both a defiant, bullying child and an uncertain, frightened adult. In response to such radical instability, Wynne-Davies suggests that Elaine's paintings are an attempt to pin down the past, and while they fail to manifest the 'real' Cordelia, they offer 'an inner and more intuitive interpretation'.[57] Crucially for Wynne-Davies, however, Atwood also observes and acknowledges that even Elaine's art remains unstable, as it is always subject to the interpretation of viewers who, to Elaine's surprise, most recently read her work as feminist and postfeminist. As Elaine reflects at the end of the novel, 'I can no longer control these paintings, or tell them what to mean' (409).

This acceptance of the dynamic, shifting nature of the paintings goes somewhat against Lorraine York's reading of the function of Elaine's art; noting that there is an 'autumnal' quality about the novel as a whole, York suggests that Elaine's paintings 'have been placed in a morgue of sorts, though it more commonly goes by the name of an art gallery'. For York, the life of the paintings lies not in the viewers who bring their own interpretations to the work but in the artist from whom they originate. When Elaine walks through the gallery, argues York, 'it's as though she is bringing life back to these paintings in the act of reviving their moments of creation and of their inspiration in her past'.[58] In a typically Atwoodian, questioning novel, such different readings perhaps best attest to the novel's own uncertainties around the ability of memory, or language, or art, to attain Elaine's desired 'unified field theory' that might bring together the disparate, shifting and often contradictory elements of a single life.

The Robber Bride

If in *Cat's Eye* Atwood constructs a tale of little girls acting as unwitting agents of the patriarchy, in *The Robber Bride* she creates instead a female villain who is voraciously self-serving and who destroys men as much as she devastates women: a fairy-tale gothic villain of mythic proportions.

Overview

The Robber Bride charts the intertwined personal histories of three middle-aged friends: Tony, an academic war historian, Charis, a gentle New Ager, and Roz, a successful businesswoman. In a closely patterned narrative, the alternating sequences are focalized through each woman in turn, as they recount their initial seduction and later betrayal by the charismatic and deeply manipulative Zenia. Unlikely companions, the women first meet at University in the 1960s and each, in turn, is targeted by Zenia: Tony in the 1960s, Charis in the 1970s and Roz in the 1980s. Now, in the present-day setting of 1990s Toronto, the three friends gather at the suggestively named Toxique café to share a regular monthly lunch date. A kind of survivors' support group established in the wake of Zenia's death five years earlier in a suitably dramatic terrorist attack in Beirut, the women provide one another with friendship and solidarity: 'they have battle scars, they've been through fire' (29). They are therefore understandably horrified when, like a vampire returning from the dead, their former friend and tormentor casually walks in.

The ensuing narrative recounts each woman's relationship with Zenia, who has a particular skill for rooting out pain and trauma and exploiting weaknesses. Through a carefully orchestrated combination of empathy and mimicry, she presents herself to each woman as an idealized reflection of themselves. Zenia variously offers each woman an opportunity to nurture and soothe the damaged child within and also presents her with a vision of herself made stronger: more powerful, more beautiful, more sensual and more exciting. Just as Tony, at one point in the novel, looks into Zenia's eyes and 'sees her own reflection: herself, as she would like to be' (167), so Charis and Roz similarly project their idealized selves onto Zenia. As Donna Bontatibus notes, the women must eventually accept that they 'unconsciously summon and will Zenia back into their lives' because each of them has unresolved issues.[59]

Like other Atwood novels, *The Robber Bride* is rich in intertextual allusions. Donna Potts identifies, among others: soap opera plots, folk tales, nursery rhymes, vampire and ghost stories, classical myths, comic books, Bible stories and murder mysteries.[60] Working in the gothic mode, the novel is full of images of twins and dark doubles, and each protagonist experiences some kind of splitting and dual identity. In childhood, Tony develops a coping mechanism that persists into adulthood, spelling words backwards and creating a bigger, tougher alter ego, Tnomerf Ynot: her name reversed. Charis is similarly twinned; as a child called Karen, she develops a method of psychic dissociation from her body to block out the violence of abuse until she is able to escape into a new life and a new name, although in moments of pain and fear, Karen always threatens to return. Roz, the mother of twins, also experiences division as she attempts to integrate her Jewish and Catholic heritage, her family's early poverty, their subsequent illegitimate wealth and her later respectable affluence. Like Tony and Charis, Roz has a surfeit of names: she is both Rosalind and Roz and carries her Jewish family name, its Anglicized revision and her married name. These unstable identities, the novel suggests, provide Zenia with a way into each woman's life. They also provide her with a ready role to inhabit, as J. Brooks Bouson observes when she suggests that, for Tony, Zenia is 'her own lawless, angry twin identity', for Charis, she is 'her split-off vulnerable and enraged child', and for Roz, she represents 'the envious and greedy aspects of her self she wants to deny'.[61]

Animating the repressed desires of the three women, stepping into gaps provided by their unresolved painful histories, Zenia – the Robber Bride – 'steals' and 'consumes' each of their men in turn. Tony's relationship with her husband West (the only male–female relationship that eventually survives Zenia) involves her twice nursing him back to well-being after being abandoned by Zenia, although the second time round, as Laurie Vickroy notes in an essay on trauma in the novel, she is 'stronger emotionally and more realistic about the man she loves'.[62] When Zenia comes knocking at Charis's door a decade later, she finds Charis living with American draft-dodger Billy, the father of Charis's then-unborn daughter; when Billy and Zenia run away together, Charis never hears from him again and is left uncertain whether he is dead or alive. And finally, when she enters Roz and Mitch's marriage, Zenia once again wreaks havoc; when she inevitably moves on and Roz refuses to allow her repentant husband to return to the family home, he kills himself, leaving Roz alone with their three children and her guilt. Tony, Charis and Roz are each targeted by Zenia through the man they love, but in each case, the man is almost incidental: the truly significant relationships in the novel are always the relationships – loyal or duplicitous – between the four women.

Eventually, the closely patterned novel concludes with the three friends back in the same café, each disclosing how she has gone alone to visit Zenia in her hotel room, each with murderous fantasy or intent. When Charis has a premonition that Zenia has fallen to her death, they return to the hotel together, only to find her lying (definitely) dead in the hotel fountain. Continuing the gothic theme of the novel, Zenia requires multiple killings to finally assure her death: suffering an overdose, falling from a balcony, drowning and a terminal cancer diagnosed post-mortem. The precise cause of death, however, remains uncertain, with each of the three women remaining under possible suspicion. The novel concludes with Tony musing on the unknowable yet intimately familiar nature of Zenia: 'Was she in any way like us? [. . .] Or, to put it the other way around: Are we in any way like her?' (470). For Phyllis Perrakis, extending a psychoanalytic reading of the novel, the women, in defeating the vampire, learn 'to celebrate the vampire's power because it is also theirs'.[63]

(Hi)storytellers: Narrative authority

In his review of the novel, Rushdie describes *The Robber Bride* as a light 'fairy tale of malicious simplicity'. Discussing the characterization of Zenia, he reflects that she is 'a perfectly credible monster', but regrets that we never see her 'as we see the other women, from the inside'.[64] That internalized perspective is limited by the novel's tripartite narrative structure to Tony, Charis and Roz, who each take turns to tell their version of events. For Bouson, this method works to provide 'a rich interplay of female voices' that forces readers to perform what she terms 'a complicated act of narrative reconstruction and psychoanalytic detection'. In piecing together three partial narrative perspectives, the reader – like the three friends in the novel – must attempt to reconstruct a complex and often seemingly contradictory history in order to decipher the enigma of Zenia. Zenia, however, suggests Bouson, ultimately resists attempts to know her.[65]

For Vickroy, the gaps and absences that make up Zenia are indicative of the fact that she represents 'a symbolic challenge to the others' endurance and self-regard' rather than ever functioning in the text as 'a fully developed character'.[66] This reading of Zenia, as more of a symbol or emblem than a psychologically coherent figure in her own right, chimes with an essay by Roxanne Fand in which she describes what she terms the 'Nietzschean Fairy-Tale' elements of *The Robber Bride*. Like Bouson, Fand also pays attention to the novel's narrative structure. In addition to the three distinct narrative voices focalized through the three friends, she identifies the overlapping presence of a seemingly omniscient narrator orchestrating the three perspectives and purposely omitting Zenia's point of view. This structural influence, she suggests, directs the reader's sympathies, much like a moralizing fairy tale. For Fand, however, the three protagonists' slow realization of their complex responses to Zenia and eventual acknowledgement of the role they each played in enabling her, ensures that the novel's moral position 'is more complex than that of the sanitized popular fairy tale'.[67]

Working alongside the novel's familiar fairy-tale elements is a particular concern with historiography. History, and the shadows it casts, is a central preoccupation of *The Robber Bride*. As Fand notes, while the three friends are given broadly equal prominence within the novel's tripartite structure, the opening and closing narrative sections are focalized through Tony the historian. As the character most consciously concerned with what Fand terms 'the problem of historical and narrative truth', Tony's prominence draws the reader's attention to those same issues.[68]

Discussing the trauma of history, Vickroy points out that Atwood purposely places the novel's various tales of parental neglect and childhood abuse in the context of the Second World War and its psychological consequences. In this manner, she suggests, 'Atwood links larger historical traumas to personal ones by showing the disastrous effects of war on parenting in the novel'.[69] We see evidence of this in each of the three friends' childhoods: Tony's mother is a traumatized and resentful war bride, while her father refuses to discuss his war record and eventually commits suicide; Charis's father dies in the war, leaving her in the care of her mentally unstable and suicidal mother; and Roz's charming but unfaithful father cuts a morally ambiguous figure as a Jewish émigré and a war profiteer whom she struggles to come to terms with throughout her life. Each woman is shaped by history – personal, national and international – and as Hilde Staels observes, it is Tony who finally recognizes their 'desire for storytelling as a necessary precondition to pacify the ghosts that haunt them'.[70]

Friendship/sisterhood/feminism

In its foregrounding of interrelated concerns around trauma, history and storytelling, *The Robber Bride* can be compared to *Bodily Harm*, *The Handmaid's Tale* and *Cat's Eye*, while its preoccupation with the complexity of female relationships also invites connections with earlier works. Briefly comparing *The Robber Bride* to *Cat's Eye*, Fand suggests that, where the earlier novel defies the feminist call to sisterhood by depicting a power struggle between women, *The Robber Bride* extrapolates this idea, taking it to further extremes. She identifies in the novel a dialogic struggle between, on the one hand, 'the centrifugal forces dividing women', and on the other, 'the centripetal power of sisterhood'.[71] Rather than resolving this tension, she suggests, the novel is propelled by the dynamism of this opposition. Atwood's novel, argues Fand, reverses gender roles and demonstrates that, while it may be fought on different terms, 'a struggle between women is as dangerous as one between men'.[72]

Published in 1993 against a backdrop of conservative retreat from many early second-wave feminist advances, *The Robber Bride* inevitably inspired many critical reflections on its response to contemporary feminist politics. In her essay on 'power feminism' in the novel, Bouson takes up this discussion, and considers how the novel chimes with the kind of analysis being put forward at the time by postfeminists such as Naomi Wolf. In her 1993 polemic, *Fire with Fire*, Wolf advocates for a new power feminism that would reject an earlier mode of 'victim feminism', which viewed women as fragile and in need of protection. According to Wolf, second-wave feminism's eagerness to celebrate women as 'naturally non-competitive, cooperative, and peace loving' led it to reject evidence of female aggression as an aberration caused by patriarchy.[73] Extending Wolf's suggestion that popular culture commonly provides an outlet for women's 'repressed fantasises of power and revenge', Bouson argues that *The Robber Bride* 'does the dream work of power feminism' by exploring the fantasy enactment of forbidden female desires.[74]

While many critics focus on the novel's depiction of female rivalry and betrayal, others point to its powerful vision of female comradery. Indeed, for Rigney, female friendship is at the heart of Atwood's novels. Atwood, she argues, 'restores women to women as friends, ultimately, though they may have suffered horrors at one another's hands'.[75] Even in *The Robber Bride*, with its overt performance of female treachery, Zenia's villainy ultimately unites her victims as co-survivors. And for Stein, similarly, while the novel is superficially about women fighting over men, it is more importantly 'the story of an evolving friendship between three women'. *The Robber Bride*, observes Stein, is 'a woman-centred book', transforming the Robber Bridegroom fairy tale of male villainy into a story about women.[76] For Bouson, however, while the novel inarguably depicts the friendship of Roz, Charis and Tony as 'nurturing and supportive', its prime concern is ultimately with the 'antagonisms, rivalries, manipulations, and betrayals' of each woman's relationship with Zenia.[77]

In an essay on 'the Lacanian double and feminist community' in *The Robber Bride*, Jean Wyatt extends this discussion of the tensions in the novel around female friendship and rivalry. She argues that *The Robber Bride* depicts the experience of intense envy: 'each of the three protagonists wants to be Zenia'. Echoing Atwood's position in 'Spotty-Handed Villainesses', Wyatt suggests that the feminist ideal of sisterhood made the existence of jealousy and competitiveness taboo. By placing envy and violence at the centre of her female characters' relations, Wyatt argues, Atwood calls on her readers 'to confront and deal with the negative feelings between women'. In this, she suggests, Atwood's novel addresses the feminist community. Atwood's three protagonists are the products of feminism, and each follows an ethics of feminist sisterhood that 'excludes all negative feelings, including envy'. Adopting a psychoanalytic reading that envy is natural (it is a healthy part of child development to envy and aspire to the power and autonomy of the parent), Wyatt suggests that the feminist prohibition on envy leads, inevitably, to repression and guilt.[78]

Hobbled by the feminist exclusion of negative emotions, each woman in turn represses her envy of Zenia and instead welcomes her, as Tony does, 'like a long-lost friend, like a sister' (114). This unquestioning act of empathy and goodness leaves Tony, like Charis and Ros, vulnerable to exploitation. While Atwood does not advocate for the abandonment of care and mutual support, *The Robber Bride*, argues Wyatt, is 'a story about restoring to a feminist community the right to envy'. When that right is denied, each woman is isolated in her repressed rage and guilt; but when envy and rage are allowed to be brought 'into the conversation, these feelings can be contextualised, seen to coexist with other, more positive emotions towards women'.[79]

Another gothic tale

Wyatt's essay on feminism and envy makes use of a familiar psychoanalytic reading of Zenia as an uncanny double, which is just one of the novel's many gothic tropes. If *Lady Oracle* provided a comic exaggeration of the genre of gothic romance, *The Robber Bride* is instead deadly serious in its depiction of violence, terror and threat, while simultaneously joyous in its uninhibited and occasionally camp depiction of Zenia's super-villainy. As Wilson observes, Zenia is 'a cannibal and a vampire: she dismembers friends, lovers, and possibly chickens for fun'.[80] Discussing this tension in the novel between its alternating modes, Fand suggests that Atwood manages to successfully create 'a dialogic interplay between fantasy and realistic believability', constructing a gothic fairy tale within a broadly realist frame.[81]

In her essay on 'border crossings' in *The Robber Bride*, Staels discusses the gothic fairy-tale roots of the novel, in which Zenia takes on the role of trickster and female counterpart of the murderous husband in the Grimm Brothers' tale of 'The Robber Bridegroom'. Zenia, argues Staels, not only steals the men of the three women but also robs the women of their 'illusory coherent identities'. Discussing the novel in terms of contemporary women's gothic writing, she suggests that such fictions explore the 'other', which is everything that represents disorder and difference, and which challenges the authority of the dominant cultural order. Consequently, Tony, Charis and Roz encounter, in the 'lawless and radically "other" but ultimately liberating Zenia', a threat to the familiar bourgeois world. For Staels, however, the novel parodies gothic conventions. While traditional gothic fiction is fascinated by dualisms and transgressions, it also ultimately exposes and condemns wrongdoing, restoring order and reconfirming the moral and social code. Contemporary postmodern gothic novels such as Atwood's instead 'emphasize the need to welcome the transgressive other as part of the self'.[82]

A number of critics, getting to grips with the nature of the transgressive other that Zenia represents, reach for a notably gothic vocabulary. For Staels, she is a 'revenant' and 'an angry spirit', taking possession of 'the ghost of banished Karen, Charis's muted and mutilated other'.[83] For Wilson instead, like Dr Jekyll's Mr Hyde, she is 'the shadow self that we must know in order not to be controlled by it'.[84] And for Palumbo, Zenia returns like an irrepressible 'ghost, a vampire, or a patched together monster'.[85] Whatever the nature of her gothic form, Zenia's villainous energy, as Rigney observes, is inextricably bound up with her gender – a connection that Rigney also extends to Atwood's other works, noting that her female characters, 'more than their comparatively benign male counterparts, are capable of virtually demonic power'.[86]

For most critics pursuing the gothic function of *The Robber Bride*, Zenia's role is explained in specifically psychoanalytic terms. This is the argument put forward by Staels, for whom Zenia's return as a vampiric, vengeful monster is 'a result of long-term denial'.[87] This reading is also developed by Palumbo, for whom the novel can be described as 'one long act of exorcism'. Each of the three protagonists, as she observes, is plagued by secret twins and unruly doubles – from Tony's unborn twin and alter ego, to Roz's multiple selves and Charis's repressed 'Karen' self – while also always twinned with their dark double, Zenia. Extending the psychoanalytic reading (and echoing Wyatt's analysis), Palumbo suggests that Zenia enacts a kind of Freudian return of the repressed. In order to exorcise their seemingly supernaturally immortal foe, each woman must address her capacity for 'conventionally nonfeminine emotions' – 'hostility, anger, and rage' – and learn to integrate rather than repress and expel such feelings. Otherwise, suggests Palumbo, that which is denied is bound to return, like an irrepressible 'ghost, a vampire, or a patched together monster'.[88] Finally, critics such as Bouson also extend this reading to implicate, not just the three central protagonists, but also the reader. Bouson contends that Atwood, in encouraging her readers to consume and enjoy Zenia's unrepentant satisfying of her monstrous appetites, pushes them to 'recognize – and thus begin to take ownership of – their disowned feelings and urges'.[89]

An essentially gothic conception of otherness and threat also underpins Eleonora Rao's essay on 'home and nation' in Atwood's work. For Rao, *The Robber Bride* is preoccupied with questions of 'home, and estrangement, national identity and belonging', constructing an uneasy and unstable opposition between a white Anglophone 'us' and an immigrant 'them'. While Zenia functions as the 'foreigner par excellence' – exotic, threatening, and other – each of the three friends also experiences feelings of homelessness and rootlessness. Like exiles, the women are divided subjects, split between their present and their past. Displaced and orphaned, they work hard to create a sense of stability and security, which Zenia threatens.[90] Rao observes that each woman builds herself a place of safety – Roz's mansion, Charis's cottage, and Tony's 'turreted fortress' (391) – but each sanctuary fails to repel Zenia's invasion. (An article by Jennifer Murray notes the echoes of the Three Little Pigs, with Zenia as the wolf attacking each house in turn.[91]) Rao touches on something of the terror that Zenia wreaks: 'The dividing line between the inside and the outside begins to falter: closed borders do not hold.'[92] Zenia disrupts the illusory stability of the other women's lives, exposing the fragility of their own status as secure insiders. For Rao, the three women's response to the threat of Zenia illuminates divisions within Canadian society and belies the Canadian self-valedictory narrative of the nation's openness to migrants. It also, she argues, warns, in true gothic manner, of the fragility of borders, of 'home', of all supposedly secure barriers intended to keep out the dangerous other.

The conclusion

The Robber Bride concludes on the neutralization of threat, the vanquishing of the vampire, the expulsion of the dangerous other. Critics, however, remain divided in their responses to Atwood's resolution. As Stein notes, the novel 'ends with a ceremonial meal and with storytelling'. The stories that they tell, she suggests, work to cement the women's friendship and to underline that history, like people, 'remains complex, multiple, and ultimately indeterminate'.[93] Wyatt also focuses on the concluding meal, which is 'structurally parallel' to the opening lunch as the Toxique, but 'represents a more substantial communion'.[94] Returning to her envy thesis, she suggests that the overly symbolic patterning of the novel's conclusion, in which each woman confesses to secretly visiting Zenia with the intention to somehow eradicate her, coupled with Zenia's coincidental death on the same day, takes the novel out of the realms of realism and into that of symbolism, where each envious women in turn 'kills' the object of her envy.

If Zenia's reincarnation at the start of the novel functions as a Freudian return of the repressed in Bouson's psychoanalytic perspective, her second death at the novel's end 'suggests her return to the watery (unconscious) element from which she has surfaced as a fantasy projection'. Bouson entertains the possibility of a constructive reading of the conclusion: having confronted Zenia and acknowledged the repressed will to power that she represents, the women are finally able to rid themselves of her 'troubling presence'. There is also, however, as Bouson suggests, a less satisfactory conclusion, whereby Zenia's death is better understood as 'a defensive need to expel, rather than assimilate, the Zenia within'.[95] Functioning in the text as a kind of cipher for female malevolence, Zenia is violently removed from the narrative. For Bouson, regardless of the actual cause of Zenia's death, the three women's shared vengeful, murderous fantasies point to their 'collective guilt' in stamping out threatening femininity.[96]

For Fand, however, who reads the novel as an exploration of what the nineteenth-century German philosopher Friedrich Nietzsche termed the 'will to power', Zenia performs a valuable function for the three protagonists. By making each woman in turn face her own 'dark impulses', she becomes, in Fand's words, 'like their Nietzschean best friend in being their best enemy'.[97] Through their various interactions, Zenia forces the women to become themselves more fully, and while the experience is painful and even violent, surviving it makes each of them stronger. The key to understanding the Nietzschean dialogic of the text, Fand argues, resides in its insistence on contradiction. The friends are 'undone by their impulse to do good – to Zenia', but also, ultimately, 'saved by that same impulse toward each other'. In this manner, she suggests, the novel both interrogates and upholds the ethic of sisterhood, much as it shows both the violence done by the will to power and the danger of denying the will to power. Zenia, argues Fand (adapting Nietzsche's term), 'has the superwoman's compulsion to succeed "over all" by regarding others as mere objects for her purposes'.[98] The goal of the three friends, therefore, is not to duplicate this monstrous narcissism, but rather to combine something of the same drive with the love and solidarity of which Zenia is incapable, thereby achieving a stronger, healthier mode of female power.

Cat's Eye and *The Robber Bride* represent significant late twentieth-century engagements with the gender politics shaped and defined by second-wave feminism. In the late 1990s and on the cusp of the twenty-first century, Atwood's lengthy, complex novels take a reflective turn, continuing to explore gender relations, but expanding the historical sweep of her narrative into the nineteenth and early-twentieth centuries.

5

History, memory and recovering the past
Alias Grace, *The Blind Assassin* and *The Penelopiad*

Atwood's novels as she approaches the end of the twentieth century and moves into the twenty-first century are increasingly ambitious, weighty volumes, self-consciously engaged with the difficulties of recovering and representing the past in the present. With *Alias Grace*, she published her first extended foray into historical fiction, writing a fictionalized account of the real-life figure Grace Marks, a young working-class Irish immigrant to Canada accused of conspiring to murder her employer and his housekeeper. In exploring the circumstances around and the responses to this mid-nineteenth-century cause célèbre, Atwood engages in both a close psychoanalytic study of an offender and broader reflections on the preoccupations of a community, a period and a nation. Similarly, with *The Blind Assassin*, she juxtaposes the personal memoir of the novel's octogenarian narrator, Iris, against an obliquely described developing social and cultural history of late-nineteenth and twentieth-century Canada. Iris, some twenty or so years older than Atwood when she was writing the novel, extends the text's reach beyond the previously described 1950s of Atwood's own childhood to provide a rich reconstruction of the 1930s and 1940s.

In this chapter, I examine some of the critical responses to these two substantial novels and also include some discussion of the 2005 text, *The Penelopiad*. This later work represents yet another mode of historical writing for Atwood, as she takes on the rewriting of Homer's classical epic, *The Odyssey*. A very different text from *Alias Grace* and *The Blind Assassin*, *The Penelopiad* nevertheless contains characteristically Atwoodian reflections on the desires and the dangers of rewriting the past that bear useful comparisons with the project she undertakes in the two earlier works. In each of the three texts, Atwood draws attention to the limits and restrictions of genre, to the fallibility of both private memory and the public historical record, and, in Coral Ann Howells's words, to 'the multiple inherited scripts through which our perceptions are structured'.[1]

In an article that focuses primarily on *The Blind Assassin*, Ruth Parkin-Gounelas comments on the length of Atwood's novels from this period. She places these later Atwood works within the context of other similarly massive recent fictions and diagnoses a kind of late-twentieth-century reaction against the mid-century minimalism of writers such as Samuel Beckett. Contemporary writers, she suggests, have retreated to the densely realized worlds of their eighteenth and nineteenth-century predecessors. And yet, she argues, 'the postmodern doorstop' novel is notable different from its Victorian ancestor, 'with its fleshed-out characters in a solid and stable world'. While a work such as *The Blind Assassin* replicates many of the qualities of the nineteenth-century realist novel, it always remains highly self-conscious of the limits of its own fictionality. As Parkin-Gounelas puts it: 'The more it adds or remembers, the less it seems to know.'[2] This same postmodern scepticism can be discerned in *Alias Grace* and *The Penelopiad*.

Alias Grace

Overview

Atwood commences the present-tense narrative of *Alias Grace* in 1859. Grace, in her early thirties, has been imprisoned for sixteen years – half of her young life. She is a 'model prisoner' (5), who repents of her sins and is entrusted with a job as maid and seamstress in the prison Governor's home, but she continues to claim amnesia of the actual event of the murders. When the novel begins, a well-intentioned group of Christians, prison reformists and those who, like the Governor's wife, have a morbid fascination with famous murderers have commissioned the services of Dr Simon Jordan, an American medic specializing in the modern treatment of 'lunatics', to undertake a kind of pre-Freudian talking cure to recover Grace's repressed memories and hopefully exonerate her of the crime.

The subsequent narrative involves Grace – 'the most duplicitous of all Atwood's female protagonists', as Barbara Hill Rigney terms her – recounting her life story to Simon in the attempt to unlock her memory.[3] Grace's account is rich with detail and the ephemera of nineteenth-century domestic life. She describes her journey to Canada and the death of her mother at sea; how she was left with a drunken father and younger siblings to care for and was relieved to escape into employment as a housemaid. In the home of Mrs Alderman Parkinson,

Grace is taken under the wing of her great friend, Mary Whitney, who is seduced and abandoned by the family's son, and eventually dies in Grace's arms from a botched abortion. Grace escapes to service in Thomas Kinnear's house, where she hopes to find another friend in the Housekeeper, Nancy. Instead, she enters a household riven with jealousies and tensions, all of which culminate in the brutal murder of Nancy and Kinnear.

Repeatedly in the novel Simon reports feeling overwhelmed by the abundance of Grace's narrative. While she claims to have no memory of the murders, she seems to have a minute recollection of 'every item of laundry she ever washed' (434). As Sandra Kumamoto Stanley observes, she provides multiple versions of herself 'which, like Scheherazade's stories, become narratives of survival'.[4] Her stories work to sustain Simon's interest in her, without ever providing the satisfaction he desires. For Karen Stein, Grace is a 'trickster' – 'She is apparently powerless, yet she contrives to liberate herself from prison through her carefully crafted storytelling.'[5] This suspected duplicity comes to a head when the narrative eventually reaches its critical point: the supposed gap in Grace's memory. When Simon is persuaded, against his better judgement, to allow a visiting Dr Jerome Dupont (recognized by Grace as a former acquaintance, Jeremiah the peddler) to attempt hypnosis, Grace appears to enter a trance in which the spirit of Mary Whitney claims to have taken possession of Grace's body at the time of the murders. Whether Grace is hypnotized against her will, possessed, coached into lying or constructing a performance that she purposely keeps from the reader remains opaque.

Subsequently, a disillusioned Simon returns to America, where he is later injured in the Civil War and loses his memory. Grace instead is eventually pardoned and marries Jamie Walsh, whom she knew as a young boy at Kinnear's. The novel ends with Grace, in her mid-forties, revealing that she may either be pregnant or sick with a tumour: an ambiguity that speaks to the novel's broader refusal to provide satisfactory answers.

Readerly desire

Alias Grace has an extended genesis in Atwood's canon. In 1974, she wrote a television screenplay about Grace Marks for CBC, entitled *The Servant Girl*. Atwood notes that she partially based this earlier depiction of Grace on an account by Susanna Moodie in her 1853 book, *Life in the Clearings*, in which she describes seeing 'a shrieking, capering' Grace incarcerated in both the Kingston Penitentiary and the Toronto Lunatic Asylum.[6] Atwood, however, later came to reconsider the motives behind Moodie's work. A well-known writer about pioneer life in the Canadian bush, Moodie's writing, suggests Sharon Rose Wilson, was deliberately designed 'to reconfirm English attitudes about the "uncivilized" life in Canada'.[7] Reflecting on Moodie's account in her 'Author's Afterword', Atwood concludes that Moodie 'can't resist the potential for literary melodrama' (538). Bringing this same critical eye to *Alias Grace*, Atwood foregrounds the many modes of readerly desire that motivate the deconstruction of a 'text' such as Grace.

Grace's story has always been sensationalized. As Stanley observes, 'with its mixture of sex and violence imbricated with class warfare' it attracted multiple lurid and highly gendered reactions from reporters and the public.[8] Jackie Shead, in her study of Atwood as a crime fiction writer, expands on this point. As it concerned a pretty young girl working in a small, relatively isolated household, the case prompted titillating speculation about the sexual arrangements of the inhabitants. The case, notes Shead, also confronted Canada's ruling classes with 'the alarming spectacle of servants rising up against their master'.[9] Class tensions were further exacerbated by sectarian divisions. Citing Revered Verringer in the novel – 'The Tories appear to have confused Grace with the Irish Question' (91) – Shead points out that, while Grace is a Protestant, her Irishness implicates her by association with Catholic rabble-rousing.

Given the wider anxieties that Grace's case seemed to excite, many critics note that Atwood's interest in her story is less to do with *what* Grace did, than with *how* she was received, and *why*. For Alison Toron, focusing on themes of prison and confinement in the novel, 'Grace's gender, class, and Irishness taint her as guilty before she has been convicted of any crime.'[10] Grace becomes a locus for competing theories around class, gender, nation and religion: each of which would 'explain' Grace in differing ways. As Stanley puts it, Grace, caught up in scandalous events, 'is examined, categorized, and imprisoned'.[11]

For Lorraine York, who has written persuasively on Atwood and celebrity, the intensity of the speculation around Grace is also key to Atwood's interest in her case. York suggests that *Alias Grace* repeats familiar themes of 'twinning, fame, and destruction: a powerful constellation in the work of Margaret Atwood'. York identifies in Atwood's fiction a recurring trope of 'the infamous woman as the evil twin of the famous star' and suggests that this imagery speaks to the writer's caution around celebrity, which can elicit hostility as well as adulation.[12] Like Joan in *Lady Oracle*, for whom fame is deeply problematic, Grace's 'celebrity' – or rather, her infamy – brings a complex array of responses. Vilified and idealized,

'Grace' becomes a composite of the various competing newspaper accounts of her character, with the 'real' Grace seeming increasingly impossible to discern.

Historical fiction

Embodying the same multiplicity that comes to epitomize Grace, the novel contains a number of competing genres and styles. Stein identifies at work in the text: 'social realism, epistolary form, Gothic fiction, and even a ballad [. . .] Jamesian ghost story, detective thriller, Gothic tale, autobiography, and Scheherazade's story'.[13] This clashing of genres and foregrounding of textuality most commonly leads critics to define the novel as postmodern, although Wilson, in her 2003 book, *Margaret Atwood's Textual Assassinations*, takes another view. Noting the 'considerable research' Atwood undertook for the novel, she suggests that *Alias Grace* 'takes seriously' themes such as double personalities, sex scandals and murder mysteries that have previously occurred in her work in the form of parody. Consequently, she argues, *Alias Grace* 'seems less experimental, less postmodern' than *The Handmaid's Tale* and *The Robber Bride*.[14] Much more prevalent, however, are readings such as that offered by Jennifer Murray in her study of the novel's quilt metaphor that identify the work as 'historiographic metafiction': a mode of postmodern writing that Linda Hutcheon defines as displaying 'theoretical self-awareness of history and fiction as human constructs'.[15]

Alias Grace is self-consciously concerned with what Murray terms 'the problematic of history and its representation'.[16] In an essay entitled 'In Search of *Alias Grace*', Atwood identifies a tension in the historical record between 'individual memory and experience' and 'collective memory and experience' and argues that fiction works best in drawing these two perspectives together. She declares, in combative mode: 'Whoever tells you that history is not about individuals, only about large trends and movements, is lying.'[17] Accordingly, *Alias Grace* works to reclaim Grace from the documented accounts of her case and provide her with an intimate, idiosyncratic voice. At the same time, as critics have noted, a broader social history can be glimpsed around the edges of Grace's narrative.

For Shead, the novel exposes darker elements of Canadian Victorian society, specifically, 'the exploitation of immigrant labour and the power politics of its class and gender relations'.[18] Wilson, like Shead, also points out that the novel is set in a very particular moment of Canadian history: after the Mackenzie rebellion, which did much to expose class tensions, and during a period of increased Irish immigration with its attendant joint anxieties around Catholicism and fears of being overrun by the lawless poor. For Wilson, the novel is both an examination of 'nineteenth century colonial attitudes about Canada, the lower classes, and the Irish' and a critique of those attitudes.[19] Reading the novel as prison literature, Toron notes that 'Grace's personal history of oppression frames her supposed crime'. This, she suggests, is typical of the genre, which is concerned with both the individual's experience of the penal system and wider social attitudes.[20] In *Alias Grace*, Atwood foregrounds the manner in which the historical cultural moment shaped both Grace and the public's response to Grace.

The servant girl

One of the social forces to which *Alias Grace* pays particularly close attention is class. When Atwood titled her 1974 screenplay *The Servant Girl*, she drew attention to labour and class relations in a manner that her later novel title does not. Nevertheless, Grace's occupation as servant is central to the novel's examination of gender, class and power. For Maria J. Lopez, examining Atwood's representation of marginalized and vulnerable groups, the novel describes 'communities of power' – scientific, legal, medical – that work, in Foucauldian terms, to discipline and punish; Grace belongs instead to 'the marginal communities of immigrants, servants, and mad people' who challenge the structures of middle- and upper-class social identity. Referring to Atwood's description of Moodie and her contemporaries visiting the lunatic asylum as if they were visiting a zoo, Lopez suggests that 'Grace, as a low-class woman, becomes the object of knowledge of a middle-to-upper-class woman'. Grace's narrative, subsequently, becomes a mode of resistance whereby she wrests back her own story, in her own voice.[21]

In an essay on 'the eroticism of class' in *Alias Grace*, Stanley also focuses closely on social hierarchies. She points to Atwood's acknowledgements, which cite Isabella Beeton's *The Book of Household Management* (1861) – a guide for middle-class women on managing domestic servants – and Mary S. Hartman's *Victorian Murderesses* (1976) – a study of murders by middle-class women – as evidence of Atwood's interest in class as a context for Grace's actions. Stanley places *Alias Grace* within a history of texts, including some of Freud's famous case studies, that eroticize 'the debased and abject servant who promises desired but forbidden knowledge to the bourgeois male'. As she observes, Grace is an enigma: simultaneously a knowing seductress and an innocent young maid – both of which constructions excite the fantasies of others. Eventually, suggests

Stanley, Grace owes her survival to 'an erotic strategy of deferral' by which she successfully moves from the servant's role of fulfilling the master's desires, to one of denying satisfaction by withholding knowledge. Although she undergoes a succession of attempts to define her – as servant, seductress, victim, murderer, prisoner, madwoman, con-woman – Grace successfully resists them all, remaining 'unknowable'.[22]

Marlene Goldman also explores the significance of Grace's status as servant and suggests that it is inextricably bound up in the text with her nationality and gender: all of which mark her out as dangerous. *Alias Grace*, she suggests, explores nineteenth-century Canadian middle- and upper-class anxieties around the Irish diaspora, class mobility and female emancipation. The novel's gothic themes of hysteria and haunting, she suggests, speak directly to gothic fiction's preoccupation with threats of invasion and corruption and its obsession with 'securing the home, the family line, and the nation state against perceived internal and external threats'. The intensity of the public scrutiny of Grace's case, suggests Goldman, was motivated by an anxious desire to keep women, the working class and the Irish in their place. Applying a historical and materialist reading to hysteria and haunting in the novel, Goldman situates Grace's story within that of a multitude of 'impoverished diasporic Irish women who were marginalized and dispossessed' when they emigrated to Canada. The ghosts that haunt *Alias Grace*, and Grace's hysterical episodes, are best read, argues Goldman, as the uncanny return of nineteenth-century Canada's repressed guilt about the abuse of working-class women like Grace, Nancy and Mary, who were left entirely vulnerable to physical and sexual exploitation by their employers.[23]

The vulnerability of working-class women at this time is also noted by Stanley. As she observes, the kind of strategies of resistance and survival that Grace, Nancy and Mary employ have serious material consequences should they go wrong. Conscious that both Mary and Nancy paid for their choices with their lives, Grace, suggests Stanley, shows a keen awareness that women like her are 'judged by their use value to the master'. Consequently, both in Kinnear's household, and later when undergoing analysis with Simon, Grace carefully preserves her value by deferring their desire to 'know' her. For Stanley, crucially, class underpins the ambiguity of the novel's conclusion. Atwood, she suggests, is reluctant to become complicit with middle-class Simon's attempt to expose and consume working-class Grace's story. Grace, therefore, remains inscrutable, eluding 'her potential colonizers, including the gaze of her avid bourgeois readers'.[24]

The quilt motif

Grace, always sewing and talking, evades those who would objectify and possess her. Describing the ubiquity of sewing, knitting and handcrafting as metaphors for history in Atwood's work, Murray observes that, in *Alias Grace*, the patchwork quilt 'emerges as the privileged motif'.[25] The novel, she argues, draws attention to the manner in which, like a quilt, it is pieced together from fragments of disparate historical documents. In *A Poetics of Postmodernism*, Hutcheon asks of documentary sources, 'can they be objectively, neutrally related? Or does interpretation inevitably enter with narrativization?'[26] Historiographic metafiction, argues Murray, is therefore caught in a paradox of desiring unimpeded access to the past while remaining aware of the impossibility of the endeavour. A similar point is made by Wilson, for whom the 'increasing documentation' commonly incorporated by postmodern fictions only 'compounds textual gaps'.[27] Accordingly, Atwood laces *Alias Grace* (as she does *The Blind Assassin*) with extracts from contemporary sources such as newspaper articles, popular songs, court proceedings, etcetera, but for all this 'evidence', the reader remains unenlightened. For Murray, Atwood uses the quilt as an expression of this paradox. Both fragmentary and unified, the quilt comes to represent the act of 'making present meaning from traces of the past'.[28]

While Murray largely focuses on quilting as a metaphor for constructing history and narrative, Wilson addresses the cultural history that Atwood's novel taps into. Grace concludes her story by describing the 'Tree of Paradise' pattern she is sewing – the first quilt she has ever made for herself – into which she is stitching material from Mary's petticoat, Nancy's dress and her own prison nightgown. Examining the history of quilt-making, Wilson notes that quilts were commonly made from fabric worn by family and friends, often on significant occasions: and so 'bits of the past become useful parts of the present'.[29] For Murray, Grace's inclusion of Mary and Nancy's fabrics is an assertion of 'solidarity among women victims'.[30] Classic quilting patterns tell stories – often biblical or folkloric – and significantly, 'quilters have traditionally been women'. Wilson suggests, therefore, that quilting was a mode of socially sanctioned communal activity for women: 'a means for women to be with other women'. Where other arts were prohibited to women as too costly or too immodest, quilting provided an accessible mode of artistic expression. This history is also taken up by Magali Cornier Michael, who notes that the relegation of quilting to domestic craft left the practice 'doubly marginalized' – excluded from both public and artistic realms.[31] As Wilson observes, however, this history of exclusion and belittlement is largely what makes quilting 'an appropriate vehicle for retelling a nineteenth-century woman's story'.[32]

Michael's essay takes up the quilting motif and reflects on its implications for the conceptualization of truth. She suggests that the novel's patchwork mode of representation, whereby different documents and voices appear alongside each other, 'undermines linearity and the cause-and-effect logic that derives from it'. For Michael, Atwood's juxtaposition of public documents alongside Grace's intimate and clearly fictionalized account, results in a 'curious leveling out' of the authority of all the novel's various texts and challenges the idea of a unified, prioritized truth.[33] Crucially, however, the novel does not lapse into relativism (whereby all versions of 'truth' are equally valid), for as Michael observes, historical accounts are fundamentally important for marginalized people as a way to retain cultural memory and bear witness to past events. *Alias Grace*, therefore, treads a line between acknowledging the existence of fact (someone *did* kill Nancy and Kinnear), while also pointing out that 'layers and layers of texts' stand between the reader and the event, and concluding that the real, material Grace 'can never be recuperated'.[34]

For Michael, Grace's quilt functions to both unsettle linear, patriarchal histories and elevate marginalized feminine narratives. Crucially, it manages to expose the power dynamics that shape the interpretation of history, while also 'retaining sight of the concrete, material bodies' (real people, to whom real things happened) at stake in narrativizations of the past.[35] Murray's reading, however, is rather more sceptical. While Wilson suggests that Grace's 'piecing together of different stories into a new pattern' is a revolutionary act, creating a new pattern 'that questions master patterns', Murray is less convinced.[36] Rather than ripping up the old patterns and constructing something entirely new, she argues, Grace can only imagine minor amendments and diversions from traditional motifs, 'a form of indecisiveness' which she reads as an essentially conservative conclusion.[37]

An anti-detective novel

If Grace's quilting adapts known patterns, her storytelling similarly revises familiar plots: most notably, the detective novel. As Shead observes, the double-murder cold-case at the heart of *Alias Grace* subverts the conventions of 'the Holmesian whodunit', particularly the assumption that the truth will eventually emerge.[38] Similarly, Earl Ingersoll describes *Alias Grace* as an 'anti-detective novel', luring readers in with the mystery of Grace's culpability, only to leave them 'without any confidence that she is clearly guilty or innocent'.[39] Hilde Staels, examining the novel's intertexts, reads the text as 'a parody' of detective fiction – a genre that began in the nineteenth century, and which traditionally functions as realism.[40] As Atwood disrupts the conventions of realism – linearity, logic, 'knowable' characters – so she undermines the foundation on which detective fiction rests. Consequently, where the novel commences with the psychoanalyst-detective's desire to achieve knowledge through logical deduction, it ends instead, as Staels notes, in 'epistemological fallibility'.[41]

John O'Neill, in an article on memory and narrative uncertainty in *Alias Grace*, also addresses the novel's departure from realism in its seeming embrace of the gothic ghost story. Focusing on Grace's unreliability and her alleged haunting by Mary, O'Neill argues that the conventional detective plot, which demands revelation and closure, is 'undermined by contact with the ghost genre'. When the dead continue to speak after death – when they can continue to offer new revelations – the comfort of a secure ending is disrupted. Consequently, in *Alias Grace*, Mary's haunting of Grace refuses the certainty that Simon seeks, opening up more questions than it answers. For O'Neill, the inaccessible truth of Grace's apparent haunting 'is the gap at the heart of *Alias Grace*' which, like Grace herself, 'resists resolution'.[42]

For Shead, Atwood proves distinctly sceptical of detective work, particularly its valorizing of a masculinist logical detachment in the Sherlockian mode. While Simon variously refers to Grace as a nut to crack (61) and an oyster to prise open (153), his attempts at scientific observation quickly unravel as Grace, defying the 'Cartesian divide between detective and subject', starts to act upon Simon, penetrating his sense of smell, his concentration and his dreams. Where Simon assumes his own neutral objectivity, Shead instead proposes that his failure to detect a unifying pattern in the scattered fragments of Grace's narrative is due to his inability to see the world from the perspective of a lower-class woman. Grace's tale, argues Shead, 'is the dirty linen of patriarchy and class injustice hung out to view', and Simon remains blind to it. Consequently, the trajectory of the novel's story of detection becomes one of 'failure and decline' rather than of progress and triumphant revelation, as Atwood undermines patriarchal Victorian ideals of rationality and moral certainty.[43]

The Blind Assassin

Atwood's tenth novel, *The Blind Assassin*, commonly elicits comparison with *Alias Grace*. For Alan Robinson, the two novels address 'similar historiographic difficulties'. Faced with a protagonist suspected of playing some role in the death of others, readers of both texts 'confront a biased, possibly unreliable narrator'.[44] Howells, instead, observes that, while both novels attempt to recover the past, *The Blind Assassin*, unlike *Alias Grace*, is 'not about things which have been forgotten but about things that have been deliberately hidden'.[45] And for Stein, much as Grace's narrative provided a glimpse of the broader cultural and political concerns of nineteenth-century Canada, so *The Blind Assassin* offers a 'social critique of the hypocrisy, injustice, classism, and sexism of the twentieth century'.[46] In these and many other analyses, critics note recurring concerns with storytelling, the entwining of personal and national histories, and the difficulties and desires involved in reconstructing the past.

Overview

The Blind Assassin is one of Atwood's most structurally complex narratives. Constructed, as Stein describes, 'like a Russian wooden doll', it contains stories nested within stories.[47] The novel is framed by a present-day narrative delivered in the last years of the twentieth century by 82-year-old Iris Chase Griffen. With a failing heart, Iris determines to write a memoir before she dies in which she will reveal family secrets, particularly those related to the suicide of her sister Laura in 1945.

Iris is what Marta Dvorak terms 'a knowledgeable narrating I'.[48] Her story stretches back to the late-nineteenth century, when Iris's grandfather built the button factory on which the Chase family fortune is founded. It proceeds through the courtship and marriage of her parents, Iris and Laura's childhood, Iris's unhappy marriage to the industrialist Richard Griffen and Iris's estrangement from her daughter Aimee, and eventually looks forward to her granddaughter, Sabrina, the imagined addressee of Iris's revelations.

The family history that Iris recounts is interspersed with details from her present life in Port Ticonderoga, Ontario, historical newspaper reports, extracts from *The Blind Assassin*, a cult novella written by Laura and published posthumously by Iris to great scandal and later acclaim, and – finally – extracted from the novella, excerpts from a series of science fiction tales of the Planet Zycron, told to Laura by her unnamed lover. As the novel proceeds, Iris is eventually revealed as the true author of the novella that she credited to her sister. Howells describes Atwood's *The Blind Assassin* novel, Laura's *The Blind Assassin* novella and the science fiction stories about blind assassins as 'three interlocking but apparently interrelated stories, all written in different styles and with different narrators'.[49] And as Robinson notes, Iris's revelation means that the novel actually contains two autobiographies by Iris: 'one written with coded obliquity during the 1940s' and one written over fifty years later, which has 'the benefit of hindsight but the added unreliability' of having been written long after the original events.[50]

Ingersoll terms *The Blind Assassin* 'a "whodunnit" – with a vengeance', in which the reader is enticed by the mystery of the opening line – 'Ten days after the war ended, my sister Laura drove a car off a bridge' (3) – and the ensuing desire to understand the motive for Laura's death.[51] To explain this event, Iris returns to her childhood. She recalls her father, Norval, returning traumatized from the Great War, having lost two brothers and an eye, and her beautiful, self-sacrificing mother, Liliana, always urging Iris to take care of her younger sister: an imposition that Iris resents. As Howells observes, Iris's identity 'is defined by her gender, her class and her role as "good sister to Laura"'.[52] When Liliana dies of a miscarriage in 1925, a young Iris overhears whispered gossip that Norval made too many sexual demands on his fragile wife. In this manner, suggests Stein, Iris internalises a gendered dichotomy of 'frail, sexless women and demanding, dangerous men' – a lesson she later takes with her into her marriage to Richard.[53]

If Iris reluctantly accepts her role as her sister's keeper, Laura – a dreamy and, to Iris, often infuriating character – is instinctively drawn to images of self-sacrifice. When the teenaged sisters meet Alex Thomas, 'an unknown young man of indeterminate social class', at a Labor Day picnic in 1934, Laura commences an intense devotion.[54] When Alex is revealed to be a communist agitator wanted by the police, the sisters combine forces to shelter him in the Chase family mansion, but subsequently, their competing feelings for him drive each to secrecy.

With the family fortune threatened, Norval marries off Iris to Richard, who Iris later reveals physically and sexually abuses both her and her sister: 'he'd got a bargain', reflects Iris, 'two for the price of one' (617). If Iris marries Richard out of a sense of familial duty, Laura submits to his sexual abuse in order – as she believes – to save Alex. For Stein, Richard remains 'a flat character, almost a caricature, a Dickensian villain': a judgement that, as Stein observes, Iris the self-reflexive memoirist also acknowledges.[55] His pantomime villainy, however, is well-suited to what becomes an increasingly gothic and melodramatic account. Richard, along with his witch-like sister,

Winifred, continues to control both sisters, and when Iris is pregnant with Aimee, Richard has Laura committed to a mental asylum, from which she escapes. Later, when a telegram arrives announcing Alex's death, Iris, knowing that Laura would be devastated at the news, informs her sister that she and Alex had been lovers. Shortly afterwards, Laura drives off a bridge and Iris remains convinced that her revelation pushed her to it.

Iris publishes her novella under Laura's name, engulfing Richard in the ensuing scandal and destroying his rising political career. When he later commits suicide in a boating 'accident', a vengeful Winifred mounts a campaign against Iris and wins custody of Aimee and, subsequently, when Aimee dies of an overdose, of Sabrina. After this succession of abuses, Iris's tell-all end-of-life memoir is, notes Robinson, her 'final act of revenge against the Griffens'.[56] By revealing her affair with Alex, Iris tells Sabrina that she is no blood relation to the Griffens and is therefore free of the tangled family history. For Howells, *The Blind Assassin* is ultimately 'the memoir of a survivor' that also potentially functions 'as public memorial, as revenge, or as exorcism'.[57]

A self-conscious storyteller

Iris, like Grace, is a self-conscious storyteller, always aware of the impact and power of her voice and the limits placed on her as a woman writer. Discussing the 'textual revenge' that Iris enacts through the writing of her memoir, Alice Ridout compares Iris's multiple thwarted attempts to tell her story to her grandfather's privately printed volume, *The Chase Industries: A History*, presented to business associates by a man with the 'freedom, power and money to authorize his own version of himself'. Unlike the poorly produced first editions of '*The Blind Assassin*', which carry a blurry image of Laura and from which Iris's name is absent, Benjamin Chase's signature is embossed in gold across the leather-bound covers of his book, confidently declaring his authorship and his authority. In contrast, Iris's novella is 'at first ignored and then viewed as transgressive'. Ridout suggests that this experience of authorial marginalization and 'the fear of not being read' is a large part of what compels Iris's second attempt at autobiography.[58]

In an essay examining the recurring trope of blindness in Atwood's fiction, Wilson also tackles the question of why Iris decides to write her final memoir. She argues that because Iris has been culpably, wilfully blind, 'lacking insight into history, current events, mythology, her father, husband, sister Laura, and her own motivations', she has endangered the safety of herself and others.[59] Realizing and regretting this in old age, Iris's second attempt at autobiography, suggests Wilson, can be understood as an attempt to rectify some of the mistakes she has made due to her lack of insight.

While blindness is obviously a prominent trope in *The Blind Assassin*, so too is muteness. The sacrificial virgins in Alex's stories have their tongues cut out so they cannot be heard screaming. So too is Iris repeatedly silenced, unable to voice her desires or speak her fears and accusations. Discussing this silencing, and the erasure of women's voices, Ridout points to a recurring motif in the novel of transient writing – children writing their names in the snow, washroom graffiti – and argues that Iris's memoir aspires to permanence. Ridout argues that Benjamin's history of the family's rising fortunes (to which Laura and Iris will both be sacrificed) silences the voices of the Chase women. In contrast, Iris's memoir is notably matrilineal, tracing a lineage from her grandmother Adelia to her granddaughter Sabrina. Iris, she suggests, is aware of the harm that writing can do, but is still more wary of 'the dangers of silence'.[60]

In defiance of the injunction on her to be silent and biddable, Iris produces an incendiary, 'palimpsestic' text in which, in Dvorak's words, 'multiple subtexts or countertexts [. . .] criss-cross one another' providing a rich, multi-voiced and subversive narrative. Where Ridout focuses on the motives driving Iris's memoir, Dvorak examines instead the methods by which Atwood constructs her 'resolutely postmodern' text.[61] By drawing attention to the story-within-a-story structure of the narrative, she suggests, the novel undermines the illusion of the framing narrative, cautioning the reader that this version, too, is yet another self-conscious act of storytelling.

Iris's memoir is carefully crafted to create intrigue and momentum. Commencing in medias res with Laura's unexplained death, Iris then proceeds to gather and order the threads of different narratives, public and private, from which she constructs her family history. Despite its close orchestration, however, Iris's narrative is also fragmented and interrupted. As Dvorak observes, Iris's present, knowing voice is frequently invaded by the narrative perspectives of multiple younger, less-knowing incarnations of Iris, which are in turn overlaid by newspaper accounts, scraps of gossip, local histories and oral narratives from various sources. For Dvorak, these multiple versions of the 'truth' eventually lead the reader to recognize that each version is only ever 'partial'.[62] Yet despite the text's typically postmodern indeterminacy, Dvorak argues that its many multidimensional strands and layers eventually combine to create a coherent 'meta-structure' that, when deciphered, is 'undeniably unifying'.[63] Unlike *Alias Grace*, which remains resolutely ambiguous, *The Blind Assassin* reveals its secrets and resolves its mysteries.

This sense of closure in *The Blind Assassin* is the focus of Ingersoll's essay on the novel, 'Waiting for the End', in which he describes the 'textual erotics' aroused in the reader by two competing desires: 'a desire for the end and a desire to postpone the end of the narrative'.[64] Using the metafictional techniques of self-conscious fiction, *The Blind Assassin*, with Iris's many observations about the difficulties of writing it, 'masquerades' as a novel being written before our eyes.[65] Iris's preoccupation with completing her memoir before her heart gives way creates a sense of urgency and elicits anxiety that Iris might not reach the ending in time. Other metafictional tropes that Ingersoll identifies include Iris's reflections on the difficulty of providing an honest account of one's own actions and her likening of her writing to spinning – a crafting trope that recalls Grace's quilting in *Alias Grace*. For Ingersoll, where readers of the earlier novel grow increasingly unsure of ever discovering what happened, *The Blind Assassin*, in contrast, seems to reassure its readers that 'the truth will ultimately be revealed'.[66]

As a self-conscious storyteller, Iris first proposes that she will strive to write for no one: as though the right hand were writing and the left hand erasing. This, she suggests, is the only way to ensure absolute integrity as a writer. With time, however, she accepts the impossibility of this attempt and starts instead to conceive of her text as addressed to Sabrina. Iris comes to recognize that there can be no full and omniscient truth, 'not because of what I've set down, but because of what I've omitted' (484). Like Dvorak, Ingersoll accepts that the novel provides significant answers; the reader, he concedes, experiences 'a tremendous sense of gratification' in confirming that Alex was Iris's lover and that she knowingly revealed this to Laura. Ingersoll, however, locates these 'facts' within the modernist mode as raising 'traditionally modernist issues such as the unreliability of narrators'. He suggests that because, by her own admission, Iris is writing for her granddaughter, her final revelations require some scepticism around motive (which the novel encourages), regarding Iris's guilt, for example, and her desire to secure her legacy. Unlike Dvorak, who identifies a fundamentally coherent structure beneath the novel's fragmentary, postmodern façade, Ingersoll suggests that *The Blind Assassin* concludes by 'offering a "truth" more indeterminate than readers might otherwise desire'.[67]

A gothic tale of victims and villains

Much as *The Blind Assassin* contains fragments of competing textual discourses, so it combines elements of competing genres. In her essay, Dvorak draws attention to the opening segment of the novel, taken from Laura's novella, in which the unnamed male narrator offers to tell a story in any mode of pulp fiction that his lover requests. 'You can have your pick', he tells her: 'jungles, tropical islands, mountains. Or another dimension of space – that's what I'm best at' (11). In this way, Dvorak suggests, Atwood highlights the manner in which genre conventions shape a narrative, and exposes 'the cultural clichés from which these fictional formulas emerge, and which they prolong'.[68] By drawing out recurring motifs of gendered violence, silencing and sacrifice across the novel's strands of romance, crime story and science fiction, she also exposes their ubiquity.

While crime, romance and science fiction are foregrounded in *The Blind Assassin*, many critics identify its primary genre as the gothic. For Robinson, the novel is characteristically Atwoodian in its depiction of a 'female protagonist's hauntings by ghosts which defy repression and must be confronted and appeased'.[69] Howells suggests the novel is 'as complicated as any Gothic romance or Victorian sensation novel'.[70] Ingersoll also draws attention to Iris's indulgence in the melodrama of gothic romance when she speculates, rather spitefully (as she half-expects Myra, the daughter of the Chase family's housekeeper, to be her first reader), as to whether Myra's biological father was not in fact Reenie's husband, but Iris's own father. This unexpected aside, argues Ingersoll, gestures towards the gothic genre's familiar tropes of master–servant relations and 'secret blood-ties', and also provides a glimpse into the 'iciness' of Iris's character as she alludes quite dispassionately to another possible sister.[71]

An extended reading of the novel's gothic aspect is offered by Stein. Where *Lady Oracle* is a comic gothic romance, *The Blind Assassin*, she suggests, is instead 'a tragic novel that uses Gothic plot devices'. These include familiar gothic conventions such as 'dreams, interrupted narration, imprisoning structures, disguises, exploration of secrets, mysterious pictures, signs, and secret or hidden rooms or other enclosures'.[72] Outlining feminist-engaged critiques of gothic fiction, which typically point to the genre's exposition of women's anxieties around imprisonment and powerlessness within a patriarchal society, Stein observes similar gothic fears at play in the stories of Laura and Iris.

Stein's essay explores the way in which Atwood uses and subverts gothic conventions. In a gothic reversal, Iris and Laura become Alex's protectors, hiding him in the attic. At the same time, notes Stein, the sisters will also experience the gothic fate of being trapped in the home of a villainous older man. Indeed, in Atwood's novel, with its many references to young men killed in war, both men and women are sometimes sacrificial victims. Gothic fiction, observes Stein, typically concludes on the freeing of the imprisoned heroine, the revelation of secret knowledge, and equilibrium as 'a young lover supersedes the older man'. In *The Blind Assassin*, instead, the young lover is long dead, and Iris frees both herself and her granddaughter from the prison of the past. Where once Iris was the blank page on which a gothic narrative of Richard's bruises was written, now she takes charge of the story, and in doing so, suggests Stein, 'registers her transformation from silence to speech, from dominated wife to independent agent'.[73] By writing in the gothic mode, Iris is able to both construct a melodramatic tale of violence and entrapment and escape its confines.

The Penelopiad

In 2005, Atwood published *The Penelopiad*. A slim volume, and a rewriting of a canonical text – a departure for Atwood – it is in many ways quite different from *Alias Grace* and *The Blind Assassin*. Nevertheless, the three texts share many concerns, specifically: the difficulties of narrating a past accessible only via myriad, unverifiable sources; the politics of storytelling (of who gets to tell their version of events); and a gendered critique of violence and power.

Overview

Described by Hilde Staels as 'a multivoiced and multiperspectival novella', *The Penelopiad* retells the story of Homer's *The Odyssey* from the perspective of Odysseus's famously faithful wife, Penelope.[74] Where Homer describes Odysseus's epic adventures on his ill-fated attempt to return to Ithaca after fighting in the Trojan War, Atwood's revision stays close to home. The narrative commences with Penelope, centuries after her death, speaking from the shadowy underworld of Hades and desirous to set the record straight. As she declares, after years of being mythologized as the wife of a legendary soldier and King, 'it's my turn to do a little story-making' (3). Penelope's life is largely taken up with domestic duties and managing female relationships – first with her beautiful and selfish cousin, the famous Helen of Troy and later with her mother-in-law and Odysseus's old nurse, both jealous of Odysseus's affections. The petty rivalries and general household management that Penelope describes are familiar in their mundanity as Atwood engages in what Howells terms a 'postmodern domestification of myth', reducing 'Odysseus's adventures with monsters and goddesses [. . .] to the level of gossip and tall tales'.[75] Crucially, however, as I point out in an essay on Atwood's revisions of classic texts, this domestic tale of women and home 'proves no less bloody, no less treacherous, and no less dramatic'.[76]

Penelope proceeds to recount her story, with which readers are familiar but which is traditionally relegated to the periphery of Odysseus's tale: how Penelope successfully maintains Odysseus's kingdom in his twenty-year absence and raises their son, Telemachus, alone; how she is pursued by the carousing, gluttonous suitors, who set up camp in her home and demand that she declare herself a widow and take another husband; and how, with the help of her twelve maids, she uses her wiles to outwit them; and finally, how Odysseus returns, tests his wife's constancy and then avenges himself on the suitors and hangs Penelope's maids as traitors. For Atwood, the hanging of the twelve maids remains the most troublesome element of Homer's narrative, and in *The Penelopiad*, she gives these violently silenced women a voice. Speaking in a succession of chorus interludes delivered in a range of musical and dramatic forms, the maids challenge Penelope from beyond the grave. Accusing her of betrayal – of inducing Odysseus to kill them so that they might never reveal her secrets – the rebellious maids challenge the upper-class authority of Penelope's narrative much as Penelope challenges the primacy of Odysseus's masculine experiences.

Is it a novel?

The disruptive, rebellious function of the maids' voices in *The Penelopiad* is given structural expression in the text through Atwood's use of the Greek chorus, whereby the maids episodically interject into Penelope's narrative, providing a destabilizing additional commentary. This practice is taken directly from the tradition of Greek theatre and is indicative of the manner in which Atwood plays with form in this text, which seems to lie on the cusp of novel and drama. Indeed, Atwood later adapted *The Penelopiad* for the stage, prompting Susanne Jung to describe it as 'quite literally situated at a crossroads of genres'.[77] Discussing the adaptation with the director, Phyllida Lloyd, Atwood explains: 'The book is in essence theatrical. It's a lot like the structure of a Greek tragedy.'[78] Developing this point, Ingersoll suggests that the text's ambiguous status as novel, novella or drama is shaped by its genesis in the Canongate Myths series of adaptations. Finding herself bound by the fundamental elements of the original plot, Ingersoll proposes that Atwood responded to this limitation by subverting the conventions of the novel genre to the point at which *The Penelopiad* might be better described, more cautiously, as 'a prose fiction version of the myth'.[79]

Ingersoll suggests that, with *The Penelopiad*, Atwood appears 'less interested in writing a novel than offering a pastiche of literary forms or genres'.[80] While the most obvious of these is the Greek chorus, the choral interludes are themselves a succession of pastiches: a rope-jumping rhyme, a lament, a popular tune, an idyll, a sea shanty, a ballad, a drama, a lecture, a trial and a love song. Examining these episodes, Jung connects Atwood's version of the Greek chorus with its many musical numbers to the more contemporary genre of musical theatre, 'so the maids literally appear as chorus line girls'.[81] Focusing on form, Ingersoll observes that Penelope's first-person narrative, which describes her life and its trials, is the most obviously novelistic element of the text. He argues, however, that at times the book becomes too contemporary – 'more reminiscent of soap opera' than classical tragedy. It is Ingersoll's contention that Penelope aspires to tragedy, but the text persistently resists her. Instead, he locates *The Penelopiad* within the genre of fictionalized memoir, which he suggests Atwood is attracted to for its 'efficacy in problematizing the search for truth' by addressing issues of memory, guilt and competing desires for both reparation and revenge – all of which pertain to Penelope's attempt to speak her story.[82]

Reclaiming voices – the twelve hanged maids

Atwood's decision to reimagine *The Odyssey* as *The Penelopiad* points to a familiar feminist literary strategy of reclaiming lost women's voices. Atwood's title, I suggest, 'wrests attention from Odysseus's *Odyssey*, placing Penelope at the centre of the narrative' and prioritizing the dutiful wife within 'the alternative "herstory" that follows'. But while this revisionary method may be well established as a means to challenge the patriarchal hegemony of Western literature, I also observe that Atwood complicates this practice. While I argue that 'To speak – to speak up, speak out, be heard, to refuse to be silent – is a feminist act', when Penelope starts to speak, so too do her maids, and they accuse her of violence, betrayal and complicity. The neat binary shift from 'his-story' to 'her-story' is complicated by the incursion of the maids' bawdy chorus of voices, which haunt Penelope throughout the text. In a typically complicated Atwoodian move, Atwood 'grants Penelope the right to reply to the patriarchal myth', but simultaneously extends that same right to the silenced and disenfranchised women who believe themselves to have been wronged by their mistress. In doing so, Atwood demonstrates that victimhood 'is not exclusive, and rarely simple'.[83]

Howells similarly locates *The Penelopiad* within a tradition of 'feminist revisionary mythmaking'. As she points out, the hanging of the maids barely gets a mention in Homer's epic, whereas Atwood's feminist revision relocates the relationship between Penelope and her maids to the centre of the story, and – in a link to *Alias Grace* and *The Blind Assassin* – makes the question of Penelope's collusion in their deaths 'the unsolved mystery at the heart of the narrative'. For Howells, 'A whiff of scandal surrounds Atwood's woman-centred revision of *The Odyssey*' which tries to get to the bottom of the text's central conundrum.[84] In the words of Atwood's introduction: 'what led to the hanging of the maids, and what was Penelope really up to?' (xxi).

While Penelope clearly remains haunted by the murdered maids, the manner and the extent to which their voices are recovered by the text remains contentious. In the tradition of Greek tragedy, Penelope is an individualized character whose monologues are interrupted by the chorus, who provide commentary and context but do not interact with the central character. Jung observes that this dramatic convention ensures that the maids remain excluded from Penelope's central prose narrative, pushed to the periphery of her text as unruly intruders. Making a similar point, Howells draws a connection with the Handmaids of *The Handmaid's Tale*, relegated to silence and to the margins of history.

Jung, however, suggests that, as outsiders, the maids also speak 'from a position of epistemic privilege'. Much to Penelope's discomfort, the maids have privileged access to the text's central matter of the 'truth' of what *really* happened.[85] Howells also makes a further connection here with Atwood's mythographic techniques in *Alias Grace*, and cites Atwood's description of herself as a historical novelist, 'digging below official versions of history to unearth "the mysterious, the buried, the forgotten, the discarded, the taboo"'.[86] If Penelope's story draws attention to the silencing of women in the Western canon, Howells points out that the story of the maids further draws attention to both gender and class, focusing on the physical and sexual exploitation of a female underclass who have no rights over their own bodies. By allowing the maids to speak – even in a peripheral, oblique and coded manner – Atwood prevents Penelope from too easily substituting one edifying myth for another.

In an article that examines feminist rewritings of *The Odyssey*, Mihoko Suzuki suggests that *The Penelopiad* raises a dilemma facing feminist adaptations of canonical texts: whether to revise and rewrite female characters who have traditionally (misogynistically) been reviled as immoral or destructive, or, instead, to 'allow agency, intelligence, and voice to female protagonists who may not be unequivocally admirable?' For Suzuki, Atwood addresses this problem through her innovative decision to bring to the fore the story of the maids. Atwood re-envisions the maids, she observes, not as silenced victims, but as 'energetic satirists of the dominant order, who literally put Odysseus on trial'. By providing the maids with a transgressive and disruptive voice, by allowing them to invade Penelope's stage, Suzuki argues that Atwood enables them to eloquently speak back to the dominant patriarchal order 'that normalized their slaughter by condemning them as unchaste and disloyal', while still leaving Penelope open to criticism and critique.[87]

Classical revisions and re-readings

Atwood's rewriting of Homer's epic has inspired comparisons with other contemporary works by women writers that ventriloquize classic mythology – works that, in Susanna Braund's words, 'ask uncomfortable or disconcerting questions' about familiar canonical texts.[88] Comparing *The Penelopiad* to Carol Ann Duffy's 1999 poetry collection, *The World's Wife*, Braund, like Howells, discusses the manner in which these contemporary interventions work to make their familiar classical sources strange by reimagining mythic tales within the limits of the prosaic and the mundane. In her article, Braund also examines Atwood's 1974 poem, 'Siren Song', from the collection *You Are Happy*, and identifies a clear feminist agenda in Atwood's reimagining of the 'quintessentially misogynistic myth' of the sirens as ruthless seducers of men. By allowing one of the Sirens to speak, thereby providing context, motivation and humour, Atwood injects 'depth and complexity' into the mythical tale.[89] In contrast, Braund suggests that the inclusion of the maids' voices in *The Penelopiad* complicates the clear feminism of the earlier revision, and she proposes that Atwood's focus on the 'utterly powerless' maids functions – in a manner previously seen in *The Robber Bride* – as a 'caution against mutual betrayal among women'.[90]

A different comparison is offered by Staels, who examines *The Penelopiad* alongside Jeanette Winterson's *Weight* (2005), which rewrites the myth of Atlas and which, like Atwood's text, mixes high and low genres, to parodic effect. In her discussion, Staels uses Hutcheon's definition of parody as 'repetition with critical difference' and notes that parody uses mimicry and imitation with serious critical purpose.[91] Staels argues that *The Penelopiad* uses both parody and 'burlesque travesty' – a more comic disruptive mode – as a means of 'liberating the protagonists from the boundaries and limitations of the ancient epic story world'.[92] Elements of burlesque travesty, she explains, are introduced into the text through anachronistic contemporary colloquialisms (e.g. when Penelope describes Helen as 'stuck-up' (20)), or in the maids' bawdy interludes. Parody, suggests Staels, enables writers like Atwood and Winterson to create a continuity with the classical world depicted in their narratives while also exposing discontinuities. In parodying and burlesquing the ancient Homeric myth, argues Staels, Atwood engages in a process of 'demythologizing': once the female characters have access to contemporary speech, and once the contradictions of Penelope and the maids' versions of events are exposed and the distinctions of high and low culture are undermined, 'the idealization of the distant past is destroyed'.[93]

For Staels, the irreverence with which Atwood treats her classical source material has a dual consequence. Penelope's down-to-earth narrative strips Homer's characters of many of their marvellous, mystical attributes and results in what Staels terms a 'depreciation of epic characters' (Odysseus has short legs; Helen is vain). But at the same time, she argues, they also undergo an 'appreciation', as the distant, mythical figures take on a new 'psychological realism and individualization'.[94] Suzuki makes a related point when she focuses on the manner in which Atwood's contemporary language brings her mythical characters sharply down to earth. For example, when Penelope declares that Circe's enchanted island was really just 'an expensive whorehouse' (84), Atwood is able, Suzuki suggests, to reinforce, in her contemporary reading, 'the shrewdness and scepticism' that are Penelope's 'defining features' in *The Odyssey*.[95] In examining the effects of language, form, parody and feminist revision, each of these critics suggests that Atwood's interventions in the classical text reinvigorate Homer's original work.

In examining *The Penelopiad* alongside *Alias Grace* and *The Blind Assassin*, this chapter skips over the intervening 2003 publication of *Oryx and Crake*. Originally intended as a stand-alone work, *Oryx and Crake* later became the first volume in the *MaddAddam* trilogy. Until the 2019 publication of *The Testaments*, which returns Atwood's readers to the Gilead of *The Handmaid's Tale*, the three dystopian *MaddAddam* novels represented Atwood's only experiment with connecting her fictional worlds and characters across texts. The next chapter examines the works of the trilogy together.

6

Atwood's dystopian futures
The *MaddAddam* trilogy

When Atwood published her eleventh novel, *Oryx and Crake*, in 2003, it was received as a significant turn to apocalyptic writing with environmental concerns at the fore. It was typically viewed as a departure in her work, not least for its primary male protagonist. In a review of the novel for the *London Review of Books*, Elaine Showalter suggested that, while the politics of *Oryx and Crake* are largely consistent with Atwood's 'pacifism, feminism, environmentalism and anti-globalism', she is 'much more forgiving of Americans and men [. . .] than in her earlier books'.[1] Like all of Atwood's previous works before the publication of *The Testaments* in 2019, the novel was initially presented as a stand-alone text, and was read as such. It was followed by four very different books (*The Penelopiad*, 2005; *Moral Disorder*, 2006; *The Tent*, 2006; and *Payback*, 2007) comprising a mythic rewriting, an 'almost a novel' story cycle, poetry, short stories and essays. In time, however, Atwood declared her intention to return to the world of *Oryx and Crake* and, with *The Year of the Flood* (2009) and *MaddAddam* (2013), she eventually completed what came to be known as the *MaddAddam* trilogy. As such, this triumvirate of texts represents something unique in Atwood's canon: a significant engagement with a unified project that stretches across a decade.

Despite the trilogy's distinctiveness, however, many critics also readily recognized that the concerns prioritized in the three novels have a long genesis in Atwood's writing. Connections were most commonly made with the dystopian aspect of *The Handmaid's Tale*, in which environmental degradation provides the backdrop to the fertility crisis that fuels the rise of Gilead. For Coral Ann Howells, reading *Oryx and Crake* alongside *The Handmaid's Tale*, the two texts represent Atwood's imaginative response to 'contemporary situations of cultural crisis'. She suggests that *Oryx and Crake* (and, consequently, the imagined world of the trilogy) can be read as a kind of sequel to *The Handmaid's Tale*. While the earlier novel is a product of the neoconservative politics of the 1980s and the later text addresses notably twenty-first-century concerns, the pollution that plagues North America in *The Handmaid's Tale* has, by the imagined time of *Oyrx and Crake*, 'escalated into worldwide climate change through global warming'.[2]

Other critics make still earlier connections, pointing to the environmental concerns raised in works such as the 1972 novel, *Surfacing*, in which 'the Americans' poison the lake and kill a heron: the symbol of victimized nature in the text. In an essay that explores the longstanding preoccupation with environmentalism in Atwood's work, Shannon Hengen draws a connection between *Surfacing*, *Life Before Man* and *Oryx and Crake* as three novels that display Atwood's 'ongoing concern with how humans fit into the environment'.[3] And in an essay that primarily focuses on *The Year of the Flood*, Miles Weafer uses the four victim positions outlined by Atwood in her 1972 thematic guide to Canadian literature, *Survival*, and applies them to the *MaddAddam* trilogy. Weafer locates Atwood's post-apocalyptic novels within a history of Canadian literary works that confront 'an unforgiving landscape and a history of colonial exploitation' – works in which an encounter with nature is not a Romantic experience of the sublime but rather a confrontation with 'hostile elements to be survived'.[4]

Moving beyond the focus on environmental damage, the trilogy's concern with biotechnology and advances in the genetic sciences placed Atwood's representation of science under scrutiny. Showalter describes *Oryx and Crake* as 'a tightly worked-out and intellectually gripping sci-fi mystery'.[5] While for Natasha Walter, reviewing *Oryx and Crake* in *The Guardian*, the novel holds a simple message: 'don't trust the scientists and the big corporations to run the world.'[6] The novel was also reviewed in *Science* magazine, suggesting a certain level of interest in Atwood's vision by the scientific community. Noting Atwood's reluctance to accept the science-fiction label, Susan Squier suggests that novels such as *Life Before Man*, *The Handmaid's Tale* and *Oryx and Crake* are more accurately described as 'inspired by the imaginative force and urgent social importance of scientific fact'. The seriousness of Atwood's literary reflections on science, argues Squier, is epitomized in her juxtaposition of the woefully underfunded Martha Graham liberal arts Academy with the lavishly equipped Watson-Crick Scientific Institute. Atwood's concern, she concludes, is to 'challenge our fascination with what science can do at the expense of what art can say'.[7]

A more combative response to Atwood's science is provided by Anthony Griffiths in a review essay for the journal *Canadian Literature*. Griffiths argues that if Atwood wants her scientific warnings to be taken seriously, then her science must stand up to scrutiny. Where Squier takes Atwood's extensive list of acknowledged sources as evidence of the depth of her research, Griffiths finds a dearth of peer-reviewed research science and argues that Atwood betrays an overreliance on the kind of sensationalist popular science that commonly circulates in the press. He argues that *Oryx and Crake* uses genetic engineering as 'a lightning rod for wrath aimed at the negative outcomes of science in general'. Targeting genetic science, however, 'is inappropriate and misleading' and fails to acknowledge the field's positive effects and the suffering it has the potential to eradicate.[8] Taking the example of the pigoons – genetically modified pigs that escape and terrorize the protagonist Jimmy – Griffiths points to the very real ecological damage done by releasing non-native imported species into new habitats and describes it as 'another instance where the imaginary problems expressed in *Oryx and Crake* distract our attention from the real ones that assail us'.[9] Responses such as Griffiths's highlight the scrutiny to which Atwood's most recent fictions are subject, particularly where they make claims to tackle real-world concerns such as biotechnology, globalization and climate change.

Oryx and Crake

Overview

Oryx and Crake commences with the protagonist Snowman, formerly known as Jimmy, scrabbling out a subsistence living on a scorched beach. Jimmy – as I will continue to refer to him, although some critics prefer Snowman – is seemingly the last man standing in the wake of an apocalyptic holocaust orchestrated by his former best friend, Crake, via a pharmaceutically released global plague. While the novel's post-apocalyptic setting lends itself to a general sense of timelessness, this is a near-future catastrophe. Jimmy describes his present as 'zero hour' (3) and the novel seems to exist in what Lee Rozelle terms 'a chronological pause between an unsustainable past and an uncertain future'.[10] In her article on *Oryx and Crake*, J. Brooks Bouson pays close attention to the novel's timeline; noting that Atwood has said elsewhere that the novel is set around Massachusetts on the East Coast of the United States, and that Jimmy is born in 1999, and is twenty-eight at the time the novel opens, Bouson dates the novel's setting as circa 2027.[11]

Although the novel commences in the immediate aftermath of Crake's catastrophic eradication of mankind, Jimmy is not alone. His depleted landscape is stalked by various genetically modified animals: splices of different species, engineered at the whim of irresponsible scientists, that present surprising and often alarming new capacities. More significantly, he keeps a resentful watch over a small community of Crakers – a genetically enhanced humanoid population bioengineered by Crake to replace and improve on irredeemable humanity. Their effect, as creatures both human and non-human, is uncanny. Crake's desire was to eradicate humanity's weaknesses – lust, competition, prejudice, aggression, greed and so forth – and his creatures are, indeed, beautiful, peaceable creatures, fostering 'post-racial, non-hierarchical vegetarianism'.[12] At the same time, as Hengen observes, the creatures are deeply unnerving, lacking 'a sense of humor or ambiguity or loss'.[13] Bouson, however, acknowledging the Crakers' weirdness, suggests that they were never really intended as a model for human improvement, but rather provide Atwood's 'satiric vision of a bioengineered posthuman future'.[14]

The slow pace of Jimmy's sun-scorched present-tense narrative contrasts with his interwoven memories, which rapidly progress from childhood into young adulthood. He charts his relationship with Crake from their school days growing up in a corporation compound, through their differing paths into higher education and eventual reunion when Crake brings Jimmy in to work for him in marketing his top-secret project, which a naïve and self-absorbed Jimmy fails to fully understands until it is much too late. As Katharine Snyder puts it, Jimmy has been 'largely unwitting, yet also wilfully unknowing' in his complicity with Crake's scheme.[15]

Oryx and Crake, as most critics observe, is a double dystopia: Jimmy's post-apocalyptic present succeeds a bleakly dystopian vision of the near future. For Walter, discussing Atwood's first foray into a male central protagonist, the novel successfully captures the perspective of a man 'brought up in an emotionally stunted environment saturated with pornography and commercialism'.[16] The world of Jimmy's youth is full of recognizable details from our present: internet pornography, fast food, videogames, advertising, voracious pharma and beauty industries, and enormous economic inequalities. It is a world in which a techno-literate elite have retreated into gated compounds, leaving the masses to fend for themselves in the largely lawless 'pleeblands' beyond. As Berthold Schoene describes it, the novel's pre-apocalyptic past is 'a dystopian hyperbole of our present'. Reflecting on the various neologisms that Atwood introduces – CorpSeCorps, rakunks, pleeblands, etcetera – Schoene suggests that, in a world in which everything is degraded, language itself 'seems battered and mushed up by advertising'.[17] Making a similar point, Gerry Canavan suggests that Jimmy and Crake grow up in 'a hyperextended, hypertrophic version of US-style consumer capitalism – our mad world, gone even madder'.[18]

In this degraded near future, Jimmy and Crake first encounter Oryx on a porn site as an exploited child sex worker from an unidentified impoverished country. Drawn to her enigmatic gaze, the boys download her picture and she becomes an object of deeply problematic desire for them both. Citing this same moment, Snyder argues that Crake and Jimmy engage in 'a form of fetishistic souvenir-collecting similar to those of the globe-trotting sex tourists whom they watch online'.[19] Later, Crake facilitates Oryx's entry into the United States, and her role remains ambiguous: she is a sex worker, romanticized by Jimmy as his girlfriend, and also Crake's collaborator, working as his assistant on the Craker project. Only ever very sketchily drawn, Oryx is, for Showalter, a vehicle for 'Atwood's indignation at child slavery, prostitution, sex tourism and other extreme forms of female victimisation'.[20] While for Bouson, she is a fitting character for the 'body-identified and sex-addicted postfeminist world of the future' that Atwood constructs.[21] Used and objectified to the last, Crake eventually orchestrates his own death by killing Oryx in front of Jimmy, knowing that Jimmy will respond by shooting him in turn.

Crake's apocalyptic plan makes provision for an unwittingly vaccinated Jimmy to survive in order to act as shepherd and guide to the Crakers in the early days of the new order. Jimmy reluctantly oversees the population's nascent culture and takes a grim satisfaction from observing the first green shoots of their seemingly irrepressible myth-making facilities. Simultaneously, the present-day frame narrative finds Jimmy rapidly running out of supplies and, having cut his foot, in desperate need of medicine. He reluctantly concludes that he must return to the 'Paradice' dome in which Crake developed his great experiment. An epic journey thus ensues through a devastated landscape stalked by predators such as wolvogs and pigoons and concludes by revealing the murder-suicide of Oryx and Crake. Upon his return to the beach, Jimmy – like Robinson Crusoe before him – discovers a footprint in the sand. Hearing voices, he spies a small group of two armed men and a woman in a clearing, and realizes he is not after all a sole survivor. The novel concludes on a pause; Jimmy, still hidden, must decide whether to run away, to kill the intruders in order to ensure the safety of the Crakers or to make his presence known and re-join human society.

Textual allusions in *Oryx and Crake*

Like so much of Atwood's work, *Oryx and Crake* is self-consciously referential of a host of literary forebears and knowingly nods to many genres. Bouson describes it as 'a complex, and game-like, multi-layered narrative' and points to the particular influence of castaway-survivor narratives, detective stories and action-thrillers, romance and of course dystopian fiction.[22] In the tradition of much classic dystopian fiction, Jimmy is a lone figure reporting on a disturbing, alien world. Rozelle, however, argues that *Oryx and Crake* only inhabits the 'dystopian' category in the broadest sense, as 'all Orwellian social, legal, and cultural apparatus has seemingly been eliminated by the novel's first chapter'.[23] Stephen Dunning suggests that while *The Handmaid's Tale* works in the dystopian tradition of George Orwell's *Nineteen Eighty-Four* – an 'oppressive regime' which maintains itself by 'inflicting pain' – the pre-apocalyptic world of *Oryx and Crake*, instead, functions in the mode of Aldous Huxley's *Brave New World*: a regime which functions by inflicting 'a hardly less humiliating pleasure'.[24]

Also discussing the extent of Atwood's dystopia, Howells draws attention to the fact that, in both *The Handmaid's Tale* and *Oryx and Crake*, Atwood uses an epigraph from Swift ('A Modest Proposal' and *Gulliver's Travels* respectively). She suggests that Jimmy, living alongside the Crakers, is a kind of Gulliver, acting as 'both mouthpiece and butt of Atwood's satire'. Where Gulliver, however, eventually becomes alienated from human beings, Jimmy instead, 'emerges as a morally responsible man and the novel's unlikely hero'.[25] As he contemplates, with both trepidation and excitement, a return to the companionship of his fellow humans, Howells suggests that Atwood opens up a small window of optimism that is absent in Swift's much bleaker work. This reading is also supported by Schoene, who concludes that *Oryx and Crake* 'never rigidifies into pure dystopia'.[26]

In addition to issues of genre, certain readily identified literary allusions recur in critical responses to the novel. A *New York Times* review by Sven Birkerts typically nods to Huxley, Shelley's *Frankenstein* and Daniel Defoe's *Robinson Crusoe*, while also discerning the influence of Samuel Beckett on the opening scenes of Jimmy, alone and muttering amid a blighted landscape.[27] Howells similarly makes a connection with Defoe in noting that, compared to Offred's prison narrative in *The Handmaid's Tale*, *Oryx and Crake* is 'closer to a wilderness or castaway narrative'.[28] Similarly, for Snyder, Jimmy is 'marooned in time, cast away between a human past and a post-human future'.[29] While Shuli Barzilai describes him as 'the remnant of a colossal shipwreck, as it were, washed up on a barely habitable and lonely planet'.[30]

If Jimmy is Crusoe, then for many critics, Crake is Frankenstein. In Bouson's words, he is 'an amalgam of the mad-impersonal-amoral scientist figures' familiar from film and prose fiction.[31] A similar point is made by Showalter, who also connects Crake to a literary lineage when she declares: 'Like all mad scientists in literature, from [H. G. Wells's] Dr Moreau to [Stanley Kubrick's] Dr Strangelove, Crake would rather destroy than create life.'[32] Bouson also observes that Atwood's characterization of Crake, which emphasizes his 'rationalistic and game-like – and utterly affectless – approach to life', draws on familiar scientist stereotypes. She suggests, however, that the novel's various allusions to autism work to medicalize this aspect of Crake's behaviour, and thus complicate the literary cliché.[33]

Others instead draw attention to Atwood's biblical allusions. Chien-Hung Chen, in an article that examines *Oryx and Crake* alongside its companion novels, notes the theme of the biblical flood and suggests that the *MaddAddam* trilogy 'is meant to mock (up) the Biblical myth of origin through a pseudo-diluvian clean-up of digital annihilation'.[34] Lorrie Moore instead traces the biblical theme through Dante's influence, observing that Jimmy, trying to make his way to 'Paradice', is a Dante-like 'pilgrim in Hell'.[35] In Howell's words, he undergoes 'a journey to the Underworld' where he must confront his ghosts in order to 'become aware of the complex dimensions of his own humanity'.[36]

Finally, an extended Shakespearian intertextual analysis is offered by Barzilai in which she reads *Oryx and Crake* as a revenge tragedy, with Crake as 'an avenging son – a latter-day Hamlet'. Crake's story, she points out, traces Hamlet's: his father is murdered; his mother marries 'Uncle Pete', the man implicated in the crime; and the son vows revenge. As in Shakespearean tragedies, the final act (Jimmy's present-day narrative) sees the stage littered with bodies. Jimmy, suggests Barzilai, is Horatio, the play's survivor who lives to tell Hamlet's tale. Whereas Hamlet's father returns as a ghost to entreat his son's revenge, in Atwood's digital future, Crake learns of Uncle Pete's betrayal via his father's emails. Citing Atwood's 1992 short story, 'Gertrude Talks Back', Barzilai suggests that Hamlet is an important intertext for Atwood – one that speaks to two recurring key themes in her work: poor parenting and revenge. Barzilai (writing before the publication of *The Year of the Flood*) also turns to *Hamlet* as a guide to reading the ambiguous conclusion of the novel; just as Hamlet/Crake procrastinates but eventually avenges his dead father, so Barzilai argues that Jimmy – who is repeatedly exhorted by Crake: 'Don't let me down' – will complete his dead friend's work and protect the Crakers from the potential violence of the strange men: 'He will step forward, spray gun raised, to complete Crake's lethally altruistic plan.'[37]

Our post-human future

Raising the spectre of yet another literary influence, Lorrie Moore proposes that, in *Oryx and Crake*'s 'whimsical fantasies of biological evolution and technology', we can trace 'the dark left hand of Ursula K. Le Guin'.[38] Despite her reservations about the term, Atwood's novel is commonly identified and discussed as science fiction, with particular attention being paid to her vision of a post-human future. Bouson commences her article on the novel by reflecting on political scientist Francis Fukuyama's warning that biotechnology might potentially push humanity into a 'posthuman' stage of history. She suggests that *Oryx and Crake* provides a 'deadly serious and darkly satiric' examination of this threat.[39] For Bouson, Crake's affectless observation that 'pretty soon, demand is going to exceed supply *for everyone*' (347) is better read as Atwood's own sincere warning. And while the Crakers, she argues, function as a kind of 'bizarre spectacle and extended authorial joke', an 'over-the-top spoof' on some of the excesses of bioengineering (the blue penises obviously spring to mind), they are also intended to sound a serious warning about the dangers of reckless genetic modification.[40] A similar point is made by Canavan, for whom the Crakers are a Swiftian satire of primitivist fantasies that would turn back the clock of civilization and have man try to start again. Instead, he argues, rather than an actual plan to save the world, the Crakers function as an allegory of 'the radical transformation of both society and subjectivity that will be necessary in order to save the planet'.[41] Atwood, argues Bouson, urges real caution around reckless scientific advancements and warns against blindly stumbling into a catastrophic future in which scientists play God and we, like Jimmy, ignore the warning signs until it is too late.

Discussing Bouson's article, Rozelle argues that her dichotomous conclusion – that it will either be 'game over for ever' or, at best, that Atwood proffers some small glimmer of hope for human survival – dismisses 'the complex viability of remaining flora and fauna that still thrive in the novel'. Indeed, Rozelle charges much Atwood criticism with a similar anthropocentrism that focuses exclusively on the actions, responsibilities and fate of the human characters and disregards the wider ecosystem. This, he suggests, results in a 'missed opportunity' to closely examine the environmental implications of Atwood's work.[42] Focusing instead on the novel's 'liminal ecologies', Rozelle argues that *Oryx and Crake* offers hope for humanity and other life forms. Where we may initially assume that Jimmy's post-apocalyptic landscape is barren and forsaken – Jimmy calls it the 'Great Emptiness' (119) – by adopting an ecocritical perspective, we can instead identify a liminal zone in which plant and animal species continue to adapt and grow. And as an equally liminal figure, stranded between the past and the future, Jimmy, suggests Rozelle, must try to imagine a new future relationship between humans and ecosystems. By focusing, not on the end of humanity, but instead on 'the fate of all life', we come to see Jimmy in a drastically new perspective as just one element within a much larger ecosystem.[43]

For Earl Ingersoll, Atwood's novel concludes that 'if traditional human qualities have to be sacrificed in order to survive, it may not be worth surviving'.[44] Responding to Ingersoll, Rozelle contends that the text, nonetheless, shows that life will continue, even if in increasingly diverse forms. He suggests that *Oryx and Crake* – perhaps despite Atwood's intentions – prioritizes man's relationship to other animals and ecosystems over the importance of 'human nature'. *Oryx and Crake*, argues Rozelle, does not simply depict 'The End', but also betrays a 'yearning for a new beginning – an ecological communitas' that might exist beyond the destruction of the world as we know it.[45] This, he suggests, is an essentially optimistic vision, and one for which Atwood is not often credited. Like Schoene, who notes that the novel ends 'in open-ended suspension', in a space of 'indeterminate potentialities', Rozelle also draws attention to the novel's open conclusion.[46] Jimmy's predicament at the end of the novel, he argues, is the same as the reader's: suspended at a 'crossroads in environmental history', we too must decide which way to jump.[47]

An ethical novel

Oryx and Crake, as Rozelle suggests, raises many ethical questions for its readers. In an essay that examines the novel's preoccupation with time and temporality, Snyder notes the disorientating nature of the narrative's chronology, in which Jimmy's past is our dystopian future. This, she suggests, creates a text that 'projects forward' from the social and political realities of our present moment, urging us to reflect on our society.[48] Snyder reads Jimmy as a traumatized figure, and she notes that the novel repeatedly juxtaposes the enormous catastrophe of human extinction against a number of smaller, personal tragedies from Jimmy's past, such as his abandonment by his mother. This overlap, she argues, is central to Atwood's purpose in the novel: by juxtaposing global horror with mundane but intense private losses and traumas, the novel challenges 'attempts to draw a *cordon sanitaire*' between the domestic and the political, the local and the global. Atwood demonstrates the futility of efforts to separate and distinguish relationships that are inextricably interconnected in what Snyder terms 'ever-widening, overlapping circles of power and obligation: the familial, the corporate, the national, the global, the non-human and the post-human'.[49] By making connections between small and large actions, Atwood resists the kind of compartmentalized thinking that – in a novel full of gated communities – underpins the collapse of ethical social behaviour.

Danette DiMarco addresses the ethics of *Oryx and Crake* in terms of its depiction of '*homo faber*' (he who labours or builds). The idealization of *homo faber* is, she suggests, an essentially capitalist perspective, which views the world and its resources in purely material terms. In her discussion, DiMarco makes use of philosopher Hannah Arendt's work, *The Human Condition*, in which Arendt describes *homo faber*'s tendency to see himself as the centre of everything and to destroy nature rather than work with it. This self-absorption leaves him blind to his interconnectedness to others and to nature. A similar conclusion is also reached by Anna Bedford in her ecofeminist reading of the novel. By 'contemplating a future of unfettered capitalism', argues Bedford, Atwood draws a connection between the 'capitalist instrumentalism that abuses and denigrates animals' and the 'pronounced commodification of human bodies' exemplified by the sex industry and child trafficking described in the novel. In both instances, the vulnerable are exploited – as raw materials or labour – for profit.[50]

For DiMarco, Crake is 'the quintessential *homo faber*', and his materialist vision of humanity would seem to dominate in the text. She proposes, however, that Jimmy represents an alternative to Crake's world building. Jimmy's adoption of the abominable snowman as an alter-ego – a liminal creature surviving on the edge of society and the wilderness, both real and unreal – points to his capacity to take up a new, previously unimagined position. There is evidence, DiMarco suggests, that Jimmy, who has always felt like an outsider, has the capacity to be ethical and compassionate and to view himself as 'embedded within the world' rather than separate from it. Consequently, when Jimmy is eventually faced with the novel's concluding options – to attack, to retreat, or to 'engage humanely' with the strangers – Atwood provides for the possibility that, in choosing the third, Jimmy may help to build a new, more equitable world than that which has previously been imagined by *homo faber*.[51]

If DiMarco seeks in Atwood's novel a reimagining of what man might become, Dunning's essay instead looks backwards, reading the novel as a call to regain something that has been lost by a ruthless and profit-driven late modernity. For Dunning, the extreme neoliberal imagined future of *Oryx and Crake* depicts a society, 'driven by base appetites and fears', which has lost its faith in the great metanarratives of religion, civil society, art and culture. Like DiMarco, he points to the novel's focus on the deleterious effects of prioritizing profit and progress over all else. For Dunning, however, Crake does not simply exemplify detached rationalism, but actually seeks 'to remedy the ills of a world in deep distress'. He likens Crake to Freud: a therapist who diagnoses the disease of unrestrained instincts. But unlike his psychoanalyst forbear, Crake's 'drastic therapy' has the technological resources to reengineer what were presumed indelible features of human nature.[52]

For Dunning, while Atwood shows a grudging admiration for Crake, she also undermines the egotism of his vision. As noted by Canavan, Bouson and others, Crake's marvellous creations are also faintly ridiculous, and their instinct for myth-making seemingly mocks his rationalist vision. Dunning points to the triangular relationship of Jimmy, Crake and Oryx as one that 'unmistakably suggests the Christian Trinity', with Crake as the creator-father, Jimmy as the sacrificial son, and Oryx as the feminine spirit.[53] In the end, argues Dunning, Crake's actions, for all his rationalism, do not make sense (why leave Jimmy and not Oryx to care for the Crakers?), suggesting that he is as motivated by jealousy and revenge as anyone else. Ultimately, suggests Dunning, Atwood shares something of Crake's pessimism, but she remains clear on what must be done if we are to avoid the worst: we cannot sacrifice qualitative value to a purely rational quantitative science. While the novel, suggests Dunning, is somewhat 'coy' about the status of the kind of origin myths and sacred stories Jimmy tells, it nevertheless affirms that 'we cannot do without such tales, not, at least, if we wish to remain even marginally human'.[54]

The Year of the Flood

Atwood's 2009 'midquel' to *Oryx and Crake* (as Canavan describes it) provides an altogether different perspective on Crake's apocalypse than that offered by Jimmy's 'last man' narrative. For Schoene, the novel's parallel chronology has the effect to 'further obfuscate the identity of Atwood's quasi-mythical envisioning as either dystopian or utopian'.[55] Its arrival, he suggests, allows for both the singularity of Jimmy's apocalyptic vision and the more hopeful plurality of alternative simultaneous experiences. Hannes Bergthaller notes that Atwood has termed *The Year of the Flood* a 'simultanial' and points out that it 'covers roughly the same time-span and follows a similar narrative pattern': commencing with a description of the current situation of the survivor-protagonists; proceeding to move backwards and forwards in time in order to explain how things arrived at the current point; before concluding on an unresolved cusp moment of reunion with others.[56] For Bouson, in an article examining the nature of Atwood's 'return to the future' with *The Year of the Flood*, the novel acts like a kind of 'repetition of a novelistic trauma' in which the author, like a victim unable to relinquish a traumatic event, seems compelled to return to her 'apocalyptic-traumatic end-of-the-world story'.[57] The return to Jimmy's world is not, however, repetitive. With this second book, Atwood widens her lens and reveals that which could not be shown from Jimmy's limited perspective, and which is hinted at in the final scenes of *Oryx and Crake*: the existence of multiple other survivors. It also moves beyond the exclusive Compounds of Jimmy's sheltered youth and into the lawless pleeblands only ever glimpsed in the earlier text. As Debrah Raschke observes, this allows Atwood to reveal what life is like for 'the 99% that make up the pleebland'.[58]

Another notable innovation of *The Year of the Flood* is the inclusion of hymns taken from '*The God's Gardeners Oral Hymnbook*' and interspersed throughout the novel. For Le Guin, reviewing the novel, the hymns 'may be read as kindly spoofs of hippy mysticism, green fervour, and religious naivety, and at the same time can be taken quite seriously'.[59] In another review, Gillian Beer also discusses these easily overlooked textual elements, and sees significance in their structural regularity. Their rhyming, she argues, is crucial: 'It knits up disorder; it discovers kinships; it solaces; it reveals. It persists to the end. These are songs to be sung, together.'[60] In an article examining the trilogy, Richard Alan Northover instead suggests that the hymns are often comic in their reinterpretation of biblical myths in ecological terms, although he notes that the Gardeners, who 'tend to take themselves quite seriously', do not find them funny.[61] In an essay that discusses the trilogy's engagement with ecological notions of sustainability and collapse, Dana Phillips argues that Atwood's primary mode is satirical and irreverent, and she points specifically to the 'tedious' hymns as an example of Atwood's 'even-handed approach to her antagonists and protagonists'.[62] Bergthaller, meanwhile, observes that the hymns work both to explain the Gardeners' theology and to provide 'an increasingly dark commentary' on the group's fate.[63]

Much as readings of the hymns range from closely analytical to vaguely bemused, so early responses to the novel were mixed. Novelist Jeanette Winterson, writing in *The New York Times*, observes that, while 'not everything in the novel works', nevertheless, 'Atwood knows how to show us ourselves', even if the mirror is disconcertingly distorted.[64] Bonnie Greer's review for *The New Statesman* argues that *The Year of the Flood*, while subtly plotted, is 'little more than a big, fat eco-pamphlet'. While the novel's various vignettes are 'beautifully realised', there is a sense, argues Greer, that Atwood is more interested in the novel's message than its characters.[65] Noting such reservations, Gina Wisker suggests that they are due in part to the slightly discordant mixture of the novel's 'post-apocalyptic, sustainability theme and its mixture of the homey arts and crafts, its quasi-religious tone, and its sometimes cartoonish characters'.[66]

Overview

In contrast to *Oryx and Crake*, *The Year of the Flood* is a notably female-centred text, focused on the experiences of two women: Toby and Ren. For Beer, reviewing the novel for *The Globe and Mail*, the alternations between Toby's third person, past-tense perspective and Ren's first person, present-tense voice add pace and variation to the novel, while also subtly exposing character differences, underlining that Toby is 'older, less exposed, less febrile than Ren'.[67] Both women are former members of the God's Gardeners: a survivalist eco-religious cult that correctly predicted the end of the world, if not the eventual manner of its ending. As Susan Watkins notes, the group offers the women 'a space of apparent safety, away from the techno-scientific corporate world'.[68] Founded by Adam One, the Gardeners are led by senior members known as Adams and Eves. For Fredric Jameson, writing in the *London Review of Books*, the Gardeners are 'perhaps the most stimulating new feature of *The Year of the Flood*'.[69]

Toby, we learn, first joined the Gardeners as a young woman, after escaping from Blanco, a brutal, sexually abusive employer. Despite what Andrew Hoogheem terms 'her strong undercurrent of skepticism' regarding the Gardener's ecotheology, she appreciates the group's offer of refuge and eventually becomes a skilled herbalist and a leading member of the group.[70] When a vengeful Blanco, years later, discovers Toby's location and mounts an attack on the Gardeners' rooftop encampment, her friends help her to escape again, securing her a job as manager of the AnooYoo day spa. This is where we first encounter Toby, waiting out the period of chaos caused by Crake's 'Waterless Flood' (7) and tending the garden that provides her with food and medicine.

Toby's narrative is interspersed with the story of Ren, a dancer and sex worker who survives Crake's apocalypse because she was serendipitously quarantined at the Scales and Tails strip club where she works. Ren's story is initially delivered from this locked biohazard room, where she has limited supplies and no way to escape. Younger than Toby, Ren first joined the God's Gardeners as a child when her mother, Lucerne, fell in love with Zeb, Adam One's brother, and ran away from the HelthWyzer Compound to be with him, bringing Ren along. As a young Gardener, Ren befriends Amanda, a street kid from the pleeblands, who also joins the group. When Ren's disillusioned mother returns to the Compounds, claiming they were kidnapped, a teenaged Ren ends up at school with Jimmy and Crake, developing an unrequited crush on Jimmy. Unhappy and unwanted, Ren runs away – at first to work with Toby, and then, when she discovers that Amanda is dating Jimmy, to the strip club in the pleeblands. Noting a familiar Atwoodian preoccupation with blending genres, Bouson adds to those already identified in *Oryx and Crake* the various romance plots of *The Year of the Flood*, specifically the love triangles between Ren, Amanda and Jimmy, and Toby, Zeb and Lucerne, as well as 'the coming-of-age story', political thriller and mystery story, as the novel hints at collusion between Crake and the male leaders of the God's Gardeners.[71]

The novel concludes on a collision of characters and events, as it is revealed that a number of the well-prepared Gardeners have survived. For Canavan, in rewarding with survival those who have chosen to change their lifestyles, the novel 'is almost as straightforwardly moralistic as a fable'.[72] Amanda and some boys from the Gardeners head to Scales and Tails to look for Ren. Freeing her, they make their way to Toby but are attacked by two Painballers: brutalized criminals and professional fighters. The men take Amanda and Ren with them for sex, but Toby manages to shoot one of them and rescue Ren. She and Ren then pursue the Painballers who still have Amanda. Just as they finally discover the group in a clearing in the woods they also come across a feverish Jimmy, and the novel converges with the conclusion of *Oryx and Crake*. They disarm the Painballers, rescue Amanda, and just as the novel ends, the Crakers approach.

Gendered futures

Watkins proposes that women's apocalyptic writing typically betrays a 'suspicion of techno-science for its destructive complicity with patriarchal and colonial enterprises'.[73] She distinguishes between 'tragic' and 'comic' modes of apocalyptic narrative: the first is catastrophic, despairing, and linear, while the second is open-ended, cyclical, and contains elements of hope. For Watkins, Ren and Toby in *The Year of the Flood* provide 'a feminine, comic reworking' of Jimmy's 'tragic masculine perspective' in *Oryx and Crake*. Refusing to accept the tragic mode, they instead continue to support and protect one another, to resist male dominance and to show empathy and humanity. For Watkins, apocalyptic narratives in the comic mode, such as *The Year of the Flood*, avoid blame and judgement and instead champion 'plural, hybrid narratives and spaces'.[74]

Other critics also observe a shifting gender politics concomitant with the change in narrative voice across the two texts. In *Oryx and Crake*, Atwood diagnosed an unhealthy division between Crake's 'masculine' scientific rationalism and the more 'feminine' traits of compassion and empathy fostered by the beleaguered arts and humanities, associated with Jimmy. Hengen suggests that Jimmy's mother, whose language speaks of 'a lost ethics and spirituality', resists the biological materialism of his father's work.[75] Jimmy's generous, artistic instincts, however, while bolstered by his mother, are, argues Hengen, largely thwarted by a society that prioritizes greed. For Howells, the gender politics of *Oryx and Crake* are further exposed by its comparison with *The Handmaid's Tale*. Where the earlier novel concludes with Offred resigning her fate into the hands of others, *Oryx and Crake* ends with Jimmy trying to decide what to do. While both are faced with uncertain outcomes, for Howells, 'that shift in balance from passivity to action codes in the gender differences' of these two very different dystopian texts.[76] With *The Year of the Flood*, Atwood does significant work to redress the masculine logic of Jimmy's male-centred narrative.

In her review of *The Year of the Flood*, Winterson observes two significant gendered tropes in the novel. Atwood, she suggests, is particularly adept at showing what happens 'when human beings (usually men) cannot love'. At worst, as with Blanco, 'brutality and sadism take over', while for others, like Crake, 'a utopian desire for perfectability replaces the lost and lonely self'. For Winterson, Crake's desire to genetically edit love and romance from human experience is less about rationalism and more about his unacknowledged desire to avoid jealousy and pain. Ultimately, she suggests, in this 'strangely lonely book' in which love and romance are absent or unsatisfactory, it is in friendship – particularly female friendships – that Atwood finds hope.[77] A similar point is made by Watkins, who observes that, despite a recurring theme of maternal neglect, the novel's focus is nevertheless on positive female relationships. As Winterson puts it: 'Atwood believes in human beings, and she likes women', and the generosity of Ren and Toby's friendship provides hope for a future beyond the end of the novel.[78]

For Bouson, while Atwood's work has always been concerned with 'the victimhood and survival of women', *The Year of the Flood* 'takes this organizing idea to a new level', depicting a world in which young 'postfeminist' women like Amanda and Ren (and like Oryx) have learned to exploit their bodies as commodities.[79] Bouson argues that Atwood exposes the metaphorical 'consumption' of women in a ruthless and predatory culture. This horror is embodied in the text by Blanco, who uses women as disposable sexual slaves before – it is rumoured – murdering them and disposing of their remains in his burger-processing machinery. To Blanco, Toby – like all women – is used to satisfy desires: 'turned into meat', both metaphorically and literally.[80]

Central to Bouson's analysis is the generational divide between middle-aged Toby and Ren, who is twenty-five when the cataclysm strikes. Bouson reads Toby as a figure of second-wave feminism, readily aware of male violence and gendered power imbalance. Ren, instead, is identified with a later, postfeminist generation. A product of postfeminist culture with its 'bottom-line corporate business culture mentality', she 'seemingly chooses, or at least accepts, her own sexual commodification and humiliation'.[81] Bouson suggests that Atwood depicts Ren and Amanda's passivity to demonstrate her fear (which also motivates *The Handmaid's Tale*) that the gains of feminism are precarious and vulnerable to attack. For Atwood, there is little difference between 'the postfeminist's embrace of her sexuality and the sexist world of the prefeminist past'.[82] Bouson concludes that *The Year of the Flood* offers two possible paths for humanity: the sexist savagery of the Painballers' rampage of torture, rape and murder, or Toby and Ren's female solidarity. That both groups survive the 'waterless flood' suggests Bouson, is Atwood's comment on the persistence of both strains of human nature.

Humanism/posthumanism

While some critics read *The Year of the Flood* as an expansion of the world of *Oryx and Crake* to encompass female experience and life in the pleeblands, others view the second novel more particularly as a development of Atwood's fundamental arguments. This is the position taken by Bergthaller in his essay on humanism and sustainability in the first two novels of the trilogy. For Bergthaller, *Oryx and Crake* ends on an impasse; traditional liberal humanism has 'pathetically failed', but the triumph of Crake's posthumanism appears 'indistinguishable from catastrophe'. With *The Year of the Flood*, Atwood attempts to resolve this deadlock by proposing 'a qualified humanism informed by evolutionary biology and disenchanted with human nature'.[83]

Discussing 'the *ecological imperative*' – that humans must acknowledge that they too are part of nature – Bergthaller identifies in both *Oryx and Crake* and *The Year of the Flood* Atwood's sense that this formula is inadequate. Crake reduces humans to animals to the point where he wishes to eradicate human nature, while the God's Gardeners tangle themselves in theological knots, turning to the biblical idea of the Fall to explain why humans must 'cultivate themselves' in order to become 'natural' again. Both of these positions fail to address a crucial element of nature, in which, as Bergthaller explains, certain species exhaust their environment to the point where they endanger their own existence. This phenomenon is perfectly 'natural'; what is *un*natural, is for a species to *consciously* limit its own engagements with its environment in order to prolong its own existence. The question raised by Atwood's novels, therefore, is 'how to tame the human animal?'[84] How do we curb humanity's natural instincts to expand and consume? Crake's solution is to restrain human nature, 'taming' the human beyond the point of remaining human, while Jimmy 'represents a humanism that fails to understand itself as a bio-political project'.[85] In *The Year of the Flood*, instead, argues Bergthaller, Atwood proposes a possible solution in the Gardeners' belief that faith can complement and moderate science. This same sense of balance underlies Atwood's belief that art and culture can sustain ethical behaviour and self-discipline, directing humanity towards its own salvation.

A useful addition to the discussion of Atwood's belief in the value and purpose of the arts is explored by Hoogheem in an essay in which he tackles the arguments of 'evocriticism' – evolutionary literary criticism. This mode of criticism looks to apply a Darwinian model of evolution to understand why humans have evolved a love for storytelling. It proposes that stories are an evolutionary tactic that enable us to make sense of the world and 'test hypotheses in safe, low-stakes settings'.[86] For Hoogheem, the Gardeners' theology – described in their hymns – supports the idea that stories and religion provide an evolutionary function: creating supportive communities, communicating knowledge and teaching necessary social values. He argues, however, that Atwood's 'ambivalent, sardonic, and ultimately fond portrayal of religion' moves beyond a simple evolutionary explanation of its function and persistence and demonstrates the need for a 'deeper, more textured' understanding of the role religion plays in human experience.[87] With the endurance of Toby and Ren (both of whom benefit from the Gardeners' teachings), Atwood makes a link between religious belief and survival that seems to support an evocritical reading, while also demonstrating that the factors that favour human survival are far more complex and potentially surprising.

Hoogheem's proposition that storytelling provides an evolutionary advantage balances a sceptical, biological view of human nature with a belief in the need for humanism. If we veer, like Crake, too close to a purely rational biological reading of humanity, then, as Bergthaller argues, it becomes difficult to argue why the survival of humanity should 'be regarded as an ethical good to begin with'? Bergthaller suggests that, for Atwood, even if 'no answer to this question could be validated by the natural sciences' we still need to find one, and this necessity, ultimately, motivates her defence of the humanities, which are so under attack in her near-future dystopian scenario.[88]

Reading the conclusion

When the closing scenes of *The Year of the Flood* converge on the final moments of *Oryx and Crake*, Atwood leaves her characters once again on the cusp of a momentous decision. For Bouson, the conclusion leaves open the possibility that the survivors might rebuild society and construct a 'new social-political utopian enclave among the dystopian ruins of the old order'.[89] Writing before the publication of *MaddAddam*, she also suggests that the faint singing that Jimmy and Ren hear at the end of the novel, which is commonly understood to announce the arrival of the Crakers, might equally herald the revelation of more human survivors, as hymn-singing God's Gardeners emerge from their safe houses. For Bergthaller, the novel provides a 'bitter-sweet, almost fairytale-like ending' in which various Gardeners survive and find each other and Blanco – the gothic villain – returns once again, only to be finally defeated. Atwood, he suggests, requires us to overlook the improbability of these events and indulge in the same kind of 'leap of faith' that the Gardeners' eco-theology requires.[90]

If the conjoined conclusions of *Oryx and Crake* and *The Year of the Flood* require some suspension of disbelief, the novels also, suggest Canavan, call on us to expand the limits of our imaginative horizons. Canavan begins his essay on the first two instalments of Atwood's trilogy with Fredric Jameson's often quoted statement that it 'is easier to imagine the end of the world than to imagine the end of capitalism'.[91] He suggests, however, that 'eco-apocalypse' is increasingly the manner in which both of these eventualities *are* being imagined, as we come to suspect that 'the one is catapulting us faster and faster towards the other'. Visions of the apocalypse such as that created by Atwood work to demonstrate that capitalism is not in fact inevitable and eternal. Consequently, argues Canavan, there is an 'unexpected utopian potency' discernible within contemporary visions of the eco-apocalypse rendered in texts such as *Oryx and Crake* and *The Year of the Flood*. Both books, he suggests, 'seek to open up new space for imagining a post-capitalist future'.[92]

MaddAddam

Overview

With the final instalment of the trilogy, Atwood brings together elements of the first two novels and draws various narrative threads towards an open-ended conclusion. Like both *Oryx and Crake* and *The Year of the Flood*, *MaddAddam* retells events leading up to Crake's apocalypse but also introduces more stories into the web of narrative. As Zeb and Toby become lovers, he recounts to her tales of his earlier life with Adam and the brothers' later ideological divergence between Adam's pacifist Gardeners and Zeb's alignment with the terrorist MaddAddamites. In this manner, Atwood fills in many of the missing details from the earlier novels.

The narrative commences, as Raschke notes, with a 'chaotic, uncomprehending camera-eye recording' of the rescue of a severely traumatized Amanda, the discovery of a feverish Jimmy and the release of the Painballers by the guileless Crakers.[93] In the confusion, the Crakers, suffering 'a major cultural misunderstanding', as Toby later terms it (13), assume that Ren and Amanda are fertile and willing participants and rape the two young women. The issue from this encounter will be the first of a new generation of inter-species children. In Bedford's ecofeminist reading, these 'hybridisations' seem 'hopeful, and part of a future that's full of singing and stories, quite removed from the fear of miscegenation that populated much early science fiction'.[94]

The novel subsequently brings together the various camps of survivors – the God's Gardeners, the MaddAddamites and the Crakers. The humans scrabble together a subsistence while searching for fellow survivors, always under threat of attack from the freed Painballers and roaming pigoons. As Jimmy convalesces, Toby takes up his mantle as storyteller and mythmaker to the Crakers, teaching one particularly inquisitive young Craker, Blackbeard, how to write. The narrative culminates in a final battle with the Painballers, in which the humans collaborate with the highly intelligent pigoons with whom the Crakers can communicate. Jimmy dies in the battle, and the remaining Painballers are executed. The novel proceeds to a conclusion, with Toby writing her account of all that happened, and then transitions into Blackbeard's narrative, as he becomes Toby's scribe. Blackbeard recounts the humans' truce with the pigoons, Toby and Zeb's marriage and the births of the first human–Craker children. In the final section, entitled 'Book', Blackbeard has taken charge of the narrative. He recounts the death of Zeb and Toby, and also the birth of more human–Craker children. For Northover, the novel is apocalyptic, 'not in the sense of the end of human history, but in the way it envisions a new age where the human oppression of nature has ended'.[95]

Narrative structure: Who speaks?

Throughout the trilogy, Atwood raises questions about narration. As Raschke puts it, her concern is with 'who sees and who tells'.[96] As Northover observes, both Jimmy in *Oryx and Crake* and Toby in *MaddAddam* question the purpose of their own storytelling and contemplate the futility of writing when the existence of future readers is doubtful. For Northover, these worries are bound up with what he calls the 'impossibility of the apocalyptic perspective' – the difficulty of imagining beyond our own end.[97] Drawing on Watkins's description of *The Year of the Flood* as functioning in the comic mode, Northover suggests that *MaddAddam* extends this alignment towards the comic in Atwood's apocalyptic tale. Although containing instances of horror and brutality, the third novel, he suggests, has a dark, ironic sense of humour. It also displays the same 'polyphony' that characterized *The Year of the Flood*, as multiple voices carry the narrative forward. Indeed, across the trilogy, Northover identifies a progressive narrative evolution, as 'control of the Word shifts from male domination through female mediation to the non-human Crakers'.[98]

With *MaddAddam*, we eventually understand that Blackbeard has transcribed the narratives that comprise both *MaddAddam* and *The Year of the Flood*, but not Jimmy's tale as told in *Oryx and Crake*. For Raschke, this revelation changes everything: 'It becomes the palimpsest for understanding what the trilogy critiques and its gestures toward remedy'.[99] Where *Oryx and Crake*, as Howells observes, tells Jimmy's story 'refracted through an omniscient narrative voice', Raschke notes that this omniscient narrator is absent from the third novel.[100] And so when Blackbeard, for example, describes the death of Toby, he admits that he can't confirm which of the three versions of her death are true, 'because I do not know' (390). The revelations of *MaddAddam*, for Raschke, compel us to reread *Oryx and Crake*. Examining the trilogy's narrative composition with close attention, Raschke puzzles over the origin of Jimmy's story in the first novel. If the Crakers are the only living witnesses to Jimmy's story, then it stands to reason that they wrote the narrative of *Oryx and Crake*. Support for this reading, she suggests, is supplied by the novel's 'odd uses of metaphor and idiom', its tendency towards literalism (when Jimmy cries, 'salt water is running down his face' [13]), and the various editorial interjections that recur, prefaced by: 'Revision' (11). This proclivity for precision exposes, argues Raschke, the presence of 'some other voice who is editing his past for consistency'.[101]

At the heart of Raschke's analysis is a critique of postmodernism. When Atwood was writing *The Handmaid's Tale*, she argues, postmodernism's multiplicity represented a subversive resistance to Gilead's fundamentalist insistence on a single, irrefutable truth. A similar multiplicity is discerned in the polyphonic *MaddAddam*. Northover, for example, notes that the novel's continuation of the story is not linear, but repeatedly circles back in time, returning to and revising previously recounted events. Consequently, he argues, the third novel 'can be considered an anti-type to the first two, rewriting them and opening up more imaginative possibilities'.[102] For Raschke, however, by the time Atwood comes to write the *MaddAddam* trilogy, postmodernism has been co-opted and neutered, and its subversive deconstruction of meaning and truth has resulted in a kind of 'cultural paralysis'. Commencing with Jimmy's childhood – a world of computer simulations, fake houses, fake food, and fake news, in which human relations are inauthentic and unsatisfying – Raschke argues that Atwood's trilogy 'dramatizes the postmodern condition gone amuck'.[103]

For Raschke, the bland plurality of the post-racial Crakers – seemingly celebrated in *MaddAddam* – represents only subordination; in their pliable passivity and inability to distinguish between true and false, the Crakers, she argues, 'are the perfect corporate citizens'.[104] Consequently, by paying attention to the narrative structure, we must recognize that the fairy-tale conclusion of *MaddAddam*, in which the earth is recovering and babies are being born, actually points us back to the start of the trilogy. 'Following the logic of the palindrome, Snowman's death at the end of *MaddAddam* is his beginning', as his narrated story comes into being sometime after his death, written by more sophisticated later Crakers. This circular ending confronts us with our complacency and drives us back to the start of *Oryx and Crake* and 'back into the seeds of our apocalypse'.[105] In this manner, for Raschke, the novel points to the continuing need for meaningful narrative in defiance of postmodernism's emptying out of the power and meaning of narrative. This is, she suggests, the moral imperative at the heart of the *MaddAddam* trilogy.

After the Anthropocene

If Raschke reads the *MaddAddam* trilogy as resisting the consequences of throwing out grand metanarratives, a number of critics instead examine the trilogy as Atwood's critique of anthropocentricism: a grand narrative whereby human beings are assumed to be the most important element of existence. In her essay on Atwood's environmentalism, Hengen identifies an evolution in the writer's thinking on this matter. Where earlier works such as *Surfacing* display an implicit assumption that the natural is superior to the artificial, Hengen suggests that, with *Oryx and Crake*, Atwood begins to contemplate a genetically engineered human, and in doing so, 'dares to look beyond her own repeated belief that human nature cannot change'. Hengen concludes, however, that Atwood remains convinced that human nature involves a complex range of physical, emotional, spiritual and emotional states, and that to 'splice out' any of those elements is to 'amputate the self as it has been known so far, and so stress nature perilously'.[106]

While Hengen points to Atwood's sense of what makes humans unique, Amelia Defalco's essay on biocapitalism focuses on Atwood's depiction of 'the fantasy of human independence and invulnerability' that underpins neoliberalism as it reaches its 'devastating endgame'. The trilogy, she suggests, indicts a 'catastrophic anthropocentricism' that relegates plants, animals, and the human body to 'marketable, utilitarian objects'. At the same time, however, the novel's vision of cross-species collaboration, she argues, 'suggests the possibility of posthumanist regeneration'.[107] A similar nod to optimism is offered by Chen, for whom the trilogy 'is a meditation on the heterogenetic human at the end of the Anthropocene'.[108] (The Anthropocene describes a geological epoch marked by man's impact on the earth, 'similar to past epochal changes caused by volcanic eruptions, continent shifts, or a meteorite strike'.[109]) Focusing on the potential opened up by this critical moment, Chen argues that Crake's apocalypse allows Atwood, over the course of the trilogy, to imagine a shift from the 'macro-politics of globalization' to the 'micro-politics of an intentional community'.[110] This shift in perspective – as 'humanity' becomes a handful of survivors – prompts a new ethical awareness in Jimmy, drawing him out of his anthropocentric assumption of his own centrality and importance. From *Oryx and Crake* to *MaddAddam*, argues Chen, Jimmy 'outgrows his being-in-and-for-itself' and eventually 'realizes being-for-others', as he relinquishes his early selfishness to finally sacrifice himself to save both his fellow surviving humans and the Crakers.[111]

Djuna Mohr proposes that the *MaddAddam* trilogy might be termed 'Anthropocene fiction', which differs from traditional science fiction with its typically 'escapist technophile and anthropocentric inclination'. Anthropocene fictions, she argues, imagine life beyond anthropocentrism, whether in terms of the posthuman or other bioforms with agency. She notes that, while *Oryx and Crake* and *The Year of the Flood* focus on the immediate aftermath of Crake's apocalypse, *MaddAddam* instead focuses on 'the transitional period of establishing a post-anthropocentric network of species'. Mohr notes a similar narrative progression across the three books as that observed by Northover: the 'privileged male narration' of *Oryx and Crake* is associated with irresponsible bioscience; *The Year of the Flood* prioritizes female experience in terms of 'victimization and resistance'; and *MaddAddam*, collated by Blackbeard, marks a shift to 'posthuman perspectives'. For Mohr, Atwood resists the logic of anthropocentrism, and the trilogy essentially 'narrates how to save an overpopulated world from humanity'.[112] This reading conflicts with that of Raschke, for whom 'The Crakers are us, adrift in the postmodern world: our current present'. Where Mohr sees a transformative advance beyond anthropocentricism, Raschke, in a notably anthropocentric analysis, sees the posthuman Crakers as both metaphors for humanity and harbingers of the death of the human: they are, she argues, 'our alien future, or more aptly our lack of future'.[113]

For Bedford, instead, a key conclusion of the trilogy involves the human characters' necessary reconceptualization of their fellow animals. As wolvogs and pigoons are variously revealed to have 'their own communities and cultures', the humans must reassess their assumed superiority.[114] This shift marks a retreat from anthropocentric instrumentalist thinking. Also discussing the pigoons' intelligence, Northover notes that only the Crakers can understand and communicate with the genetically modified pigs, and suggests that the humans' exclusion from this communication signals 'a loss of power' and 'the beginning of a more just dispensation'. When humans are no longer the supreme purveyors of language, they 'have to negotiate and share power with other animals'.[115] This is part of a process of radical decentring of the human narrative in the text. It also involves the realization that, from a purely ecological point of view, as Bedford notes, the wiping out of humanity 'is not a tragedy, and can only be dystopian from an anthropocentric perspective'.[116] And as Northover observes, by giving the last chapter to Blackbeard, Atwood ensures that the non-human Crakers 'literally have the last word'.[117]

Critics have variously found the *MaddAddam* trilogy bleak and cautiously optimistic. Philips, for example, sees in the characters' scavenging and reusing of the scraps of industrially produced goods recovered from the devastated landscape a familiar industriousness that threatens to restart the same processes that brought humanity to the brink of environmental collapse. For this reason, she argues, the trilogy describes 'a doom cycle'.[118] In large part, what optimism is discerned is gleaned from the vision of inter-species cooperation and the vision of a radically changed but vital future for humanity. In an essay that examines the persistent theme of breakfast in the final novel, Shelley Boyd suggests that the meal symbolizes Atwood's 'guarded optimism' that there will, ultimately, be 'near-future worlds (and meals) not unlike our own'. That the survivors continue to come together and share a meal, often of necessity made from incongruous and unappetizing ingredients, demonstrates, she proposes, their capacity to 'imagine and reimagine themselves into the future'.[119] The nature of that reimagining is crucial, however. As Mohr observes, where Crake thought he could remodel the world and make it better, the text rejects his vision. In its place, Atwood offers a post-anthropocentric world comprised of 'a network of species, respect for nature and the Other, communication and cooperation'.[120] On this basis, the trilogy offers a vision of a new humanity that can remain humane.

Conclusion

The preceding chapters have testified to the richness and diversity of the critical readings available on Margaret Atwood's work. Inevitably, the sheer volume of material has necessitated certain choices around selection. Some useful resources have been addressed only briefly, while others have been examined more closely, often because they are indicative or exemplary of a particular focus or method adopted by a number of critics. My intention has always been to provide a breadth of analyses while also giving full attention to the more influential or paradigm-shifting approaches to Atwood's writing.

More significant still, in terms of the choices made in shaping this guide, has been the focus on Atwood's most prominent long-form fictions. Again, given the enormous volume of Atwood's creative production, every editor and critic who attempts some kind of overview of her work must tackle questions of coverage and selection. Most typically, edited companion collections such as Coral Ann Howells's *The Cambridge Companion to Margaret Atwood*, or more thematic approaches such as Karma Waltonen's *Margaret Atwood's Apocalypses*, focus primarily on Atwood's novels while including a small number of chapters that examine her short fiction and poetry. Some collections, such as John Moss and Tobi Kozakewich's *Margaret Atwood: The Open Eye* (2006), do provide a substantial number of essays that examine works other than the novels, but this is much rarer. Certainly, by far the majority of journal articles and book chapters on Atwood's work tend to address her major novels. Within this book, the most significant omissions, I would suggest, are some of the more recent substantial works, which are necessarily currently attended by a limited amount of critical analysis. In particular, *Moral Disorder* (2006), *Stone Mattress* (2014), *The Heart Goes Last* (2015) and *Hag-Seed* (2016) develop familiar thematic and genre preoccupations and provide for potentially fruitful comparisons with earlier works. And most recently, *The Testaments* (2019), Atwood's much-anticipated sequel to *The Handmaid's Tale*, will undoubtedly attract a significant amount of critical attention in the years to come.

One notable early critical response to three of these works is provided by Howells's article, 'True Trash: Genre Fiction Revisited in *Stone Mattress*, *The Heart Goes Last* and *Hag-Seed*'. Discussing Atwood's predilection for 'true trash' – a term she takes from the title of a short story in the 1991 collection, *Wilderness Tips* – Howells examines the manner in which these recent works make use of popular genres to produce 'transgressive entertainments'. This triumvirate of texts, all published within three years, reprise, as Howells observes, previous experiments with gothic romance and gothic horror, vampire fiction, fantasy, dystopia, crime fiction and thrillers. Paraphrasing an observation recently made by Atwood that 'this age of anxiety and uncertainty about the future is not the time for realistic fiction', Howells makes a connection between the dark tales of *Stone Mattress*, the sometimes farcical dystopia of *The Heart Goes Last* and the ghostly magical comedy of her Shakespearean rewriting in *Hag-Seed*. Each of these works, suggests Howells, while they vary in form and focus, uses popular, often fantastical, genres to make astute, ethical observations about the politics of the present day.[1]

Stone Mattress: Nine Wicked Tales

In *Stone Mattress*, the first book Atwood published after completing her epic *MaddAddam* trilogy, we see, as Howells observes, a notable shift in perspective and scale from the global apocalypse to more local, intimate stories of individuals, many of whom are ageing and suddenly faced with their own mortality. This is a theme that Helen Snaith picks up in her examination of *Stone Mattress* from a feminist perspective on gerontology. Snaith suggests that with these 'wicked tales', Atwood appropriates the landscape of dystopia and 'deliberately subverts the standardised behaviours of old age', showing older women who centre their sexuality within their narratives and seek revenge on men who have wronged them in the past.[2]

Stone Mattress concludes with a darkly satiric dystopian tale titled 'Torching the Dusties', in which a terrorist movement called 'Our Turn', composed of disenfranchised and frustrated youths, turn their anger on the older generation, attacking and setting alight retirement homes. In an ageist society in which the ageing body is itself a form of dystopia, Snaith examines the manner in which Atwood's elderly female protagonists use technology to transcend bodily limitations and explore 'a virtual utopia' in cyberspace.[3] In stories such as 'Alphinland', in which Constance, an elderly writer of fantasy fictions, creates and maintains an online virtual reality, technology provides Constance with the freedom and mobility that are increasingly absent to her in the real world.

In its centring of ageing protagonists, *Stone Mattress* can be connected to other works by Atwood in which old age is an increasingly prevalent theme. This recurring interest has been observed in critical works such as Teresa Gibert's essay on the aesthetics of ageing in Atwood's fiction, Pilar Sánchez Calle's article on ageing and death in Atwood's *The Door*, and Susan Watkins's comparative examination of ageing in the fictions of Penelope Lively, Doris Lessing and Atwood.[4] It is also key to Amelia Defalco's analysis of issues around the ethics of care raised by Atwood in the short story cycle, *Moral Disorder*.[5] I also discuss ageing as a crucial paradigm in Atwood's work in a 2017 article that compares the depiction of old age in *The Blind Assassin* and *Moral Disorder*. Drawing connections with a much earlier 1983 short story, 'The Victory Burlesk', in which the narrator is horrified to be confronted by an ageing stripper, I suggest that each of these later works represents an 'essentially ethical attempt' to inhabit old age, 'a phenomenon most commonly seen from without'.[6] As Atwood herself grows older, the theme of ageing recurs in her work and will arguably become increasingly pertinent to critical responses.

The Heart Goes Last

Following her darkly satirical extrapolation of the generation gap in *Stone Mattress*, a similarly bleak exploration of contemporary anxieties is provided by *The Heart Goes Last*: another Atwoodian dystopia that feels, at times, a little too close to home. The novel commences in a post-economic-crash America. A litany of banking crisis, redundancies, foreclosures and widespread destitution has left formerly middle-class protagonists Stan and Charmaine living in their car and trying to evade the criminal gangs that roam the lawless streets. In desperation, and fuelled by nostalgia for a safer, happier age, the couple sign up to a 'social experiment' that involves dividing their time between living in a picket-fence fantasy of fifties suburbia and incarceration in a privately run prison.

The novel itself has an interesting genesis, first written and published in serial form in 2012 by the eBook publisher Byliner as a four-part serial entitled *Positron*, before being revised and published as *The Heart Goes Last* in 2015. The project combined Atwood's interest in both the nineteenth-century tradition of publishing novels in serial form and the possibilities opened up for writing and writers by new technologies. (I discuss this in the introduction to my 2017 interview with Atwood.[7]) This idiosyncratic genesis perhaps resulted in what many reviewers saw as the somewhat uneven tone of the novel, which veers from its opening scenes of broadly realist dystopia through an at times disorientating array of genres and eventually concludes in comedy and farce involving Elvis impersonators and sex robots. In a fairly typical summation, Lionel Shriver, writing in *The Financial Times*, affirms Atwood's skill and experience, but nevertheless proposes that the novel is 'overextended' and suffers from shaky foundations.[8] For Howells, however, despite the carnivalesque chaos, *The Heart Goes Last* 'engages with serious ethical questions about institutional power versus individual freedom and free will'.[9]

A rare extended discussion of *The Heart Goes Last* is provided by Tim Engles in his book, *White Male Nostalgia in Contemporary North American Literature*. Engles argues that white male power 'weaponizes nostalgia' in its attempt to regain its lost status and dominance. He suggests that, in its exposition of the ravages of neoliberalism, *The Heart Goes Last* imagines an America in which white people are reduced to the kind of precarious living conditions 'long endured by many of their subordinated ethnoracial others'.[10] The promised manicured security of the suburban community appeals to Stan and Charmaine in much the same way that conservative political parties play on nostalgia for security and status in white men who have suffered from economic precarity, and who struggle with the increased visibility of women and ethnic minorities. Such nostalgia, argues Engles, works to displace anger that would be better directed at the class system and economic structure onto groups of non-white 'others', or women. Accordingly, Stan gets angry at Charmaine when he finds himself unemployed and reliant on her pay cheque. For Engles, Stan's fantasies about 'Jasmine', a mysterious other woman, stem from a 'nostalgia that includes restoration of himself as head-of-the-home breadwinner'.[11] While Stan tells himself that his fantasies are prompted by his wife's lack of sexual passion, Engles points to the sexbot trope in the novel as a metaphor for the emasculation of men in a neoliberal economy that demands an unrealistic enactment of heteronormative masculinity. Feeling powerless and resentful, men look to assert their masculinity over an entirely compliant woman. Ultimately, suggests Engles, Atwood demonstrates that the weaponizing of nostalgia to prop up the failing neoliberal economy is bad for both men and women.

Hag-Seed

The Heart Goes Last, although grounded in a highly contemporary world of mortgage debt, casualized labour and for-profit prisons, is also a Shakespearian revision of sorts, 'a place of illusion, masquerade, and mistaken identities' influenced by *A Midsummer Night's Dream*.[12] As such, it has something in common with *Hag-*

Seed, Atwood's rewriting of *The Tempest*. Again, there is little available criticism on this relatively recent text. In an essay on Atwood's revisions of classic texts, I compare it to *The Penelopiad* and read it as a highly self-conscious adaptation: 'a novel about a man producing a play about a man producing a play.' Where *The Penelopiad* follows a familiar strategy of rewriting classic works from the perspective of peripheral and largely silent characters, with *Hag-Seed*, Atwood adopts a quite different approach, in which her protagonist directs a production of Shakespeare's play as part of a prison education programme. I argue that the anxiety around revision glimpsed at times in *The Penelopiad* is absent in *Hag-Seed*. After the performance, the prisoner-actors imagine new after-lives for Shakespeare's characters, and Atwood provides a celebratory conclusion, in which 'the readers have become writers and have claimed the text for themselves'.[13]

Other critics also focus on *Hag-Seed*'s Shakespearian revisions. In an article that considers how Atwood strives to balance innovation and fidelity in her reading of Shakespeare's play, Sofía Muñoz-Valdivieso suggests that *The Tempest*'s combination of comedy, tragedy and romance, which would appear to make it difficult to adapt, actually chimes well with Atwood's own proclivity for genre-shifting texts. Her article focuses on the strategies of adaptation that Atwood employs in order to achieve a text that is 'a contemporary double of the original' while still managing to be 'its own creature'.[14]

For Philip Smith, instead, Atwood is less interested in Shakespeare 'than in what we do with him'. In an article that reads *Hag-Seed* alongside *Bodily Harm*, Smith suggests that the earlier novel, with its claustrophobic island setting and postcolonial power struggles, is another Atwoodian reading of *The Tempest*. In his discussion, Smith is notably sceptical of transhistorical readings of Shakespeare's 'timelessness' and suggests instead that *Hag-Seed* offers 'an extended counter-thesis to an essentialist view of Shakespeare'.[15] Atwood, he argues, emphasizes the artifice, free will and desire that contribute to the characters' discovery of personal connections with the play and its apparent resemblance to their lives. Once again, Atwood is read as a highly self-conscious, sceptical writer always concerned to examine and test cultural assumptions.

The Atwood phenomenon

The speed at which Atwood continues to produce substantial, significant works is dizzying. And in recent years, her work has also encompassed increasingly diverse formats and collaborations, from the multimedia book tour of *The Year of the Flood* in 2009, at which the God's Gardeners hymns, set to music by composer Orville Stoeber, were sung by local choirs, through *The Happy Zombie Sunrise Home*, a serialized novel co-authored with Naomi Alderman and published on Wattpad in 2012, to *Angel Catbird*, Atwood's graphic novel series illustrated by Johnny Christmas and Tamra Bonvillain (2016–17). Most recently, the 2019 publication of *The Testaments* was a genuine literary phenomenon, with a midnight bookshop launch in central London, at which Atwood was cheered, followed the next day with an event at the National Theatre screened live to 1,000 cinemas across the world. The success of *The Testaments* was built, in large part, on the renewed interest in *The Handmaid's Tale* inspired by the successful 2017 Hulu television adaptation of the novel. This has, in turn, given rise to a rich new seam of Atwood studies focusing on adaptation: a topic usefully explored by Eva-Marie Kröller, in her essay 'The Hulu and MGM Adaptation of *The Handmaid's Tale*', and in *Adapting Margaret Atwood: The Handmaid's Tale and Beyond*, edited by Shannon Wells-Lassagne and Fiona McMahon. Perfectly timed to capture this moment of popular and critical interest, the launch of *The Testaments* represents a new high-water mark of Atwood's cultural impact.

Discussing *The Testaments* in a review for *The Conversation*, Watkins notes the manner in which *The Handmaid's Tale* has been reread in recent years in light of the #MeToo movement, the Trump administration and charges of 'fake news'. Where the 1985 novel concluded on the deeply troubling scepticism of the Gileadean Studies conference, Watkins suggests that, in 2019, 'Atwood replaces that incredulity with a much clearer sense of the validity of women's stories'.[16] A similar point is made by Sophie Gilbert in her review for *The Atlantic*, in which she also contextualizes Atwood's unexpected return to Gilead against the adoption of the Handmaid's uniform as a symbol of protest in the #MeToo era: 'A movement has swept her up', suggests Gilbert, 'though she hadn't set out to write for one'.[17]

While it seems to expand exponentially, what Graham Huggan termed in 2001 the 'Atwood phenomenon' has been building for many years, inspiring something of a sub-genre of Atwood criticism in itself.[18] In an early essay on the theme, 'Celebrity, or a Disneyland of the Soul: Margaret Atwood and the Media', Susanne Becker, for example, discusses Atwood's developing relationship with the media and its fascination with her.[19] The topic is further explored in Huggan's *The Postcolonial Exotic: Marketing the Margins*, in which he addresses the material and symbolic economies of cultural value surrounding the marketing of postcolonial writers such as Salman Rushdie, V. S. Naipaul and Michael

Ondaatje, and devotes a chapter to Atwood. Focusing on ideas of exoticism and celebrity glamour, Huggan describes the 'global image-making machinery' that has contributed to the turning of Atwood into a 'national icon and cultural celebrity'.[20] Huggan points to several factors, including Atwood's tireless promotion of her own work, her ability to speak eloquently (and quotably) on a variety of topics, and her controversial and fraught twin reputation as both the most famous Canadian writer and a spokesperson for feminist issues. (Laura Moss also discusses Atwood's branding as a Canadian icon abroad in a 2006 essay[21]). Each of these elements, suggests Huggan, accumulate cultural capital, eventually attaining the point at which Atwood's name alone sells books.

Huggan's work is extended by Lorraine York's influential studies of Atwood's celebrity in *Literary Celebrity in Canada* (2007) and *Margaret Atwood and the Labour of Literary Celebrity* (2013). In the earlier work, York places Atwood within a national context, reading her fame alongside that of fellow Canadian writers, Michael Ondaatje and Carol Shields. For York, Atwood's often wry self-consciousness about her fame sets her apart from Ondaatje and Shields, and she identifies in Atwood a 'powerfully shrewd and subtly uneasy' engagement with her own celebrity.[22] Examining the depiction of characters such as Joan in *Lady Oracle* and Elaine in *Cat's Eye*, who name and satirize the voracious appetite for artistic celebrities, York's concern is less, she explains, with why Atwood is so famous, and more with how she and her books are read in terms of her fame.

In her later work instead, York's focus is more on the idea of literary celebrity as the product of the labour of many parties – publishers, editors, agents, publicists and so forth – all working alongside the writer. As the public face of a professional industry that works hard to achieve the seemingly ephemeral status of fame, York identifies in Atwood a 'nuanced and strategic approach to literary production'. The book pays attention to peripheral but crucial aspects of the writer's work, such as Atwood's relationships with her agent and editor, her Toronto office and her use of social media. Atwood's writerly celebrity, suggest York, exists somewhere in between her existence as 'both economic labourer and mystic creator'.[23]

As Atwood moves into her eighties, with little indication of any inclination to slow down, both her labour and her creativity remain formidable. And as her longstanding concern with equality, liberty and human rights is met by an equally compelling preoccupation with impending climate catastrophe, she challenges her critics to keep up – to rise to the challenge of evaluating, critiquing and examining her complex, ethical, urgent fictions.

Notes

Introduction

1. Margaret Atwood, 'Margaret Dorothy Killam Atwood', *The Globe and Mail*, 23 April 2007. https://www.theglobeandmail.com/life/margaret-dorothy-killam-atwood/article684022/. Accessed 17 May 2020.
2. Coral Ann Howells, *Margaret Atwood* (Houndmills: Macmillan, 1996), pp. 3–4.
3. Heidi Slettedahl Macpherson, *The Cambridge Introduction to Margaret Atwood* (Cambridge: Cambridge University Press, 2010), p. 2.
4. Pauline Butling and Susan Rudy, *Writing in Our Time: Canada's Radical Poetries in English (1957–2003)* (Waterloo: Wilfrid Laurier University Press, 2005).
5. Paul Groetsch, 'Margaret Atwood: A Canadian Nationalist', in Reingard M. Nischik (ed.), *Margaret Atwood: Works and Impact* (Rochester: Camden House, 2000), p. 169.
6. Groetsch (2000), p. 175.
7. Margaret Atwood, 'After Survival . . . Excerpts from a Speech Delivered at Princeton University, 19 April 1985', *The CEA Critic* 50 (Fall 1987), p. 38. Cited in Groetsch (2000), p. 176.
8. Linda Sandler, 'Preface', *Margaret Atwood: A Symposium*. Ed. Linda Sandler, *The Malahat Review: An International Quarterly of Life and Letters* 41 (January 1977), p. 5.
9. Slettedahl Macpherson (2010), p. 5.
10. Robert Sharp, 'Margaret Atwood Awarded 2016 PEN Pinter Prize', *English PEN*, 16 June 2016. www.englishpen.org/events/atwood-pen-pinter-prize-2016/. Accessed 14 March 2019.
11. Nathalie Cook, *Margaret Atwood: A Biography* (Toronto: ECW Press, 1998), pp. 19–20.
12. Rosemary Sullivan, *The Red Shoes: Margaret Atwood Starting Out* (Toronto: Harper Flamingo, 1998), p. 6.
13. Fiona Tolan, '"I Could Say That Too": An Interview with Margaret Atwood', *Contemporary Women's Writing* 11.3 (November 2017), p. 461.
14. Margaret Atwood, *Negotiating with the Dead: A Writer on Writing* (Cambridge: Cambridge University Press, 2002), p. 7.
15. Atwood (2002), p. 13.

Chapter 1

1. Marge Piercy, 'Margaret Atwood: Beyond Victimhood' (1973), in Judith McCombs (ed.), *Critical Essays on Margaret Atwood* (Boston: G.K. Hall, 1988), p. 54.
2. Margaret Atwood, 'Introduction' to *The Edible Woman* (London: Virago, 1988), pp. 7–8.
3. Atwood (1988).
4. Fiona Tolan, *Margaret Atwood: Feminism and Fiction* (Amsterdam: Rodopi, 2007), p. 10.
5. Linda Sandler, 'Interview with Margaret Atwood', *The Malahat Review: An International Quarterly of Life and Letters* 41 (January 1977), p. 11.
6. Graeme Gibson, 'Dissecting the Way a Writer Works' (1972), in Earl G. Ingersoll (ed.), *Margaret Atwood: Conversations* (Ontario: Ontario Review, 1990), p. 12.
7. Rowland Smith, 'Margaret Atwood: The Stoic Comedian', *The Malahat Review: An International Quarterly of Life and Letters* 41 (January 1977), p. 137.
8. Jane Rule, 'Life, Liberty and the Pursuit of Normalcy: The Novels of Margaret Atwood', *The Malahat Review: An International Quarterly of Life and Letters* 41 (January 1977), p. 44.
9. Gregory Fitz Gerald and Kathryn Crabbe, 'Evading the Pigeonholers' (1979), in Earl G. Ingersoll (ed.), *Margaret Atwood: Conversations* (Ontario: Ontario Review, 1990), p. 132.
10. Linda Rogers, 'Margaret the Magician', *Canadian Literature* 60 (Spring 1974), p. 83.
11. Jane Miller, 'Self-Deprecating', Review. *The Times Literary Supplement* 3527 (2 October 1969), p. 1122.
12. Millicent Bell, 'The Girl on the Wedding Cake', Review. *New York Times Book Review* (18 October 1970), p. 26.
13. T. D. MacLulich, 'Atwood's Adult Fairy Tale: Lévi-Strauss, Bettelheim, and *The Edible Woman*', in Judith McCombs (ed.) *Critical Essays on Margaret Atwood* (Boston: G.K. Hall, 1988), p. 180.
14. Jerome H. Rosenberg, 'On Reading the Atwood Papers in the Thomas Fisher Library', *The Malahat Review: An International Quarterly of Life and Letters* 41 (January 1977), p. 191.
15. Rule (1977), p. 42.
16. Smith (1977), p. 134.
17. Smith (1977), p. 138.
18. Catherine McLay, 'The Dark Voyage: *The Edible Woman* as Romance', in Arnold E. Davidson and Cathy N. Davidson (eds), *The Art of Margaret Atwood: Essays in Criticism* (Toronto: Anansi, 1981), pp. 124, 125.

19 McLay (1981), p. 126.
20 McLay (1981), p. 131.
21 Sherrill Grace, *Violent Duality: A Study of Margaret Atwood* (Montreal: Véhicule Press, 1980), p. 3.
22 Grace (1980), p. 93.
23 Grace (1980), p. 93.
24 Sharon Rose Wilson, *Margaret Atwood's Fairy-Tale Sexual Politics* (Jackson: University Press of Mississippi, 1993), pp. 82, 85.
25 Wilson (1993), pp. 94, 94, 95.
26 MacLulich (1988), p. 183.
27 MacLulich (1988), pp. 187, 184, 188.
28 Rogers (1974), p. 84.
29 Sarah Sceats, *Food, Consumption and the Body in Contemporary Women's Fiction* (Cambridge: Cambridge University Press, 2000), pp. 96, 97.
30 Sceats (2000), p. 98.
31 Sceats (2000), p. 99.
32 Paul Delany, '*Surfacing*: Clearing a Canadian Space', Review. *New York Times Book Review* (4 March 1973), p. 441.
33 Margaret Laurence, 'Review of *Surfacing*' (1973), in Judith McCombs (ed.), *Critical Essays on Margaret Atwood* (Boston: G.K. Hall, 1988), pp. 46, 47.
34 Margaret Atwood, 'A Reply', *Signs: Journal of Women in Culture and Society* 2.2 (1976), p. 340.
35 Delany (1973), p. 441.
36 Eli Mandel, 'Atwood Gothic', in Judith McCombs (ed.), *Critical Essays on Margaret Atwood* (Boston: G.K. Hall, 1988), p. 118.
37 Margaret Atwood, *Survival: A Thematic Guide to Canadian Literature* (Toronto: House of Anansi Press, 2012), p. 32.
38 Marion Wynne-Davies, *Margaret Atwood* (Tavistock: Northcote House, 2009), p. 11.
39 Laurence (1973), p. 47.
40 Carol Christ, 'Margaret Atwood: The Surfacing of Women's Spiritual Quest and Vision', *Signs: Journal of Women in Culture and Society* 2.2 (Winter 1976), p. 317.
41 Piercy (1973), p. 44. Cited in Christ (1976), p. 317.
42 Christ (1976), p. 318.
43 Christ (1976), p. 324.
44 Judith Plaskow, 'On Carol Christ on Margaret Atwood: Some Theological Reflections', *Signs: Journal of Women in Culture and Society* 2.2 (Winter 1976), p. 331.
45 Plaskow (1976), p. 337.
46 Plaskow (1976), pp. 337, 338.
47 Atwood (1976), p. 340.

48 Mandel (1988), p. 118.
49 Mandel (1988), p. 118.
50 Cynthia Sugars, '"Saying Boo to Colonialism": *Surfacing*, Tom Thomson, and the National Ghost', in John Moss and Tobi Kozakewich (eds), *Margaret Atwood: The Open Eye* (Ottawa: University of Ottawa Press, 2006), p. 152.
51 Grace (1980), p. 98.
52 Grace (1980), p. 99.
53 Grace (1980), p. 101.
54 Sandler (1977), pp. 13–14.

Chapter 2

1 Marion Wynne-Davies, *Margaret Atwood* (Tavistock: Northcote House, 2009), pp. vii, 26, vii.
2 Kathryn VanSpanckeren, 'Introduction', in Kathryn VanSpanckeren and Jan Garden Castro (eds), *Margaret Atwood: Vision and Forms* (Carbondale and Edwardsville: Southern Illinois University Press, 1988), p. xx.
3 Ellen McWilliams, *Margaret Atwood and the Female Bildungsroman* (Farnham: Ashgate, 2009), p. 82.
4 Barbara Hill Rigney, *Margaret Atwood* (Basingstoke: Macmillan, 1987), p. 63.
5 Sofia Sanchez-Grant, 'The Female Body in Margaret Atwood's *The Edible Woman* and *Lady Oracle*', *Journal of International Women's Studies* 9.2 (March 2009), p. 84.
6 Nathalie Cooke, *Margaret Atwood: A Critical Companion* (Westport: Greenwood, 2004), p. 79.
7 Molly Hite, *The Other Side of the Story: Structures and Strategies of Contemporary Feminist Narratives* (Ithaca: Cornell University Press, 1989), p. 127.
8 Annette Kolodny, 'Margaret Atwood and the Politics of Narrative', in Arnold E. Davidson (ed.), *Studies on Canadian Literature: Introductory and Critical Essays* (New York: MLA, 1990), p. 94.
9 Colette Tennant, *Reading the Gothic in Margaret Atwood's Novels* (New York: Edwin Mellen, 2003), p. 66.
10 Joanna Russ, 'Somebody's Trying to Kill Me and I Think It's My Husband: The Modern Gothic', in Juliann Fleenor (ed.), *The Female Gothic* (Montreal: Eden Press, 1983), p. 44. Cited in Tennant (2003), p. 67.
11 Tennant (2003), p. 70.
12 Marjorie Fee, *The Fat Lady Dances: Margaret Atwood's Lady Oracle* (Toronto: ECW, 1993), p. 59.
13 Fee (1993), pp. 64, 63.

14 Graves, cited in Marilyn Patton, '*Lady Oracle*: The Politics of the Body', *ARIEL: A Review of International English Literature* 22.4 (October 1991), p. 30.
15 Patton (1991), p. 31.
16 Hite (1989), p. 139.
17 Patton (1991), p. 32.
18 Patton (1991), p. 37.
19 Sharon Rose Wilson, *Margaret Atwood's Fairy-Tale Sexual Politics* (Jackson: University of Mississippi Press, 1993), p. 121.
20 Wilson (1993), p. 133.
21 Margaret Atwood, *Survival: A Thematic Guide to Canadian Literature* (Toronto: House of Anansi Press, 2012), p. 235.
22 Shuli Barzilai, '"Say That I Had a Lovely Face": The Grimms' "Rapunzel," Tennyson's "Lady of Shalott," and Atwood's *Lady Oracle*', *Tulsa Studies in Women's Literature* 19.2 (Autumn 2000), pp. 235, 237.
23 Barzilai (2000), p. 331.
24 Barzilai (2000), p. 250.
25 Coral Ann Howells, *Margaret Atwood* (New York: St Martin's Press, 1996), p. 88.
26 Wynne-Davies (2009), p. 27.
27 Wynne-Davies (2009), p. 29.
28 Barbara Amiel, 'Life After Surviving', *Maclean's* (15 October 1979), p. 66. Cited in Carol Beran, *Living Over the Abyss: Margaret Atwood's Life Before Man* (Toronto: ECW, 1993), p. 17.
29 Wynne-Davies (2009), p. 31.
30 Elizabeth Meese, 'An Interview with Margaret Atwood', *Black Warrior Review* 12.1 (1985), pp. 88–108, 89. Cited in Kolodny (1990), p. 96.
31 Beran (1993), p. 25.
32 Marilyn French, 'Spouses and Lovers', Review. *The New York Times*, 3 February 1980. www.nytimes.com. Accessed 18 December 2018.
33 Gayle Greene, '*Life Before Man*: Can Anything Be Saved?', in Kathryn VanSpanckeren and Jan Garden Castro (eds), *Margaret Atwood: Vision and Forms* (Carbondale and Edwardsville: Southern Illinois University Press, 1988), pp. 65, 67.
34 Karen Stein, 'It's About Time: Temporal Dimensions in Margaret Atwood's *Life Before Man*', in Sarah A. Appleton (ed.), *Once upon a Time: Myth, Fairy Tales and Legends in Margaret Atwood's Writings* (Newcastle upon Tyne: Cambridge Scholars, 2008), p. 98.
35 Stein (2008), p. 99.
36 Kolodny (1990), pp. 91–2.
37 Kolodny (1990), p. 95.
38 Sherrill Grace, *Violent Duality: A Study of Margaret Atwood* (Montreal: Véhicule Press, 1980), pp. 135, 137.

39 Kolodny (1990), p. 95.
40 Kolodny (1990), p. 96.
41 Stein (2008), p. 96.
42 Stein (2008), p. 97.
43 Stein (2008), p. 111.
44 Emma Parker, 'You Are What You Eat: The Politics of Eating in the Novels of Margaret Atwood', *Twentieth Century Literature* 41.3 (Autumn 1995), pp. 352, 353.
45 Sarah Sceats, *Food, Consumption and the Body in Contemporary Women's Fiction* (Cambridge: Cambridge University Press, 2004), p. 21.
46 Parker (1995), pp. 360, 363.
47 Parker (1995), p. 364.
48 Patton (1991), pp. 158, 160.
49 Parker (1995), p. 364.
50 Hill Rigney (1987), p. 99.
51 Hill Rigney (1987), p. 104.
52 Marilyn Patton, 'Tourists and Terrorists: The Creation of *Bodily Harm*', *Papers on Language & Literature* 28.2 (Spring 1992), p. 151.
53 Diana Brydon, 'Atwood's Postcolonial Imagination: Rereading *Bodily Harm*', in Lorraine M. York (ed.), *Various Atwoods: Essays on the Later Poems, Short Fiction, and Novels* (Toronto: Anansi, 1995), p. 109.
54 Kolodny (1990), pp. 96, 97.
55 Simone Drichel, 'Regarding the Other: Postcolonial Violations and Ethical Resistance in Margaret Atwood's *Bodily Harm*', *MFS: Modern Fiction Studies* 54.1 (Spring 2008), pp. 312.
56 Patton (1992), p. 154.
57 Ildiko de Papp Carrington, 'Another Symbolic Descent', *Essays on Canadian Writing* 26 (1983), p. 46.
58 Patton (1992), p. 161.
59 Patton (1992), p. 165.
60 Helen Tiffin, '"Everyone Is in Politics": Margaret Atwood's *Bodily Harm* and Blanche D'Alpuget's *Turtle Beach*. Part II: Voice and Form', in Russell McDougall and Gillian Whitlock (eds), *Australian/Canadian Literatures in English: A Comparative Perspective* (Melbourne: Methuen, 1987), p. 125.
61 Brydon (1995), p. 112.
62 Drichel (2008), p. 27.
63 Drichel (2008), p. 23.
64 Kate Marantz, 'Making It (In)Visible: The Politics of Absence in Margaret Atwood's *Bodily Harm*', *Studies in Canadian Literature/Études en Literature Canadienne* 41.2 (2016), p. 138.

65 Marantz (2016), pp. 139, 149.
66 Frank Davey, *Margaret Atwood: A Feminist Poetics* (Vancouver: Talonbooks, 1984), p. 70.
67 Jerome H. Rosenberg, *Margaret Atwood* (Boston: Twayne, 1984), p. 131.
68 Rosenberg (1984), p. 131.
69 Rosenberg (1984), p. 133.
70 Kolodny (1990), p. 98.
71 Davey (1984), p. 57.
72 Davey (1984), p. 61.
73 Davey (1984), pp. 78, 79.

Chapter 3

1 Margaret Atwood, 'Haunted by *The Handmaid's Tale*', *The Guardian*, 20 January 2012. https://www.theguardian.com/books/2012/jan/20/handmaids-tale-margaret-atwood. Accessed 26 March 2019.
2 Margaret Atwood, 'What *The Handmaid's Tale* Means in the Age of Trump', *The New York Times*, 10 March 2017.
3 Danuta Kean, 'Prescient About the President: Which Writers Can Help Us to Read Trump?' *The Guardian*, 24 January 2017. https://www.theguardian.com/books/2017/jan/24/prescient-about-the-president-which-writers-can-help-us-read-trump. Accessed 26 March 2019.
4 Fiona Tolan, '"I Could Say That, Too": An Interview with Margaret Atwood', *Contemporary Women's Writing* 11.3 (November 2017), p. 452.
5 Alexandra Alter, 'Uneasy About the Future, Readers Turn to Dystopian Classics', *The New York Times*, 27 January 2017, www.nytimes.com/2017/01/27/business/media/dystopian-classics-1984-animal-farm-the-handmaids-tale.html?_r=0. Accessed 29 September 2017.
6 Atwood (2012), n.p.
7 Margaret Atwood, *The Handmaid's Tale* (London: Vintage, 1996), p. 324.
8 Earl Ingersoll, 'Margaret Atwood's *The Handmaid's Tale*: Echoes of Orwell', *Journal of the Fantastic in the Arts* 5.4 (1993), p. 64.
9 Coral Ann Howells, *Margaret Atwood* (Houndmills: Macmillan, 1996), p. 128.
10 Ingersoll (1993), p. 65.
11 Ingersoll (1993), p. 67.
12 Angela Laflen, '"From a Distance It Looks Like Peace": Reading Beneath the Fascist Style of Gilead in Margaret Atwood's *The Handmaid's Tale*', *Studies in Canadian Literature/Études en Literature Canadienne* 32.1 (2007), p. 87.
13 Laflen (2007), p. 94.

14 Mary McCarthy, 'The Handmaid's Tale', Review. *The New York Times. Books*, 9 February 1986. http://movies2.nytimes.com/books/00/03/26/specials/mccarthy-atwood.html. Accessed 18 December 2018.
15 Atwood (1997), p. 98.
16 Lorna Sage, 'Projections from a Messy Present', Review. *Times Literary Supplement*, 21 March 1986, p. 307.
17 John Updike, 'Expeditions to Gilead and Seegard', Review. *The New Yorker*, 12 May 1986, p. 121.
18 Updike (1986), p. 123.
19 Howells (1996), p. 127.
20 Atwood, unpublished essay. Cited in Howells (1996), p. 129.
21 'An interview with Margaret Atwood on her novel *The Handmaid's Tale*', No author. No date. Everyman's Library. http://www.randomhouse.com/knopf/classics//catalog/display.pperl?isbn=9780307264602&view=qa. Accessed 26 March 2019.
22 See, for example, Ursula K. Le Guin, '*The Year of the Flood* by Margaret Atwood', *The Guardian*, 29 August 2009. https://www.theguardian.com/books/2009/aug/29/margaret-atwood-year-of-flood. Accessed 26 March 2019.
23 Gina Wisker, *Atwood's The Handmaid's Tale: A Reader's Guide* (London: Continuum, 2010), p. 122.
24 Coral Ann Howells, 'Margaret Atwood's Dystopian Visions: *The Handmaid's Tale* and *Oryx and Crake*', in Coral Ann Howells (ed.), *The Cambridge Companion to Margaret Atwood* (Cambridge: Cambridge University Press, 2006), p. 161.
25 Barbara Hill Rigney, *Margaret Atwood* (Houndmills: Macmillan, 1987), pp. 103–4.
26 Madonne Miner, '"Trust Me": Reading the Romance Plot in Margaret Atwood's *The Handmaid's Tale*', *Twentieth Century Literature* 37.2 (Summer 1991), p. 150.
27 Miner (1991), p. 160.
28 Miner (1991), p. 161.
29 Tae Yamamoto, 'How Can a Feminist Read *The Handmaid's Tale*? A Study of Offred's Narrative', in John Moss and Tobi Kozakewich (eds), *Margaret Atwood: The Open Eye* (Ottawa: University of Ottawa Press, 2006), p. 195.
30 Miner (1991), p. 164.
31 Mervyn Rothstein, 'No Balm in Gilead for Margaret Atwood', Interview. *The New York Times. Books*, 17 February 1986. http://movies2.nytimes.com/books/00/09/03/specials/atwood-gilead.html. Accessed 18 December 2018.
32 Elizabeth Meese, 'The Empress Has No Clothes' (1985), in Earl G. Ingersoll (ed.), *Margaret Atwood: Conversations* (Princeton: Ontario Review, 1990), p. 183. Cited in Shirley Neuman, '"Just a Backlash": Margaret Atwood, Feminism and *The Handmaid's Tale*', *University of Toronto Quarterly* 75.3 (Summer 2006), p. 858.
33 Wisker (2010), p. 3.
34 Theodore F. Sheckels, *The Political in Margaret Atwood's Fiction: The Writing on the Wall of the Tent* (Farnham: Ashgate, 2012), p. 78.

35 Susan Faludi, *Backlash: The Undeclared War against American Women*. 1991 (London: Vintage, 1993).
36 Neuman (2006), p. 858.
37 Neuman (2006), p. 861.
38 Gayle Greene, 'Choice of Evils', Review. *The Women's Review of Books* 3.10 (July 1986), p. 14.
39 Neuman (2006), pp. 861–2.
40 Fiona Tolan. 'Feminist Utopias and Questions of Liberty: Margaret Atwood's *The Handmaid's Tale* as Critique of Second Wave Feminism', *Women: A Cultural Review* 16.1 (Spring 2005), p. 19.
41 Tolan (2005), p. 23.
42 Greene (1986), p. 10.
43 Tolan (2005), p. 31.
44 Neuman (2006), p. 866.
45 Marta Dvorak, 'What is Real/Reel? Margaret Atwood's "Rearrangement of Shapes on a Flat Surface," Or Narrative as Collage', *Études Anglaises* 51.4 (October 1988), p. 448.
46 Howells (2006), p. 168.
47 Dvorak (1988), p. 449.
48 Mario Klarer, 'Orality and Literacy as Gender-Supporting Structures in Margaret Atwood's *The Handmaid's Tale*', *Mosaic* 28.4 (December 1995), p. 130.
49 Klarer (1995), pp. 134, 136.
50 Wisker (2010), p. 18.
51 Wisker (2010), p. 19.
52 Wisker (2010), p. 21.
53 Jennifer A. Wagner-Lawlor, 'From Irony to Affiliation in Margaret Atwood's *The Handmaid's Tale*', *Critique: Studies in Contemporary Fiction* 45.1 (2003), pp. 83, 84.
54 Wagner-Lawlor (2003), pp. 85, 93.
55 Dvorak (1988), pp. 449, 450, 456.
56 Greene (1986), p. 14.
57 Howells (1996), pp. 126, 127.
58 Howells (1996), p. 137.
59 Yamamoto (2006), pp. 199, 203.
60 Allan Weiss, 'Offred's Complicity and the Dystopian Tradition in Margaret Atwood's *The Handmaid's Tale*', *Studies in Canadian Literature / Études en Literature Canadienne* 34.1 (2009), p. 120.
61 J. Broooks Bouson, *Brutal Choreographies: Oppositional Strategies and Narrative Design in the Novels of Margaret Atwood* (Amherst: University of Massachusetts Press, 1993), p. 154.
62 Weiss (2009), p. 137.

63 Patricia A. Stapleton, 'Suicide as Apocalypse in *The Handmaid's Tale*', in Karma Waltonen (ed.), *Margaret Atwood's Apocalypses* (Newcastle upon Tyne: Cambridge Scholars, 2015), pp. 35, 38.
64 Neuman (2006), p. 864.
65 Neuman (2006), p. 864.
66 Rigney (1987), pp. 115, 116, 120.
67 Howells (2006), p. 165.
68 Stapleton (2015), p. 38.
69 Arnold E. Davidson, 'Future Tense: Making History in *The Handmaid's Tale*', in Kathryn VanSpanckeren and Jan Garden Castro (eds), *Margaret Atwood: Visions and Forms* (Carbondale: Southern Illinois UP, 1988), p. 113.
70 Davidson (1988), p. 114.
71 Rothstein (1986).
72 Hilde Staels, 'Margaret Atwood's *The Handmaid's Tale*: Resistance Through Narrating', *English Studies* 76.5 (1995), p. 464.
73 Staels (1995), pp. 456, 464.
74 Howells (1996), p. 146.
75 Davidson (1988), pp. 119, 120.
76 Howells (1996), pp. 146, 135, 147, 146.

Chapter 4

1 Marion Wynne-Davies, *Margaret Atwood* (Tavistock: Northcote House, 2010), pp. 5, 44.
2 Karen Stein, *Margaret Atwood Revisited* (New York: Twayne, 1999), p. 86.
3 Alice M. Palumbo, 'On the Border: Margaret Atwood's Novels', in Reingard M. Nischik (ed.), *Margaret Atwood: Works and Impact* (Rochester: Camden House, 2000), pp. 81–2.
4 Barbara Hill Rigney, 'Alias Atwood: Narrative Games and Gender Politics', in Reingard M. Nischik (ed.), *Margaret Atwood: Works and Impact* (Rochester: Camden House, 2000), p. 161.
5 Margaret Atwood, 'Spotty-Handed Villainesses: Problems of Female Bad Behaviour in the Creation of Literature', *Curious Pursuits: Occasional Writing 1970–2005* (London: Virago, 2005), p. 172.
6 Atwood (2005), p. 180.
7 Atwood (2005), p. 185.
8 Wynne-Davies (2010), pp. 42, 6.
9 Earl G. Ingersoll, 'Waltzing Again', in Earl G. Ingersoll (ed.), *Margaret Atwood: Conversations* (Princeton: Ontario Review Press, 1990), p. 236.

10 Molly Hite, 'Optics and Autobiography in Margaret Atwood's *Cat's Eye*', *Twentieth Century Literature* 41.2 (Summer 1995), p. 136.
11 Ingersoll (1990), p. 236.
12 Julie Brown, 'Our Ladies of Perpetual Hell: Witches and Fantastic Virgins in Margaret Atwood's *Cat's Eye*', *Journal of the Fantastic in the Arts* 4.3 (1991), p. 40.
13 Chinmoy Banerjee, 'Atwood's Time: Hiding Art in *Cat's Eye*', *MFS: Modern Fiction Studies* 36.4 (Winter 1990), p. 513.
14 Laura Martocci, 'Girl World and Bullying: Intersubjective Shame in Margaret Atwood's *Cat's Eye*', in Patricia Moran and Erica L. Johnson (eds), *The Female Face of Shame* (Bloomington: Indiana University Press, 2016), p. 150.
15 Hite (1995), p. 138.
16 Hite (1995), p. 139.
17 Martocci (2016), p. 153.
18 Kiriaki Massoura, '"I Look At It and See My Life Entire": Language, Third-Eye Vision and Painting in Margaret Atwood's *Cat's Eye*', *British Journal of Canadian Studies* 17.2 (September 2004), p. 211.
19 Banerjee (1990), p. 516.
20 Banerjee (1990), p. 517.
21 Banerjee (1990), p. 516.
22 Wynne-Davies (2010), p. 47.
23 Banerjee (1990), p. 520.
24 Marta Dvorak, 'Margaret Atwood's *Cat's Eye*: or the Trembling Canvas', *Études Anglaises* 54.3 (2001), p. 300.
25 Earl G. Ingersoll, 'Margaret Atwood's *Cat's Eye*: Re-Viewing Women in a Postmodern World', *ARIEL: A Review of International English Literature* 22.4 (October 1991), pp. 17, 19.
26 Hite (1995), p. 135.
27 Hite (1995), p. 153.
28 Margaret Atwood, *On Writers and Writing*. 2002 (London: Virago, 2003).
29 Wynne-Davies (2010), p. 46.
30 Ingersoll (1991), p. 19.
31 Stein (1999), pp. 88, 87.
32 Jill Ker Conway, *When Memory Speaks: Reflections on Autobiography* (New York: Knopf, 1998), p. 7.
33 Stein (1999), p. 90.
34 Salman Rushdie, 'The Best Fears of Our Lives: *The Robber Bride*', Review. *The Independent*, 17 October 1993. https://www.independent.co.uk/arts-entertainment/book-review-the-best-fears-of-our-lives-the-robber-bride-margaret-atwood-bloomsbury-1499-pounds-1511278.html. Accessed 18 December 2018.
35 Dvorak (2001), p. 300.
36 Ingersoll (1990), p. 236.

37 Hite (1995), p. 137.
38 Ingersoll (1991), p. 21.
39 Hite (1995), p. 145.
40 Ingersoll (1991), p. 21.
41 Ingersoll (1991), p. 21.
42 Hite (1995), p. 145.
43 Massoura (2004), p. 212.
44 Massoura (2004), p. 212.
45 Wynne-Davies (2010), p. 51.
46 Brown (1991), p. 42.
47 Massoura (2004), p. 210.
48 Dvorak (2001), p. 300.
49 Sharon R. Wilson, 'Margaret Atwood's Visual Art', *Essays on Canadian Writing* 50 (Fall 1993), p. 129.
50 Reingard M. Nischik, *Engendering Gender: The Works of Margaret Atwood* (Ottawa: University of Ottawa Press, 2009).
51 Brown (1991), pp. 40–1.
52 Brown (1991), p. 46.
53 Dvorak (2001), p. 300.
54 Massoura (2004), p. 210.
55 Dvorak (2001), p. 305.
56 Hite (1995), pp. 139, 164.
57 Wynne-Davies (2010), p. 48.
58 Lorraine York, 'Biography/Autobiography', in Coral Ann Howells (ed.), *The Cambridge Companion to Margaret Atwood* (Cambridge: Cambridge University Press, 2006), p. 36.
59 Donna Bontatibus, 'Reconnecting with the Past: Personal Hauntings in Margaret Atwood's *the Robber Bride*', *Papers on Language and Literature* 34 (1998), p. 359.
60 Donna L. Potts, '"The Old Maps are Dissolving": Intertextuality and Identity in Atwood's *The Robber Bride*', *Tulsa Studies in Women's Literature* 18.2 (Autumn 1999), p. 281.
61 J. Brooks Bouson, 'Slipping Sideways into the Dreams of Women: The Female Dream Work of Power Feminism in Margaret Atwood's *The Robber Bride*', *Lit: Literature Interpretation Theory* 6.3–4 (1995), p. 151.
62 Laurie Vickroy, 'You're History: Living with Trauma in *The Robber Bride*', in J. Brooks Bouson (ed.), *Margaret Atwood: The Robber Bride, The Blind Assassin, Oryx and Crake* (London: Continuum, 2010), p. 57.
63 Phyllis Sternberg Perrakis, 'Atwood's *The Robber Bride*: The Vampire as Intersubjective Catalyst', *Mosaic* 30.3 (September 1997), p. 167.
64 Rushdie (1993), n.p.
65 Bouson (1995), p. 151.

66 Vickroy (2010), p. 50.
67 Roxanne J. Fand, 'Margaret Atwood's *The Robber Bride*: The Dialogic Moral of a Nietzschean Fairy Tale', *Critique: Studies in Contemporary Fiction* 45.1 (2003), p. 68.
68 Fand (2003), p. 73.
69 Vickroy (2010), p. 53.
70 Hilde Staels, 'Parodic Border Crossings in *The Robber Bride*', in J. Brooks Bouson (ed.) *Margaret Atwood: The Robber Bride, The Blind Assassin, Oryx and Crake* (London: Continuum, 2010), p. 39.
71 Fand (2003), p. 69.
72 Fand (2003), p. 72.
73 Naomi Wolf, *Fire with Fire: The New Female Power and How It Will Change the 21st Century* (New York: Random House, 1993), p. 136.
74 Bouson (1995), pp. 149–50.
75 Rigney (2000), p. 163.
76 Stein (1999), p. 96.
77 Bouson (1995), p. 150.
78 Jean Wyatt, 'I Want to be You: Envy, the Lacanian Double, and Feminist Community in Margaret Atwood's *The Robber Bride*', *Tulsa Studies in Women's Literature* 17.1 (Spring 1998), pp. 37, 38, 52.
79 Wyatt (1998), pp. 52, 59.
80 Sharon R. Wilson, 'Mythological Intertexts in Margaret Atwood's Work', in Reingard M. Nischik (ed.), *Margaret Atwood: Works and Impact* (Rochester: Camden House, 2000), p. 224.
81 Fand (2003), p. 73.
82 Staels (2010), pp. 36, 38, 40.
83 Stein (1999), pp. 40, 41, 42.
84 Wilson (2000), p. 224.
85 Palumbo (2000), p. 83.
86 Rigney (2000), p. 162.
87 Staels (2010), p. 43.
88 Palumbo (2000), pp. 82–3.
89 Bouson (1995), p. 151.
90 Eleonora Rao, 'Home and Nation in Margaret Atwood's Later Fiction', in Coral Ann Howells (ed.), *The Cambridge Companion to Margaret Atwood* (Cambridge: Cambridge University Press, 2006), pp. 102, 103.
91 Jennifer Murray, 'Questioning the Triple Goddess: Myth and Meaning in Margaret Atwood's *The Robber Bride*', *Canadian Literature* 173 (Summer 2002), pp. 72–90.
92 Rao (2006), p. 106.
93 Stein (1990), p. 102.
94 Wyatt (1998), p. 58.

95 Bouson (1995), p. 162.
96 Bouson (1995), p. 161.
97 Fand (2003), p. 72.
98 Fand (2003), p. 75.

Chapter 5

1. Coral Ann Howells, 'Transgressing Genre: A Generic Approach to Margaret Atwood's Novels', in Reingard M. Nischik (ed.), *Margaret Atwood: Works and Impact* (Rochester: Camden House, 2000), p. 153.
2. Ruth Parkin-Gounelas, 'Margaret Atwood's *The Blind Assassin*: The Psychoanalysis of Duplicity', *MFS: Modern Fiction Studies* 50.3 (Fall 2004), p. 681.
3. Barbara Hill Rigney, 'Alias Atwood: Narrative Games and Gender Politics', in Reingard M. Nischik (ed.) *Margaret Atwood: Works and Impact* (Rochester: Camden House, 2000), p. 157.
4. Sandra Kumamoto Stanley, 'The Eroticism of Class and the Enigma of Margaret Atwood's *Alias Grace*', *Tulsa Studies in Women's Literature* 22.2 (Autumn 2003), p. 380.
5. Karen Stein, 'Talking Back to Bluebeard: Atwood's Fictional Storytellers', in Sharon Rose Wilson (ed.), *Margaret Atwood's Textual Assassinations: Recent Poetry and Fiction* (Columbus: Ohio State University Press, 2003a), p. 164.
6. Margaret Atwood, 'Author's Afterword', in *Alias Grace* (London: Virago, 1997), p. 539.
7. Sharon Rose Wilson, 'Quilting as Narrative Art: Metafictional Construction in *Alias Grace*', in Sharon Rose Wilson (ed.), *Margaret Atwood's Textual Assassinations: Recent Poetry and Fiction* (Columbus: Ohio State University Press, 2003), p. 122.
8. Stanley (2003), p. 372.
9. Jackie Shead, *Margaret Atwood: Crime Fiction Writer – The Reworking of a Popular Genre* (Farnham: Ashgate, 2015), p. 87.
10. Alison Toron, 'The Model Prisoner: Reading Confinement in *Alias Grace*', *Canadian Literature* 208 (Spring 2011), p. 16.
11. Stanley (2003), p. 372.
12. Lorraine York, 'Biography/Autobiography', in Coral Ann Howells (ed.), *The Cambridge Companion to Margaret Atwood* (Cambridge: Cambridge University Press, 2006), pp. 36, 37.
13. Karen Stein, *Margaret Atwood Revisited* (New York: Twayne, 1999), p. 103.
14. Wilson (2003), p. 121.
15. Linda Hutcheon, *A Poetics of Postmodernism: History, Theory, Fiction* (London: Routledge, 1988), p. 5.
16. Jennifer Murray, 'Historical Figures and Paradoxical Patterns: The Quilting Metaphor in Margaret Atwood's *Alias Grace*', *Studies in Canadian Literature* 26.1 (March 2001), p. 64.

17 Margaret Atwood, 'In Search of *Alias Grace:* On Writing Canadian Historical Fiction', *The American Historical Review* 103.5 (December 1998), pp. 1504–5.
18 Shead (2015), p. 88.
19 Wilson (2003), pp. 122–3.
20 Toron (2011), p. 15.
21 Maria J. Lopez, '"You Are One of Us": Communities of Marginality, Vulnerability, and Secrecy in Margaret Atwood's *Alias Grace*', *ESC: English Studies in Canada* 38.2 (June 2012), p. 158.
22 Stanley (2003), pp. 371, 373, 374.
23 Marlene Goldman, *DisPossession: Haunting in Canadian Fiction* (Montreal & Kingston: McGill-Queen's University Press, 2012), pp. 149, 152.
24 Stanley (2003), pp. 376, 383.
25 Murray (2001), p. 65.
26 Hutcheon (1988), p. 122.
27 Wilson (2003), p. 122.
28 Murray (2001), p. 66.
29 Wilson (2003), p. 125.
30 Murray (2001), p. 79.
31 Magali Cornier Michael, 'Rethinking History as Patchwork: The Case of Atwood's *Alias Grace*', *Modern Fiction Studies* 47.2 (Summer 2001), p. 426.
32 Wilson (2003), p. 125.
33 Michael (2001), p. 421.
34 Michael (2001), p. 425.
35 Michael (2001), p. 441.
36 Wilson (2003), p. 123.
37 Murray (2001), p. 81.
38 Shead (2015), p. 88.
39 Earl Ingersoll, 'Waiting for the End: Closure in Margaret Atwood's *The Blind Assassin*', *Studies in the Novel* 35.4 (Winter 2003), p. 543.
40 Hilde Staels, 'Intertexts of Margaret Atwood's *Alias Grace*', *Modern Fiction Studies* 46.2 (Summer 2000), p. 428.
41 Staels (2000), p. 432.
42 John O'Neill, 'Dying in a State of Grace: Memory, Duality and Uncertainty in Margaret Atwood's *Alias Grace*', *Textual Practice* 27.4 (2013), pp. 663, 655.
43 Shead (2015), pp. 94, 96, 89.
44 Alan Robinson, '"Alias Laura": Representations of the Past in Margaret Atwood's *The Blind Assassin*', *The Modern Language Review* 101.2 (April 2006), p. 348.
45 Coral Ann Howells, *Margaret Atwood*. 2nd edn. (Houndmills, Basingstoke: Palgrave Macmillan, 2005), p. 155.

46 Karen Stein, 'A Left-Handed Story: *The Blind Assassin*', in Sharon Rose Wilson (ed.), *Margaret Atwood's Textual Assassinations: Recent Poetry and Fiction* (Columbus: Ohio State University Press, 2003b), p. 136.
47 Stein (2003b), p. 135.
48 Marta Dvorak, 'The Right Hand Writing and the Left Hand Erasing in Margaret Atwood's *The Blind Assassin*', *Commonwealth: Essays and Studies* 25.1 (Autumn 2002), p. 60.
49 Howells (2005), p. 156.
50 Robinson (2006), p. 348.
51 Ingersoll (2003), p. 543.
52 Howells (2005), p. 159.
53 Stein (2003b), p. 139.
54 Howells (2005), p. 159.
55 Stein (2003b), p. 148.
56 Robinson (2006), p. 349.
57 Howells (2005), pp. 155, 156.
58 Alice Ridout, '"Without Memory, There Can Be No Revenge": Iris Chase Griffen's Textual Revenge in Margaret Atwood's *The Blind Assassin*', *Margaret Atwood Studies* 2.2 (December 2008), pp. 14–15.
59 Sharon R. Wilson, 'Blindness and Survival in Margaret Atwood's Major Novels', in Coral Ann Howells (ed.), *The Cambridge Companion to Margaret Atwood* (Cambridge: Cambridge University Press, 2006), p. 185.
60 Ridout (2008), pp. 16, 23.
61 Dvorak (2002), pp. 59, 68.
62 Dvorak (2002), p. 60.
63 Dvorak (2002), p. 68.
64 Ingersoll (2003), p. 544.
65 Ingersoll (2003), p. 546.
66 Ingersoll (2003), p. 549.
67 Ingersoll (2003), p. 555.
68 Dvorak (2002), p. 65.
69 Robinson (2006), p. 347.
70 Howells (2005), p. 156.
71 Ingersoll (2003), p. 554.
72 Stein (2003b), pp. 138, 137.
73 Stein (2003b), p. 151.
74 Hilde Staels, '*The Penelopiad* and *Weight*: Contemporary Parodic and Burlesque Transformations of Classical Myths', *College Literature* 6.4 (Fall 2009), p. 106.
75 Coral Ann Howells, '"We Can't Help but Be Modern": *The Penelopiad*', in S. A. Appleton (ed.), *Once Upon a Time: Myth, Fairy Tales and Legends in Margaret Atwood's Writings* (Newcastle upon Tyne: Cambridge Scholars, 2008), p. 65.

76 Fiona Tolan, 'Atwood's Revision of Classic Texts', in Coral Ann Howells (ed.), *The Cambridge Companion to Margaret Atwood*. 2nd edn. (Cambridge: Cambridge University Press, 2021).
77 Susanne Jung, '"A Chorus Line": Margaret Atwood's *Penelopiad* at the Crossroads of Narrative, Poetic and Dramatic Genres', *Connotations* 24.1 (2014/2015), p. 42.
78 Phyllida Lloyd, 'She's Left Holding the Fort', *The Guardian*, 26 October 2005. www.guardian.co.uk/stage/2005/oct/26/theatre.classics. Accessed 9 February 2019.
79 Earl G. Ingersoll, 'Flirting with Tragedy: Margaret Atwood's *The Penelopiad* and the Play of the Text', *Intertexts* 12.1–2 (Spring 2008), p. 111.
80 Ingersoll (2008), p. 112.
81 Jung (2014/2015), p. 44.
82 Ingersoll (2008), pp. 118, 125.
83 Tolan (2021), n.p.
84 Howells (2008), pp. 59, 62, 57.
85 Jung (2014/2015), p. 58.
86 Howells (2008), p. 64.
87 Mihoko Suzuki, 'Rewriting the *Odyssey* in the Twenty-First Century: Mary Zimmerman's *Odyssey* and Margaret Atwood's *Penelopiad*', *College Literature* 34.2 (Spring 2007), pp. 270, 275, 272.
88 Susanna Braund, '"We're Here Too, the Ones Without Names." A Study of Female Voices as Imagined by Margaret Atwood, Carol Ann Duffy, and Marguerite Yourcenar', *Classical Reception Journal*, 4.2 (2012), p. 190.
89 Braund (2012), p. 194.
90 Braund (2012), p. 206.
91 Linda Hutcheon, *A Theory of Parody: The Teachings of Twentieth-Century Art Forms* (London and New York: Methuen, 1985), p. 32.
92 Staels (2009), p. 101.
93 Staels (2009), pp. 104, 106.
94 Staels (2009), p. 106.
95 Suzuki (2007), p. 269.

Chapter 6

1 Elaine Showalter, 'The Snowman Cometh', *London Review of Books* 25.14 (24 July 2003). https://www.lrb.co.uk/v25/n14/elaine-showalter/the-snowman-cometh n.p.
2 Coral Ann Howells, 'Margaret Atwood's Dystopian Visions: *The Handmaid's Tale* and *Oryx and Crake*', in Coral Ann Howells (ed.), *The Cambridge Companion to Margaret Atwood* (Cambridge: Cambridge University Press, 2006), p. 161.

3. Shannon Hengen, 'Margaret Atwood and Environmentalism', in Coral Ann Howells (ed.), *The Cambridge Companion to Margaret Atwood* (Cambridge: Cambridge University Press, 2006), p. 80.
4. Miles Weafer, 'Writing from the Margin: Victim Positions in Atwood's *The Year of the Flood*', in Karma Waltonen (ed.), *Margaret Atwood's Apocalypses* (Newcastle upon Tyne: Cambridge Scholars, 2015), pp. 57–8.
5. Showalter (2003), n.p.
6. Natasha Walter, 'Pigoons Might Fly', *The Guardian*, 10 May 2003. https://www.theguardian.com/books/2003/may/10/bookerprize2003.bookerprize n.p.
7. Susan Squier, 'A Tale Meant to Inform, Not to Amuse', *Science* 302.5648 (14 November 2003), pp. 1154–5.
8. Anthony Griffiths, 'Genetics according to *Oryx and Crake*', *Canadian Literature* 181 (2004), p. 192.
9. Griffiths (2004), p. 194.
10. Lee Rozelle, 'Liminal Ecologies in Margaret Atwood's *Oryx and Crake*', *Canadian Literature* 206 (Autumn 2010), p. 63.
11. J. Brooks Bouson, '"It's Game Over Forever": Atwood's Satiric Vision of a Bioengineered Posthuman Future in *Oryx and Crake*', *Journal of Commonwealth Literature* 39.3 (September 2004), p. 140.
12. Rozelle (2010), p. 69.
13. Hengen (2006), p. 83.
14. Bouson (2004), p. 139.
15. Katherine V. Snyder, '"Time to Go": The Post-Apocalyptic and the Post-Traumatic in Margaret Atwood's *Oryx and Crake*', *Studies in the Novel* 43.4 (Winter 2011), p. 471.
16. Walter (2003), n.p.
17. Berthold Schoene, 'Getting World Going in Margaret Atwood's *Oryx and Crake*', *Senses and Society* 8.1 (2013), p. 98.
18. Gerry Canavan, 'Hope, But Not for Us: Ecological Science Fiction and the End of the World in Margaret Atwood's *Oryx and Crake* and *The Year of the Flood*', *LIT: Literature Interpretation Theory* 23.2 (2012), p. 140.
19. Snyder (2011), p. 482.
20. Showalter (2003), n.p.
21. Bouson (2004), p. 147.
22. Bouson (2004), p. 141.
23. Rozelle (2010), p. 63.
24. Stephen Dunning, 'Margaret Atwood's *Oryx and Crake*: The Terror of the Theraputic', *Canadian Literature* 186 (2005), p. 86.
25. Howells (2006), p. 169.
26. Schoene (2013), p. 98.
27. Sven Birkerts, 'Present at the Re-Creation', *The New York Times*, 18 May 2003. https://www.nytimes.com/2003/05/18/books/present-at-the-re-creation.html n.p.

28 Howells (2006), p. 170.
29 Snyder (2011), p. 472.
30 Shuli Barzilai, '"Tell My Story": Remembrance and Revenge in Margaret Atwood's *Oryx and Crake* and Shakespeare's *Hamlet*', *Critique: Studies in Contemporary Fiction* 50.1 (Fall 2008), p. 88.
31 Bouson (2004), p. 145.
32 Showalter (2003), n.p.
33 Bouson (2004), p. 146.
34 Chien-Hung Chen, 'Micro-biopolitics at the End of the Anthropocene: Margaret Atwood's *MaddAddam* Trilogy', *Mosaic* 51.3 (September 2018), p. 189.
35 Lorrie Moore, 'Bioperversity: Margaret Atwood's Genetically Engineered Nightmare', *The New Yorker*, 19 May 2003. https://www.newyorker.com/magazine/2003/05/19/bioperversity n.p.
36 Howells (2006), p. 170.
37 Barzilai (2008), p. 108.
38 Moore (2003), n.p.
39 Bouson (2004), p. 140.
40 Bouson (2004), pp. 141, 151.
41 Canavan (2012), p. 152.
42 Rozelle (2010), p. 63.
43 Rozelle (2010), p. 64.
44 Earl G. Ingersoll, 'Survival in Margaret Atwood's Novel, *Oryx and Crake*', *Extrapolation* 45.2 (2004), p 167.
45 Rozelle (2010), p. 70.
46 Schoene (2013), p. 101.
47 Rozelle (2010), p. 71.
48 Snyder (2011), p. 471.
49 Snyder (2011), p. 473.
50 Anna Bedford, 'Survival in the Post-Apocalypse: Ecofeminism in *MaddAddam*', in Karma Waltonen (ed.), *Margaret Atwood's Apocalypses* (Newcastle upon Tyne: Cambridge Scholars, 2015), pp. 76, 80.
51 Danette DiMarco, 'Paradice Lost, Paradise Regained: *homo faber* and the Makings of a New Beginning in *Oryx and Crake*', *Papers on Language and Literature* 41.2 (2005), pp. 170, 188, 171.
52 Dunning (2005), pp. 87, 89, 94.
53 Dunning (2005), p. 95.
54 Dunning (2005), p. 98.
55 Schoene (2013), p. 98.
56 Hannes Bergthaller, 'Housebreaking the Human Animal: Humanism and the Problem of Sustainability in Margaret Atwood's *Oryx and Crake* and *The Year of the Flood*', *English Studies* 91.7 (November 2010), p. 738.

57 J. Brooks Bouson, '"We're Using Up the Earth. It's Almost Gone": A Return to the Post-Apocalyptic Future in Margaret Atwood's *The Year of the Flood*', *Journal of Commonwealth Literature* 46.1 (2011), p. 10.
58 Debrah Raschke, 'Margaret Atwood's *MaddAddam* Trilogy: Postmodernism, Apocalypse, and Rapture', *Studies in Canadian Literature* 39.2 (2014), p. 22.
59 Ursula K. Le Guin, '*The Year of the Flood* by Margaret Atwood', *The Guardian*, 29 August 2009. https://www.theguardian.com/books/2009/aug/29/margaret-atwood-year-of-flood. n.p.
60 Gillian Beer, 'Review: *The Year of the Flood* by Margaret Atwood', *The Globe and Mail*, 11 September 2009. https://www.theglobeandmail.com/arts/books-and-media/review-the-year-of-the-flood-by-margaret-atwood/article4292431/. n.p.
61 Richard Alan Northover, 'Ecological Apocalypse in Margaret Atwood's *MaddAddam* Trilogy', *Studia Neophilologica* 88 (2016), p. 83.
62 Dana Phillips, 'Collapse, Resilience, Stability and Sustainability in Margaret Atwood's *MaddAddam* Trilogy', in Adeline Johns-Putra, John Parham and Louise Squires (eds), *Literature and Sustainability: Concept, Text and Culture* (Manchester: Manchester University Press, 2017), p. 147.
63 Bergthaller (2010), p. 738.
64 Jeanette Winterson, 'Strange New World', *The New York Times*, 17 September 2009. https://www.nytimes.com/2009/09/20/books/review/Winterson-t.html. n.p.
65 Bonnie Greer, 'The Year of the Flood', *New Statesman*, 17 September 2009. https://www.newstatesman.com/books/2009/09/flood-atwood-novel-crake-world. n.p.
66 Gina Wisker, *Margaret Atwood: An Introduction to Critical Views of Her Fiction* (Houndmills: Palgrave Macmillan, 2012), p. 176.
67 Beer (2009), n.p.
68 Susan Watkins, 'Future Shock: Rewriting the Apocalypse in Contemporary Women's Fiction', *Literature Interpretation Theory* 23.2 (2012), p. 122.
69 Fredric Jameson, 'Then You Are Them', *London Review of Books* 31.17 (10 September 2009), pp. 7–8.
70 Andrew Hoogheem, 'Secular Apocalypses: Darwinian Criticism and Atwoodian Floods', *Mosaic: An Interdisciplinary Critical Journal* 45.2 (June 2012), p. 59.
71 Bouson (2011), p. 11.
72 Canavan (2012), p. 155.
73 Watkins (2012), p. 119.
74 Watkins (2012), pp. 132, 135.
75 Hengen (2006), p. 83.
76 Howells (2006), p. 170.
77 Winterson (2009), n.p.
78 Winterson (2009), n.p.
79 Bouson (2011), p. 12.

80 Bouson (2011), p. 13.
81 Bouson (2011), p. 14.
82 Bouson (2011), p. 15.
83 Bergthaller (2010), p. 729.
84 Bergthaller (2010), p. 732.
85 Bergthaller (2010), p. 737.
86 Hoogheem (2012), p. 56.
87 Hoogheem (2012), p. 57.
88 Bergthaller (2010), p. 742.
89 Bouson (2011), p. 23.
90 Bergthaller (2010), p. 741.
91 Frederic Jameson, 'Future City', *New Left Review*, 21 May–June 2003. https://newleftreview.org/issues/II21. n.p.
92 Canavan (2012), p. 139.
93 Raschke (2014), p. 24.
94 Bedford (2015), p. 91.
95 Northover (2016), p. 91.
96 Raschke (2014), p. 23.
97 Northover (2016), p. 82.
98 Northover (2016), p. 85.
99 Raschke (2014), p. 23.
100 Howells (2006), p. 171.
101 Raschke (2014), p. 24.
102 Northover (2016), p. 91.
103 Raschke (2014), p. 23.
104 Raschke (2014), pp. 31–2.
105 Raschke (2014), pp. 27, 29.
106 Hengen (2006), p. 74.
107 Amelia Defalco, 'MaddAddam, Biocapitalism, and Affective Things', *Contemporary Women's Writing* 11.3 (November 2017), pp. 434–5.
108 Chen (2018), p. 93.
109 Dunja M. Mohr, 'Anthropocene Fiction: Narrating the "Zero Hour" in Margaret Atwood's *MaddAddam* Trilogy', in Ursula Mathis-Moser and Marie J. Carrière (eds), *Writing Beyond the End Times? The Literatures of Canada and Quebec* (Innsbruck: Innsbruck University Press, 2017), p. 26.
110 Chen (2018), p. 180.
111 Chen (2018), p. 188.
112 Mohr (2017), pp. 27–8.
113 Raschke (2014), p. 36.
114 Bedford (2015), p. 83.

115 Northover (2016), p. 93.
116 Bedford 92015), p. 88.
117 Northover (2016), p. 94.
118 Phillips (2017), p. 157.
119 Shelley Boyd, 'Ustopian Breakfasts: Margaret Atwood's *MaddAddam*', *Utopian Studies* 26.1 (2005), p. 162.
120 Mohr (2017), p. 37.

Conclusion

1 Coral Ann Howells, 'True Trash: Genre Fiction Revisited in Margaret Atwood's *Stone Mattress*, *The Heart Goes Last*, and *Hag-Seed*', *Contemporary Women's Writing* 11.3 (November 2017), pp. 298–9.
2 Helen Snaith, 'Dystopia, Gerontology and the Writing of Margaret Atwood', *Feminist Review* 116.1 (2017), p. 119.
3 Snaith (2017), p. 125.
4 Teresa Gibert, 'The Aesthetics of Ageing in Margaret Atwood's Fiction', in Brian J. Worsfold (ed.), *Women Ageing Through Literature and Experience* (Lleida: University of Lleida Press, 2005), pp. 31–42; Pilar Sánchez Calle, 'Writing, Aging and Death in Margaret Atwood's *The Door*', *ES Review* 39 (2018), pp. 135–56; Susan Watkins, '"Summoning Your Youth at Will": Memory, Time, and Aging in the Work of Penelope Lively, Margaret Atwood, and Doris Lessing', *Frontiers: A Journal of Women Studies* 34.2 (2013), pp. 222–44.
5 Amelia Defalco, 'Moral Obligation, Disordered Care: The Ethics of Caregiving in Margaret Atwood's *Moral Disorder*', *Contemporary Literature* 52.2 (Summer 2011), pp. 236–63.
6 Fiona Tolan, 'Ageing and Subjectivity in Margaret Atwood's Fiction', *Contemporary Women's Writing* 11.3 (November 2017), p. 337.
7 Fiona Tolan, '"I Could Say That Too": An Interview with Margaret Atwood', *Contemporary Women's Writing* 11.3 (November 2017), p. 455.
8 Lionel Shriver, '*The Heart Goes Last* by Margaret Atwood', *The Financial Times*, 25 September 2015. https://www.ft.com/content/bd29a288-5e2b-11e5-9846-de406ccb37f2. n.p.
9 Howells (2017), p. 305.
10 Tim Engles, *White Male Nostalgia in Contemporary North American Literature* (Cham: Springer, 2018), pp. 225, 224.
11 Engles (2018), p. 229.
12 Howells (2017), p. 306.

13 Fiona Tolan, 'Margaret Atwood's Rewriting of Classic Texts', in Coral Ann Howells (ed.), *The Cambridge Companion to Margaret Atwood*. 2nd edn. (Cambridge: Cambridge University Press, 2021).
14 Sofía Muñoz-Valdivieso, 'Shakespeare Our Contemporary in 2016: Margaret Atwood's Rewriting of *The Tempest* in *Hag-Seed*', *Sederi – Yearbook of the Spanish and Portuguese Society for English Renaissance Studies* 27 (2017), p. 125.
15 Philip Smith, 'Margaret Atwood's Tempests: Critiques of Shakespearian Essentialism in *Bodily Harm* and *Hag-Seed*', *Margaret Atwood Studies* 11 (2017), pp. 30, 33.
16 Susan Watkins, 'Review: *The Testaments* – Margaret Atwood's Sequel to *The Handmaid's Tale*', *The Conversation*, 12 September 2019. https://theconversation.com/review-the-testaments-margaret-atwoods-sequel-to-the-handmaids-tale-123465. n.p.
17 Sophie Gilbert, 'Margaret Atwood Bears Witness', *The Atlantic*, December 2019. https://www.theatlantic.com/magazine/archive/2019/12/margaret-atwood-bears-witness/600796/. n.p.
18 Graham Huggan, *The Postcolonial Exotic: Marketing the Margins* (London: Routledge, 2001), p. 211.
19 Susanne Becker, 'Celebrity, or a Disneyland of the Soul: Margaret Atwood and the Media', in Reingard M. Nischik (ed.) *Margaret Atwood: Works and Impact* (Rochester: Camden House, 2000), pp. 28–40.
20 Huggan (2001), p. 210.
21 Laura Moss, 'Margaret Atwood: Branding a Canadian Abroad', in John Moss and Tobi Kozakewich (eds), *Margaret Atwood: The Open Eye* (Ottawa: University of Ottawa Press, 2006), pp. 19–33.
22 Lorraine York, *Literary Celebrity in Canada* (Toronto: University of Toronto Press, 2007), p. 101.
23 Lorraine York, *Margaret Atwood and the Labour of Literary Celebrity* (Toronto: University of Toronto Press, 2013), pp. 24, 195.

Select bibliography

Works by Atwood

(Where applicable, details are given of editions used for quotations in this guide.)

Novels

The Edible Woman. 1969 (London: Virago, 1988).
Surfacing. 1972 (London: Virago, 1979).
Lady Oracle. 1976 (London: Virago, 1982).
Life Before Man. 1979 (London: Vintage, 1996).
Bodily Harm. 1981 (London: Vintage, 1996).
The Handmaid's Tale. 1985 (London: Vintage, 1996).
Cat's Eye. 1988 (London: Virago, 1990).
The Robber Bride. 1993 (London: Virago, 1994).
Alias Grace. 1996 (London: Virago, 1997).
The Blind Assassin. 2000 (London: Virago, 2001).
Oryx and Crake. 2003 (London: Virago, 2009).
The Penelopiad (Edinburgh: Canongate, 2005).
The Year of the Flood (London: Bloomsbury, 2009).
MaddAddam (London: Bloomsbury, 2013).
The Heart Goes Last (London: Bloomsbury, 2015).
Hag-Seed. 2016 (London: Vintage, 2017).
The Testaments (London: Bloomsbury, 2019).

Short stories

Dancing Girls and Other Stories. 1977 (London: Vintage, 1996).
Bluebeard's Egg and Other Stories. 1983 (London: Vintage, 1996).
Murder in the Dark. 1983 (London: Virago, 1994).
Wilderness Tips. 1991 (London: Bloomsbury, 1995).
Good Bones (London: Virago, 1992).
Moral Disorder (London: Bloomsbury, 2006).
The Tent (London: Bloomsbury, 2006).
Stone Mattress (London: Bloomsbury, 2014).

Poetry

Double Persephone (Toronto: Hawkshead Press, 1961).
The Circle Game. 1964 (Toronto: House of Anansi, 1967).
The Animals in That Country. 1968 (Oxford: Oxford University Press, 1969).
The Journals of Susanna Moodie (Oxford: Oxford University Press, 1970).
Procedures for Underground (Oxford: Oxford University Press, 1970).
Power Politics (Toronto: House of Anansi, 1971).
You Are Happy (Oxford: Oxford University Press, 1974).
Two-Headed Poems (Oxford: Oxford University Press, 1978).
True Stories (Oxford: Oxford University Press, 1981).
Interlunar (Oxford: Oxford University Press, 1984).
Morning in the Burned House (London: Virago, 1995).
Eating Fire: Selected Poetry 1965–1995 (London: Virago, 1998).
The Door (London: Virago, 2007).
Dearly (London: Chatto & Windus, 2020).

Non-fiction

Survival: A Thematic Guide to Canadian Literature. 1972 (Toronto: House of Anansi, 2012).
Second Words: Selected Critical Prose (Toronto: House of Anansi, 1982).
Strange Things: The Malevolent North in Canadian Literature (Oxford: Oxford University Press, 1995).
Negotiating with the Dead: A Writer on Writing (Cambridge: Cambridge University Press, 2002).
Moving Targets: Writing with Intent 1982–2004 (Toronto: House of Anansi, 2004).
Curious Pursuits: Occasional Writing (London: Virago, 2005).
Writing with Intent: Essays, Reviews, Personal Prose 1983–2005 (New York: Carroll & Graf, 2005).
Payback: Debt and the Shadow Side of Wealth (Toronto: House of Anansi, 2008).
In Other Worlds: SF and the Human Imagination (London: Virago, 2011).

Graphic novels

Angel Catbird, with Johnnie Christmas and Tamra Bonvillain (Milwaukie: Dark Horse Books, 2016)
Angel Catbird: To Castle Catula, with Johnnie Christmas and Tamra Bonvillain (Milwaukie: Dark Horse Books, 2017).
Angel Catbird: The Catbird Roars, with Johnnie Christmas and Tamra Bonvillain (Milwaukie: Dark Horse Books, 2017).

War Bears. Vols. 1–3, with Ken Steacy (Milwaukie: Dark Horse Books, 2018).
The Handmaid's Tale: The Graphic Novel, with Renée Nault (London: Jonathan Cape, 2019).

Children's fiction

Up in the Tree (Toronto: McClelland & Stewart, 1978).
Anna's Pet, with Joyce Barkhouse (Halifax: Lorimer, 1980).
For the Birds (Toronto: Douglas & McIntyre, 1990).
Princess Prunella and the Purple Peanut (New York: Workman Publishing, 1995).
Rude Ramsay and the Roaring Radishes (London: Bloomsbury, 2003).
Bashful Bob and Doleful Dorinda (London: Bloomsbury, 2004).
Wandering Wenda and Widow Wallop's Wunderground Washery (Toronto: McArthur, 2011).

Books about Atwood

Appleton, Sarah A. *Once upon A Time: Myth, Fairy Tales and Legends in Margaret Atwood's Writings* (Newcastle upon Tyne: Cambridge Scholars, 2008).
Beran, Carol. *Living Over the Abyss: Margaret Atwood's Life before Man* (Toronto: ECW, 1993).
Bouson, Brooks J. *Brutal Choreographies: Oppositional Strategies and Narrative Design in the Novels of Margaret Atwood* (Amherst: University of Massachusetts Press, 1993).
Bouson, Brooks J (ed.). *Margaret Atwood: The Robber Bride, The Blind Assassin, Oryx and Crake* (London: Continuum, 2010).
Carrington, Ildikó de Papp. *Margaret Atwood and Her Works* (Toronto: ECW Press, 1987).
Cooke, Nathalie. *Margaret Atwood: A Biography* (Toronto: ECW Press, 1998).
Cooke, Nathalie. *Margaret Atwood: A Critical Companion* (Westport: Greenwood, 2004).
Davey, Frank. *Margaret Atwood: A Feminist Poetics* (Vancouver: Talonbooks, 1984).
Davidson, Arnold E. and Cathy N. Davidson (eds) *The Art of Margaret Atwood: Essays in Criticism* (Toronto: House of Anansi, 1981).
Fee, Marjorie. *The Fat Lady Dances: Margaret Atwood's Lady Oracle* (Toronto: ECW, 1993).
Grace, Sherrill. *Violent Duality: A Study of Margaret Atwood* (Montreal: Véhicule Press, 1980).
Grace, Sherrill and Lorraine Weir (eds). *Margaret Atwood: Language, Text, and System* (Vancouver: University of British Columbia Press, 1983).

Hengen, Shannon. *Margaret Atwood's Power: Mirrors, Reflections and Images in Select Fiction and Poetry* (Toronto: Second Story Press, 1993).
Howells, Coral Ann. *Margaret Atwood*. 2nd edn (Houndmills: Palgrave Macmillan, 2005).
Howells, Coral Ann (ed.). *The Cambridge Companion to Margaret Atwood* (Cambridge: Cambridge University Press, 2006).
Howells, Coral Ann (ed.). *The Cambridge Companion to Margaret Atwood*. 2nd edn (Cambridge: Cambridge University Press, 2021).
Ingersoll, Earl G. *Margaret Atwood: Conversations* (Princeton: Ontario Review Press, 1990).
Ingersoll, Earl G. *Waltzing Again: New and Selected Conversations with Margaret Atwood* (Princeton: Ontario Review Press, 2006).
Macpherson, Heidi Slettedahl. *The Cambridge Introduction to Margaret Atwood* (Cambridge: Cambridge University Press, 2010).
McCombs, Judith (ed.). *Critical Essays on Margaret Atwood* (Boston: G. K. Hall, 1988).
McWilliams, Ellen. *Margaret Atwood and the Female Bildungsroman* (Farnham: Ashgate, 2009).
Mendez-Egles, Beatrice. *Margaret Atwood: Reflection and Reality* (Edinburg: Pan American University Press, 1987).
Moss, John and Tobi Kozakewich (eds). *Margaret Atwood: The Open Eye* (Ottawa: University of Ottawa Press, 2006).
Nicholson, Colin (ed.). *Margaret Atwood: Writing and Subjectivity: New Critical Essays* (Basingstoke: Macmillan, 1994).
Nischik, Reingard M (ed.). *Margaret Atwood: Works and Impact* (Toronto: House of Anansi, 2002).
Nischik, Reingard M. *Engendering Genre: The Works of Margaret Atwood* (Ottawa: University of Ottawa Press, 2009).
Rao, Eleonora. *Strategies for Identity: The Fiction of Margaret Atwood* (New York: Peter Lang, 1993).
Reynolds, Margaret. *Margaret Atwood: The Essential Guide to Contemporary Literature* (London: Vintage, 2002).
Reynolds, Margaret and Jonathan Noakes. *Margaret Atwood: The Handmaid's Tale, Bluebeard's Egg, The Blind Assassin* (London: Vintage, 2012).
Rigney, Barbara Hill. *Margaret Atwood* (Basingstoke: Macmillan, 1987).
Rosenberg, Jerome H. *Margaret Atwood* (Boston: Twayne, 1984).
Shead, Jackie. *Margaret Atwood: Crime Fiction Writer – The Reworking of a Popular Genre* (Farnham: Ashgate, 2015).
Sheckels, Theodore F. *The Political in Margaret Atwood's Fiction: The Writing on the Wall of the Tent* (Farnham: Ashgate, 2012).
Stein, Karen. *Margaret Atwood Revisited* (New York: Twayne, 1999).
Sullivan, Rosemary. *The Red Shoes: Margaret Atwood Starting Out* (Toronto: HarperCollins, 1998).

Tennant, Colette. *Reading the Gothic in Margaret Atwood's Novels* (New York: Edwin Mellen, 2003).

Tolan, Fiona. *Margaret Atwood: Feminism and Fiction* (Amsterdam: Rodopi, 2007).

VanSpanckeren, Kathryn and Jan Garden Castro (eds). *Margaret Atwood: Vision and Forms* (Carbondale: Southern Illinois University Press, 1988).

Waltonen, Karma (ed.). *Margaret Atwood's Apocalypses* (Newcastle upon Tyne: Cambridge Scholars, 2015).

Wells-Lassagne, Shannon and Fiona McMahon (eds). *Adapting Margaret Atwood: The Handmaid's Tale and Beyond* (Cham: Palgrave Macmillan, 2021).

Wilson, Sharon Rose. *Margaret Atwood's Fairy-Tale Sexual Politics* (Jackson: University of Mississippi Press, 1993).

Wilson, Sharon Rose (ed.). *Margaret Atwood's Textual Assassinations: Recent Poetry and Fiction* (Columbus: Ohio State University Press, 2003).

Wisker, Gina. *Atwood's The Handmaid's Tale: A Reader's Guide* (London: Continuum, 2010).

Wisker, Gina. *Margaret Atwood: An Introduction to Critical Views of Her Fiction* (Houndmills: Palgrave Macmillan, 2012).

Wynne-Davies, Marion. *Margaret Atwood* (Tavistockl: Northcote House, 2009).

York, Lorraine. *Margaret Atwood and the Labour of Literary Celebrity* (Toronto: University of Toronto Press, 2013).

Books with substantial discussion of Atwood

Banerjee, Suparna. *Science, Gender and History: The Fantastic in Mary Shelley and Margaret Atwood* (Newcastle upon Tyne: Cambridge Scholars, 2014).

Engles, Tim. *White Male Nostalgia in Contemporary North American Literature* (Cham: Springer, 2018).

Goldman, Marlene. *DisPossession: Haunting in Canadian Fiction* (Montreal & Kingston: McGill-Queen's University Press, 2012).

Howells, Coral Ann. *Contemporary Canadian Women's Fiction: Refiguring Identities* (Houndmills: Palgrave, 2003).

Huggan, Graham. *The Postcolonial Exotic: Marketing the Margins* (London: Routledge, 2001).

Perrakis, Phyllis Sternberg. *Adventures of the Spirit: The Older Woman in the Works of Doris Lessing, Margaret Atwood, and Other Contemporary Women Writers* (Columbus: Ohio State University Press, 2007).

Ridout, Alice. *Contemporary Women Writers Look Back: From Irony to Nostalgia* (London: Continuum, 2012).

Sceats, Sarah. *Food, Consumption and the Body in Contemporary Women's Fiction* (Cambridge: Cambridge University Press, 2000).

Sheckels, Theodore F. *The Island Motif in the Fiction of L.M. Montgomery, Margaret Laurence, Margaret Atwood, and other Canadian Women Novelists* (New York: Peter Lang, 2003).
Macpherson, Heidi Slettedahl. *Courting Failure: Women and the Law in Twentieth-Century Literature* (Akron: University of Akron Press, 2007).
Watkins, Susan. *Contemporary Women's Post-Apocalyptic Fiction* (London: Palgrave Macmillan, 2020).
York, Lorraine. *Literary Celebrity in Canada* (Toronto: University of Toronto Press, 2007).

Book chapters and critical essays

General, or covering more than one title

Becker, Susanne. 'Celebrity, or a Disneyland of the Soul: Margaret Atwood and the Media', in Reingard M. Nischik (ed.), *Margaret Atwood: Works and Impact* (Rochester: Camden House, 2000), pp. 28–40.
Gibert, Teresa. 'The Aesthetics of Ageing in Margaret Atwood's Fiction', in Brian J. Worsfold (ed.), *Women Ageing Through Literature and Experience* (Lleida: University of Lleida Press, 2005), pp. 31–42.
Hengen, Shannon. 'Margaret Atwood and Environmentalism', in Coral Ann Howells (ed.), *The Cambridge Companion to Margaret Atwood* (Cambridge: Cambridge University Press, 2006), pp. 72–85.
Howells, Coral Ann. 'Transgressing Genre: A Generic Approach to Margaret Atwood's Novels', in Reingard M. Nischik (ed.), *Margaret Atwood: Works and Impact* (Rochester: Camden House, 2000), pp. 139–53.
Howells, Coral Ann. 'Margaret Atwood's Dystopian Visions: *The Handmaid's Tale* and *Oryx and Crake*', in Coral Ann Howells (ed.), *The Cambridge Companion to Margaret Atwood* (Cambridge: Cambridge University Press, 2006), pp. 161-75.
Howells, Coral Ann. 'True Trash: Genre Fiction Revisited in Margaret Atwood's *Stone Mattress*, *The Heart Goes Last*, and *Hag-Seed*', *Contemporary Women's Writing* 11.3 (November 2017), pp. 297–315.
Irvine, Lorna. 'Murder and Mayhem: Margaret Atwood Deconstructs', *Contemporary Literature* 29.2 (Summer 1988), pp. 265–76.
Moss, Laura. 'Margaret Atwood: Branding a Canadian Abroad', in John Moss and Tobi Kozakewich (eds), *Margaret Atwood: The Open Eye* (Ottawa: University of Ottawa Press, 2006), pp. 19–33.
Palumbo, Alice M. 'On the Border: Margaret Atwood's Novels', in Reingard M. Nischik (ed.), *Margaret Atwood: Works and Impact* (Rochester: Camden House, 2000), pp. 81–2.
Parker, Emma. 'You Are What You Eat: The Politics of Eating in the Novels of Margaret Atwood', *Twentieth Century Literature* 41.3 (Autumn 1995), pp. 349–68.

Rao, Eleonora. 'Home and Nation in Margaret Atwood's Later Fiction', in Coral Ann Howells (ed.), *The Cambridge Companion to Margaret Atwood* (Cambridge: Cambridge University Press, 2006), pp. 100–13.

Sanchez-Grant, Sofia. 'The Female Body in Margaret Atwood's *The Edible Woman* and *Lady Oracle*', *Journal of International Women's Studies* 9.2 (March 2008), pp. 77–92.

Smith, Philip. 'Margaret Atwood's Tempests: Critiques of Shakespearian Essentialism in *Bodily Harm* and *Hag-Seed*', *Margaret Atwood Studies* 11 (2017), pp. 29–40.

Snaith, Helen. 'Dystopia, Gerontology and the Writing of Margaret Atwood', *Feminist Review* 116.1 (2017), pp. 118–32.

Stein, Karen. 'Talking Back to Bluebeard: Atwood's Fictional Storytellers', in Sharon Rose Wilson (ed.), *Margaret Atwood's Textual Assassinations: Recent Poetry and Fiction* (Columbus: Ohio State University Press, 2003), pp. 154–71.

Tolan, Fiona. 'Ageing and Subjectivity in Margaret Atwood's Fiction', *Contemporary Women's Writing* 11.3 (November 2017), pp. 336–53.

Tolan, Fiona. 'Atwood's Revision of Classic Texts', in Coral Ann Howells (ed.), *The Cambridge Companion to Margaret Atwood*. 2nd edn (Cambridge: Cambridge University Press, 2021).

Wilson, Sharon R. 'Margaret Atwood's Visual Art', *Essays on Canadian Writing* 50 (Fall 1993), pp. 129–73.

Wilson, Sharon R. 'Mythological Intertexts in Margaret Atwood's Work', in Reingard M. Nischik (ed.), *Margaret Atwood: Works and Impact* (Rochester: Camden House, 2000), pp. 215–28.

Wilson, Sharon R. 'Blindness and Survival in Margaret Atwood's Major Novels', in Coral Ann Howells (ed.), *The Cambridge Companion to Margaret Atwood* (Cambridge: Cambridge University Press, 2006), pp. 176–90.

York, Lorraine 'Biography/Autobiography', in Coral Ann Howells (ed.), *The Cambridge Companion to Margaret Atwood* (Cambridge: Cambridge University Press, 2006), pp. 28–42.

About *The Edible Woman*

Bajwa, Poonam. 'Margaret Atwood's *The Edible Woman* and the Commercialization of Literary Scholarship', *Studies in Canadian Literature* 35.2 (2010), pp. 145–64.

Bouson, Brooks J. 'The Anxiety of Being Influenced: Reading and Responding to Character in Margaret Atwood's *The Edible Woman*', *Style* 24.2 (July 1990), pp. 228–41.

Greene, Gayle. 'Margaret Atwood's *The Edible Woman*: "Rebelling Against the System"', in Beatrice Mendez-Egle (ed.), *Margaret Atwood: Reflection and Reality* (Edinburg: Pan American University Press, 1987), pp. 95–115.

MacLulich, T. D. 'Atwood's Adult Fairy Tale: Lévi-Strauss, Bettelheim, and *The Edible Woman*', in Judith McCombs (ed.) *Critical Essays on Margaret Atwood* (Boston: G.K. Hall, 1988), pp. 179–97.

McLay, Catherine. 'The Dark Voyage: *The Edible Woman* as Romance', in Arnold E. Davidson and Cathy N. Davidson (eds), *The Art of Margaret Atwood: Essays in Criticism* (Toronto: Anansi, 1981), pp. 123–38.

Patterson, Jayne. 'The Taming of Externals: A Linguistic Study of Character Transformation in Margaret Atwood's *The Edible Woman*', *Studies in Canadian Literature* 7.2 (Summer 1982), pp. 141–50.

About *Surfacing*

Christ, Carol. 'Margaret Atwood: The Surfacing of Women's Spiritual Quest and Vision', *Signs: Journal of Women in Culture and Society* 2.2 (Winter 1976), pp. 316–30.

Davidson, Arnold E. and Cathy N. Davidson. 'The Anatomy of Margaret Atwood's *Surfacing*', *ARIEL: A Review of International English Literature* 10.3 (July 1979), pp. 38–54.

Fiamengo, Janice. '"It Looked at Me with Its Mashed Eye": Animal and Human Suffering in *Surfacing*', in John Moss and Tobi Kozakewich (eds), *Margaret Atwood: The Open Eye* (Ottawa: University of Ottawa Press, 2006), pp. 171–84.

Granofsky, Ronald. 'Fairy-Tale Morphology in Margaret Atwood's *Surfacing*', *Mosaic* 23.4 (1990), pp. 51–65.

Kapuscinski, Kiley. 'Negotiating the Nation: The Reproduction and Reconstruction of the National Imaginary in Margaret Atwood's *Surfacing*', *English Studies in Canada* 33.3 (September 2007), pp. 95–123.

Murray, Jennifer. 'For the Love of a Fish: A Lacanian Reading of Margaret Atwood's *Surfacing*', *LIT: Literature, Interpretation, Theory* 26.1 (2015), pp. 1–21.

Plaskow, Judith. 'On Carol Christ on Margaret Atwood: Some Theological Reflections', *Signs: Journal of Women in Culture and Society* 2.2 (Winter 1976), pp. 331–9.

Sugars, Cynthia. '"Saying Boo to Colonialism": *Surfacing*, Tom Thomson, and the National Ghost', in John Moss and Tobi Kozakewich (eds), *Margaret Atwood: The Open Eye* (Ottawa: University of Ottawa Press, 2006), pp. 137–58.

Thomas, Sue. 'Mythic Reconception and the Mother/Daughter Relationship in Margaret Atwood's *Surfacing*', *Ariel* 19.2 (April 1988), pp. 73–85.

Tolan, Fiona. 'Guilt and Responsibility in the Community and the Self: An Examination of Mutual Responsibility in Margaret Atwood's *Surfacing*', *British Journal of Canadian Studies* 17.1 (2004), pp. 105–16.

Trigg, Tina. 'A Silhouette of Madness: Reading Atwood's *Surfacing*', in John Moss and Tobi Kozakewich (eds), *Margaret Atwood: The Open Eye* (Ottawa: University of Ottawa Press, 2006), pp.159–70.

About *Lady Oracle*

Barzilai, Shuli. '"Say That I Had a Lovely Face": The Grimms' "Rapunzel," Tennyson's "Lady of Shalott," and Atwood's *Lady Oracle*', *Tulsa Studies in Women's Literature* 19.2 (Autumn 2000), pp. 231–54.

Barzilai, Shuli. 'The Bluebeard Syndrome in Atwood's *Lady Oracle*: Fear and Femininity', *Marvels & Tales* 19.2 (2005), pp. 249–73.

Kozakewich, Tobi. 'Having It Both Ways? Romance, Realism, and Irony in *Lady Oracle*'s Adulterous Affairs', in John Moss and Tobi Kozakewich (eds), *Margaret Atwood: The Open Eye* (Ottawa: University of Ottawa Press, 2006), pp. 185–94.

Patton, Marilyn. '*Lady Oracle*: The Politics of the Body', *ARIEL: A Review of International English Literature* 22.4 (October 1991), pp. 29–48.

Szalay, Edina. 'The Gothic as Maternal Legacy in Margaret Atwood's *Lady Oracle*', *Neohelicon* 28.1 (2001), pp. 216–33.

Thieme, John. 'A Female Houdini: Popular Culture in Margaret Atwood's *Lady Oracle*', *Kunapipi* 14.1 (1992), pp. 71–80.

About *Life Before Man*

Afrougheh, Shahram and Kalantari Mandana. 'A Study of Hélène Cixous' Concepts of Neuter and Other in Margaret Atwood's *Life Before Man*', *International Journal of Applied Linguistics and English Literature* 3.3 (2014), pp. 104–11.

Greene, Gayle. '*Life Before Man*: Can Anything Be Saved?', in Kathryn VanSpanckeren and Jan Garden Castro (eds), *Margaret Atwood: Vision and Forms* (Carbondale: Southern Illinois University Press, 1988), pp. 65–84.

Stein, Karen. 'It's About Time: Temporal Dimensions in Margaret Atwood's *Life Before Man*', in Sarah A. Appleton (ed.), *Once upon a Time: Myth, Fairy Tales and Legends in Margaret Atwood's Writings* (Newcastle upon Tyne: Cambridge Scholars, 2008), pp. 95–113.

About *Bodily Harm*

Brydon, Diana. 'Atwood's Postcolonial Imagination: Rereading *Bodily Harm*', in Lorraine M. York (ed.), *Various Atwoods: Essays on the Later Poems, Short Fiction, and Novels* (Toronto: Anansi, 1995), pp. 89–116.

Drichel, Simone. 'Regarding the Other: Postcolonial Violations and Ethical Resistance in Margaret Atwood's *Bodily Harm*', *MFS: Modern Fiction Studies* 54.1 (Spring 2008), pp. 31–2.

Hansen, Elaine Tuttle. 'Fiction and (Post) Feminism in Atwood's *Bodily Harm*', *Novel* 19.1 (1985), pp. 5–21.

Irvine, Lorna. 'The Here and Now of *Bodily Harm*', in Kathryn VanSpanckeren and Jan Garden Castro (eds), *Margaret Atwood: Vision and Forms* (Carbondale: Southern Illinois University Press, 1988), pp. 85–100.

Lucking, David. 'In Pursuit of the Faceless Stranger: Depths and Surfaces in Margaret Atwood's *Bodily Harm*', *Studies in Canadian Literature* 15.1 (1990), pp. 76–93.

Marantz, Kate. 'Making It (In)Visible: The Politics of Absence in Margaret Atwood's *Bodily Harm*', *Studies in Canadian Literature/Études en Literature Canadienne* 41.2 (2016), p. 138.

Mycak, Sonia. 'Divided and Dismembered: The Decentred Subject in Margaret Atwood's *Bodily Harm*', *Canadian Review of Comparative Literature* 20.3 (1993), pp. 469–78.

Patton, Marilyn. 'Tourists and Terrorists: The Creation of *Bodily Harm*', *Papers on Language & Literature* 28.2 (Spring 1992), p. 151.

Rubenstein, Roberta. 'Pandora's Box and Female Survival: Margaret Atwood's *Bodily Harm*', in Judith McCombs (ed.), *Critical Essays on Margaret Atwood* (Boston: G. K. Hall, 1988), pp. 259–75.

About *The Handmaid's Tale*

Davidson, Arnold E. 'Future Tense: Making History in *The Handmaid's Tale*', in Kathryn VanSpanckeren and Jan Garden Castro (eds), *Margaret Atwood: Visions and Forms* (Carbondale: Southern Illinois University Press, 1988), pp. 113–21.

Dvorak, Marta. 'What is Real/Reel? Margaret Atwood's "Rearrangement of Shapes on a Flat Surface," Or Narrative as Collage', *Études Anglaises* 51.4 (October 1988), pp. 448–60.

Hammer, Stephanie Barbé. 'The World as It will Be? Satire and Technology of Power in *The Handmaid's Tale*', *Modern Language Studies* 20.2 (1990), pp. 39–49.

Hooker, Deborah. '(Fl)orality, Gender, and the Environmental Ethos of Atwood's *The Handmaid's Tale*', *Twentieth Century Literature* 52.3 (Fall 2006), pp. 275–305.

Ingersoll, Earl. 'Margaret Atwood's *The Handmaid's Tale*: Echoes of Orwell', *Journal of the Fantastic in the Arts* 5.4 (1993), pp. 64–72.

Klarer, Mario. 'Orality and Literacy as Gender-Supporting Structures in Margaret Atwood's *The Handmaid's Tale*', *Mosaic* 28.4 (December 1995), pp. 129–42.

Kröller, Eva-Marie. 'The Hulu and MGM Television Adaptation of *The Handmaid's Tale*', in Coral Ann Howells (ed.), *The Cambridge Companion to Margaret Atwood*. 2nd edn (Cambridge: Cambridge University Press, 2021), pp. 189–205.

Laflen, Angela. '"From a Distance it Looks Like Peace": Reading Beneath the Fascist Style of Gilead in Margaret Atwood's *The Handmaid's Tale*', *Studies in Canadian Literature / Études en Literature Canadienne* 32.1 (2007), pp. 82–105.

Miner, Madonne. '"Trust Me": Reading the Romance Plot in Margaret Atwood's *The Handmaid's Tale*', *Twentieth Century Literature* 37.2 (Summer 1991), pp. 148–68.

Neuman, Shirley. '"Just a Backlash": Margaret Atwood, Feminism and *The Handmaid's Tale*', *University of Toronto Quarterly* 75.3 (Summer 2006), pp. 857–68.

Staels, Hilde. 'Margaret Atwood's *The Handmaid's Tale*: Resistance Through Narrating', *English Studies* 76.5 (1995), pp. 455–67.

Stapleton, Patricia A. 'Suicide as Apocalypse in *The Handmaid's Tale*', in Karma Waltonen (ed.), *Margaret Atwood's Apocalypses* (Newcastle upon Tyne: Cambridge Scholars, 2015), pp. 27–39.

Tolan, Fiona. 'Feminist Utopias and Questions of Liberty: Margaret Atwood's *The Handmaid's Tale* as Critique of Second Wave Feminism', *Women: A Cultural Review* 16.1 (Spring 2005), pp. 18–32.

Wagner-Lawlor, Jennifer A. 'From Irony to Affiliation in Margaret Atwood's *The Handmaid's Tale*', *Critique: Studies in Contemporary Fiction* 45.1 (2003), pp. 83–96.

Weiss, Allan. 'Offred's Complicity and the Dystopian Tradition in Margaret Atwood's *The Handmaid's Tale*', *Studies in Canadian Literature / Études en Literature Canadienne* 34.1 (2009), pp. 120–41.

Yamamoto, Tae. 'How Can a Feminist Read *The Handmaid's Tale*? A Study of Offred's Narrative', in John Moss and Tobi Kozakewich (eds), *Margaret Atwood: The Open Eye* (Ottawa: University of Ottawa Press, 2006), pp. 195–206.

About *Cat's Eye*

Banerjee, Chinmoy. 'Atwood's Time: Hiding Art in *Cat's Eye*', *MFS: Modern Fiction Studies* 36.4 (Winter 1990), pp. 513–22.

De Jong, Nicole. 'Mirror Images in Margaret Atwood's *Cat's Eye*', *NORA: Nordic Journal of Feminist and Gender Research* 6.2 (September 1998), pp. 97–107.

Derry, Ken. 'Blood on the Wall: Christianity, Colonialism, and the Mimetic Conflict in Margaret Atwood's *Cat's Eye*', *Religion & Literature* 48.3 (Autumn 2016), pp. 91–112.

Dvorak, Marta. 'Margaret Atwood's *Cat's Eye*: or the Trembling Canvas', *Études Anglaises* 54.3 (2001), pp. 299–309.

Hite, Molly. 'Optics and Autobiography in Margaret Atwood's *Cat's Eye*', *Twentieth Century Literature* 41.2 (Summer 1995), pp. 135–59.

Ingersoll, Earl G. 'Margaret Atwood's *Cat's Eye*: Re-Viewing Women in a Postmodern World', *ARIEL: A Review of International English Literature* 22.4 (October 1991), pp. 17–27.

Massoura, Kiriaki. '"I Look at It and See My Life Entire": Language, Third-Eye Vision and Painting in Margaret Atwood's *Cat's Eye*', *British Journal of Canadian Studies* 17.2 (September 2004), pp. 210–22.

Potvin, Liza. 'Voodooism and Female Quest Patters in Margaret Atwood's *Cat's Eye*', *Journal of Popular Culture* 36.3 (January 2003), pp. 636–50.

Ross, Rob. 'A Paler Shade of Green: Suburban Nature in Margaret Atwood's *Cat's Eye*', *Studies in Canadian Literature* 39.1 (2014), pp. 98–120.

About *The Robber Bride*

Bouson, J. Brooks. 'Slipping Sideways into the Dreams of Women: The Female Dream Work of Power Feminism in Margaret Atwood's *The Robber Bride*', *Lit: Literature Interpretation Theory* 6.3–4 (1995), pp. 149–66.

Fand, Roxanne J. 'Margaret Atwood's *The Robber Bride*: The Dialogic Moral of a Nietzschean Fairy Tale', *Critique: Studies in Contemporary Fiction* 45.1 (2003), pp. 65–81.

Perrakis, Phyllis Sternberg. 'Atwood's *The Robber Bride*: The Vampire as Intersubjective Catalyst', *Mosaic* 30.3 (1997), pp. 151–68.

Potts, Donna L. '"The Old Maps are Dissolving": Intertextuality and Identity in Atwood's *The Robber Bride*', *Tulsa Studies in Women's Literature* 18.2 (1999), pp. 281–92.

Staels, Hilde. 'Parodic Border Crossings in *The Robber Bride*', in J. Brooks Bouson (ed.), *Margaret Atwood: The Robber Bride, The Blind Assassin, Oryx and Crake* (London: Continuum, 2010), pp. 36–49.

Tolan, Fiona. 'Sucking the Blood Out of Second Wave Feminism: Postfeminist Vampirism in Margaret Atwood's *The Robber Bride*', *Gothic Studies* 9.2 (November 2007), pp. 45–57.

Vickroy, Laurie. 'You're History: Living with Trauma in *The Robber Bride*', in J. Brooks Bouson (ed.), *Margaret Atwood: The Robber Bride, The Blind Assassin, Oryx and Crake* (London: Continuum, 2010), pp. 50–65.

Wyatt, Jean. 'I Want to be You: Envy, the Lacanian Double, and Feminist Community in Margaret Atwood's *The Robber Bride*', *Tulsa Studies in Women's Literature* 17.1 (Spring 1998), pp. 37–64.

About *Alias Grace*

Defalco, Amelia. 'Haunting Physicality: Corpses, Cannibalism, and Carnality in Margaret Atwood's *Alias Grace*', *University of Toronto Quarterly* 75.2 (Spring 2006), pp. 771–83.

Hutchison, Lorna. 'The Book Reads Well: Atwood's *Alias Grace* and the Middle Voice', *Pacific Coast Philology* 38 (2003), pp. 40–59.

Lopez, Maria J. '"You are One of Us": Communities of Marginality, Vulnerability, and Secrecy in Margaret Atwood's *Alias Grace*', *ESC: English Studies in Canada* 38.2 (June 2012), pp. 157–77.

Mannon, Bethany Ober. 'Fictive Memoir and Girlhood Resistance in Margaret Atwood's *Alias Grace*', *Critique: Studies in Contemporary Fiction* 55.5 (2014), pp. 551–66.

Michael, Magali Cornier. 'Rethinking History as Patchwork: The Case of Atwood's *Alias Grace*', *Modern Fiction Studies* 47.2 (Summer 2001), pp. 421–47.

Murray, Jennifer. 'Historical Figures and Paradoxical Patterns: The Quilting Metaphor in Margaret Atwood's *Alias Grace*', *Studies in Canadian Literature* 26.1 (Spring 2001), pp. 64–83.

O'Neill, John. 'Dying in a State of Grace: Memory, Duality and Uncertainty in Margaret Atwood's *Alias Grace*', *Textual Practice* 27.4 (2013), pp. 651–70.

Staels, Hilde. 'Intertexts of Margaret Atwood's *Alias Grace*', *Modern Fiction Studies* 46.2 (Summer 2000), pp. 427–50.

Stanley, Sandra Kumamoto. 'The Eroticism of Class and the Enigma of Margaret Atwood's *Alias Grace*', *Tulsa Studies in Women's Literature* 22.2 (Autumn 2003), pp. 371–86.

Wilson, Sharon Rose. 'Quilting as Narrative Art: Metafictional Construction in *Alias Grace*', in Sharon Rose Wilson (ed.), *Margaret Atwood's Textual Assassinations: Recent Poetry and Fiction* (Columbus: Ohio State University Press, 2003), pp. 121–34.

About *The Blind Assassin*

Dvorak, Marta. 'The Right Hand Writing and the Left Hand Erasing in Margaret Atwood's *The Blind Assassin*', *Commonwealth: Essays and Studies* 25.1 (Autumn 2002), pp. 59–68.

Ingersoll, Earl G. 'Waiting for the End: Closure in Margaret Atwood's *The Blind Assassin*', *Studies in the Novel* 35.4 (Winter 2003), pp. 543–58.

Michael, Magali Cornier. 'Narrative Multiplicity and the Multi-layered Self in *The Blind Assassin*', in J. Brooks Bouson (ed.), *Margaret Atwood: The Robber Bride, The Blind Assassin, Oryx and Crake* (London: Continuum, 2010), pp. 88–102.

Parkin-Gounelas, Ruth. 'Margaret Atwood's *The Blind Assassin*: The Psychoanalysis of Duplicity', *MFS: Modern Fiction Studies* 50.3 (Fall 2004), pp. 681–700.

Ridout, Alice. '"Without Memory, There Can Be No Revenge": Iris Chase Griffen's Textual Revenge in Margaret Atwood's *The Blind Assassin*', *Margaret Atwood Studies* 2.2 (December 2008), pp. 14–25.

Robinson, Alan. '"Alias Laura": Representations of the Past in Margaret Atwood's *The Blind Assassin*', *The Modern Language Review* 101.2 (April 2006), pp. 347–59.

Stein, Karen. 'A Left-Handed Story: *The Blind Assassin*', in Sharon Rose Wilson (ed.), *Margaret Atwood's Textual Assassinations: Recent Poetry and Fiction* (Columbus: Ohio State University Press, 2003), pp. 135–53.

Tolan, Fiona. '"Was I My Sister's Keeper?": *The Blind Assassin* and Problematic Feminisms', in J. Brooks Bouson (ed.), *Margaret Atwood: The Robber Bride, The Blind Assassin, Oryx and Crake* (London: Continuum, 2010), pp. 73–87.

About the *MaddAddam* trilogy

Barzilai, Shuli. '"Tell My Story": Remembrance and Revenge in Margaret Atwood's *Oryx and Crake* and Shakespeare's *Hamlet*', *Critique: Studies in Contemporary Fiction* 50.1 (Fall 2008), pp. 87–110.

Bedford, Anna. 'Survival in the Post-Apocalypse: Ecofeminism in *MaddAddam*', in Karma Waltonen (ed.), *Margaret Atwood's Apocalypses* (Newcastle upon Tyne: Cambridge Scholars, 2015), pp. 71–92.

Bergthaller, Hannes. 'Housebreaking the Human Animal: Humanism and the Problem of Sustainability in Margaret Atwood's *Oryx and Crake* and *The Year of the Flood*', *English Studies* 91.7 (November 2010), pp. 728–43.

Bouson, J. Brooks. '"It's Game Over Forever": Atwood's Satiric Vision of a Bioengineered Posthuman Future in *Oryx and Crake*', *Journal of Commonwealth Literature* 39.3 (September 2004), pp. 139–56.

Bouson, J. Brooks. '"We're Using Up the Earth. It's Almost Gone": A Return to the Post-Apocalyptic Future in Margaret Atwood's *The Year of the Flood*', *Journal of Commonwealth Literature* 46.1 (2011), pp. 9–26.

Boyd, Shelley. 'Ustopian Breakfasts: Margaret Atwood's *MaddAddam*', *Utopian Studies* 26.1 (2005), pp. 160–82.

Canavan, Gerry. 'Hope, But Not for Us: Ecological Science Fiction and the End of the World in Margaret Atwood's *Oryx and Crake* and *The Year of the Flood*', *LIT: Literature Interpretation Theory* 23.2 (2012), pp. 138–59.

Chen, Chien-Hung. 'Micro-biopolitics at the End of the Anthropocene: Margaret Atwood's *MaddAddam* Trilogy', *Mosaic* 51.3 (September 2018), pp. 179–98.

Defalco, Amelia. 'MaddAddam, Biocapitalism, and Affective Things', *Contemporary Women's Writing* 11.3 (November 2017), pp. 432–51.

DiMarco, Danette. 'Paradise Lost, Paradise Regained: *Homo faber* and the Makings of a New Beginning in *Oryx and Crake*', *Papers on Language and Literature* 41.2 (2005), pp. 170–95.

Dunning, Stephen. 'Margaret Atwood's *Oryx and Crake*: The Terror of the Therapeutic', *Canadian Literature* 186 (2005), pp. 86–101.

Griffiths, Anthony. 'Genetics according to *Oryx and Crake*', *Canadian Literature* 181 (2004), pp. 192–5.

Hoogheem, Andrew. 'Secular Apocalypses: Darwinian Criticism and Atwoodian Floods', *Mosaic: An Interdisciplinary Critical Journal* 45.2 (June 2012), pp. 55–71.

Ingersoll, Earl G. 'Survival in Margaret Atwood's Novel, *Oryx and Crake*', *Extrapolation* 45.2 (2004), pp. 162–75.

Mohr, Dunja M. 'Anthropocene Fiction: Narrating the "Zero Hour" in Margaret Atwood's *MadAddam* Trilogy', in Ursula Mathis-Moser and Marie J. Carrière (eds), *Writing Beyond the End Times? The Literatures of Canada and Quebec* (Innsbruck: Innsbruck University Press, 2017), pp. 25–45.

Northover, Richard Alan. 'Ecological Apocalypse in Margaret Atwood's *MaddAddam* Trilogy', *Studia Neophilologica* 88 (2016), pp. 81–95.

Raschke, Debrah. 'Margaret Atwood's *MaddAddam* Trilogy: Postmodernism, Apocalypse, and Rapture', *Studies in Canadian Literature* 39.2 (2014), pp. 22–44.

Rozelle, Lee. 'Liminal Ecologies in Margaret Atwood's *Oryx and Crake*', *Canadian Literature* 206 (Autumn 2010), pp. 61–72.

Schoene, Berthold. 'Getting World Going in Margaret Atwood's *Oryx and Crake*', *Senses and Society* 8.1 (2013), pp. 96–105.

Snyder, Katherine V. '"Time to Go": The Post-Apocalyptic and the Post-Traumatic in Margaret Atwood's *Oryx and Crake*', *Studies in the Novel* 43.4 (Winter 2011), pp. 470–89.

Weafer, Miles. 'Writing from the Margin: Victim Positions in Atwood's *The Year of the Flood*', in Karma Waltonen (ed.), *Margaret Atwood's Apocalypses* (Newcastle upon Tyne: Cambridge Scholars, 2015), pp. 57–70.

About *The Penelopiad*

Braund, Susanna. '"We're Here Too, the Ones Without Names." A Study of Female Voices as Imagined by Margaret Atwood, Carol Ann Duffy, and Marguerite Yourcenar', *Classical Reception Journal* 4.2 (2012), pp. 190–208.

Howells, Coral Ann. '"We Can't Help but Be Modern": *The Penelopiad*', in S. A. Appleton (ed.), *Once upon a Time: Myth, Fairy Tales and Legends in Margaret Atwood's Writings* (Newcastle upon Tyne: Cambridge Scholars, 2008), pp. 57–72.

Ingersoll, Earl G. 'Flirting with Tragedy: Margaret Atwood's *The Penelopiad* and the Play of the Text', *Intertexts* 12.1–2 (Spring 2008), pp. 111–28.

Jung, Susanne '"A Chorus Line": Margaret Atwood's *Penelopiad* at the Crossroads of Narrative, Poetic and Dramatic Genres', *Connotations* 24.1 (2014/2015), pp. 41–62.

Staels, Hilde. '*The Penelopiad* and *Weight*: Contemporary Parodic and Burlesque Transformations of Classical Myths', *College Literature* 6.4 (Fall 2009), pp. 100–18.

Suzuki, Mihoko. 'Rewriting the *Odyssey* in the Twenty-First Century: Mary Zimmerman's *Odyssey* and Margaret Atwood's *Penelopiad*', *College Literature* 34.2 (Spring 2007), pp. 263–78.

Index

Adapting Margaret Atwood: The Handmaid's Tale and Beyond (Wells-Lassagne and McMahon)   150
Alderman, Naomi
   Happy Zombie Sunrise Home   150
Alias Grace (Atwood)   5, 7, 75, 76, 99–109, 113, 118
   anti-detective novel   107–8
   historical fiction   103–4
   overview   100–1
   quilt motif   106–7
   readerly desire   101–3
   servant girl   104–5
Amnesty International   6
Anderson, Hans Christian
   'Red Shoes, The'   37, 38
Angel Catbird (Atwood)   150
Animals in That Country, The (Atwood)   5
Anthropocene fiction   141–4
anthropocentrism   128, 142, 143
apocalyptic narrative, 'tragic' and 'comic' modes of   134
Arendt, Hannah
   Human Condition, The   130
Atwood, Carl   2
Atwood, Margaret Eleanor
   Alias Grace   5, 7, 75, 76, 99–109, 113, 118
   Angel Catbird   150
   Animals in That Country, The   5
   biography of   2–7
   Blind Assassin, The   5, 7, 17, 33, 99, 100, 106, 109–15, 118, 147
   Bodily Harm   7, 42, 45–52, 59, 66, 76, 92, 149
   'Boys at the Lab, The'   2
   Cat's Eye   2, 5, 7, 33, 40, 75–88, 92, 97, 151
   Circle Game, The   1, 27
   Curious Pursuits   76

Dearly   3
Door, The   147
Double Persephone   1, 5
Edible Woman, The   1, 3, 7, 9–20, 28–9, 32, 37, 40, 42–4, 52
'English Metaphysical Romance, The'   2
'Gertrude Talks Back'   127
God's Gardeners Oral Hymnbook, The   132
Governor General's Award   1
Hag-Seed   7, 145, 146, 148–9
Handmaid's Tale, The   5, 7, 17, 31, 42, 46, 47, 52, 53–73, 75–7, 92, 103, 118, 120–2, 126, 135, 136, 140, 145, 150
Happy Zombie Sunrise Home   150
Heart Goes Last, The   7, 145–8
'In Search of *Alias Grace*'   103
Journals of Susanna Moodie, The   27
Lady Oracle   7, 15, 19, 31–44, 46, 47, 52, 60, 83, 94, 102, 114, 151
Life Before Man   7, 19, 31, 39–47, 52, 59, 122
MaddAddam   7, 73, 120–2, 127, 138–44, 147
Moral Disorder   2, 145, 147
Morning in the Burned House   82
Negotiating with the Dead: A Writer on Writing   6, 13
On Writers and Writing   82
Oryx and Crake   5, 7, 58, 59, 120–36, 138, 140–2
Penelopiad, The   7, 99, 100, 115–20, 149
Positron   147
Robber Bride, The   5, 7, 17–18, 75–7, 119
Robber Bridegroom, The   49
Selected Poems II   82
Servant Girl, The   104
'Siren Song'   119

'Spotty-Handed Villainesses: Problems of Female Bad Behaviour in the Creation of Literature' 76
Stone Mattress 7, 145–7
Surfacing 2, 3, 9, 13, 22–9, 31–3, 40, 42, 43, 122, 141
Survival: A Thematic Guide to Canadian Literature 3, 4, 10, 22, 24, 27, 31, 32, 38
Testaments, The 5, 10, 73, 120, 121, 145, 150
True Stories 59
'Victory Burlesk, The' 147
Year of the Flood, The 7, 121, 122, 127, 131–8, 140, 142, 150
You Are Happy 27, 119
Atwood: A Biography (Cooke) 6
Atwoodian 1, 31, 75, 80, 88, 99, 114, 117, 134, 147, 149
Atwood persona, the 13
Atwood phenomenon, the 7, 149–51
'Atwood's Adult Fairy Tale: Lévi-Strauss, Bettelheim, and *The Edible Woman*' (MacLulich) 17
Austen, Jane 6

Backlash: The Undeclared War Against American Women (Faludi) 62
Banerjee, Chinmoy 78–80
Barzilai, Shuli 36, 38, 39, 127
Beauvoir, Simone de
 Second Sex, The 10
Becker, Susanne
 'Celebrity, or a Disneyland of the Soul: Margaret Atwood and the Media' 150
Beckett, Samuel 100
Bedford, Anna 130, 139, 143
Beer, Gillian 132
Beeton, Isabella
 Book of Household Management, The 104
Bell, Millicent 14
Bell Jar, The (Plath) 22
Bentham, Jeremy 87
Beran, Carol 41
 Living Over the Abyss: Margaret Atwood's Life Before Man 40
Berger, John
 Ways of Seeing 87

Bergthaller, Hannes 131, 132, 136, 137
Bettelheim, Bruno 19
Birkerts, Sven 126
Blind Assassin, The (Atwood) 5, 7, 17, 33, 99, 100, 106, 109–15, 118, 147
 gothic tale of victims and villains 113–15
 overview 109–11
 self-conscious storyteller 111–13
Bodily Harm (Atwood) 7, 42, 45–52, 59, 66, 76, 92, 149
 healing comedy 51–2
 overview 46–8
 postcolonial novel 48–50
 responsibility 50–1
 touch 50–1
Bonvillain, Tamra 150
Booker Prize for Fiction 5
Book of Household Management, The (Beeton) 104
Bouson, J. Brooks 68, 92, 97, 123–6, 128, 131–2, 134–6
'Boys at the Lab, The' (Atwood) 2
bpNichol 3
Braund, Susanna 119
Brave New World (Huxley) 126
Brown, Julie 78, 85, 86
Brydon, Diana 46, 49, 50
Butling, Pauline
 Writing in Our Time 3
Byliner 147

Calle, Pilar Sánchez 147
Cambridge Companion to Margaret Atwood, The (Howells) 5, 145
Cambridge Introduction to Margaret Atwood, The (Macpherson) 3
Canada/Canadian 15, 19, 23
 cultural production 3
 Governor General's Award 1
 multiculturalism 4
 nationalism 2, 4
Canada Council 3, 4
Canadian Literature 13, 122
Canavan, Gerry 124, 131
Carrington, Ildikó de Papp 49
catastrophic anthropocentricism 142
Cat's Eye (Atwood) 2, 5, 7, 33, 40, 75–88, 92, 97, 151

art and representation 85–8
fictional autobiography 81–3
overview 78–81
Women Beware Women 83–5
celebrity 102, 150
 cultural 151
 glamour 151
 literary 151
'Celebrity, or a Disneyland of the Soul: Margaret Atwood and the Media' (Becker) 150
Centennial Commission Poetry Competition 5
Chen, Chien-Hung 127
Chevalier dans l'Ordre des Arts et des Lettres 5
Christ, Carol P.
 Diving Deep and Surfacing 25
 'Margaret Atwood: The Surfacing of Women's Quest and Spiritual Vision' 25
Christmas, Johnnie 150
Circle Game, The (Atwood) 1
 'This is a Photograph of Me' 27
Clockwork Orange, A 57
Cohen, Leonard 23
comic romance 52
Commonwealth Writers' Best Book Prize 5
communities of power 104
Conversation, The 150
Conway, Jill Ker 82–3
Cooke, Nathalie
 Atwood: A Biography 6
 Margaret Atwood: A Critical Companion 33, 40
crime fiction 102, 146
Critical Essays on Margaret Atwood (McCombs) 5
Curious Pursuits (Atwood) 76

Dante 127
Darwinian model of evolution 137
Davey, Frank 51
 Margaret Atwood: A Feminist Poetics 52
Davidson, Arnold 71, 72
 'Future Tense: Making History in *The Handmaid's Tale*' 71

Dearly (Atwood) 3
Defalco, Amelia 142, 147
Defoe, Daniel
 Robinson Crusoe 126
Delany, Paul 22, 23
detective fiction 32, 108
Dick, Philip K.
 Man in the High Castle, The 54
DiMarco, Danette 130
Diving Deep and Surfacing (Christ) 25
Door, The (Atwood) 147
Double Persephone (Atwood) 1, 5
Drichel, Simone 47–50
Duffy, Carol Ann
 World's Wife, The 119
Dunaway, Faye 53
Dunning, Stephen 126, 130–1
Duvall, Robert 53
Dvorak, Marta 64–6, 81, 83, 85–7, 109, 112–14
dystopia 7, 52–4, 57–9, 63, 64, 66, 68, 70, 73, 120–44, 146, 147

ecological carelessness 31
ecological imperative 136
ecology 23, 24, 31, 123, 128, 129, 132, 143
Edible Woman, The (Atwood) 1, 3, 7, 9–20, 28–9, 32, 37, 40, 42–4, 52
 body, the 19–20, 22
 consumption 19–20
 early reception 13–15
 fairy-tale gothic 15–17
 fairy-tale imagery 17–19
 feminist readings 24
 overview 11–13
 romance plot 15–17
Eliot, George
 Middlemarch 39
Engendering Genre: The Works of Margaret Atwood (Nischik) 86
Engles, Tim
 White Male Nostalgia in Contemporary North American Literature 148
'English Metaphysical Romance, The' (Atwood) 2
English National Opera 53
environmental damage 122
environmentalism 121, 122, 141

Evaristo, Bernadine 5
excessive materialism 31

fairy tale 1, 12, 14, 29, 32, 36, 37, 39, 49, 59, 77, 91, 93, 141
  gothic 15–17, 88, 94
  imagery 17–19, 38
Faludi, Susan
  Backlash: The Undeclared War Against American Women 62
fanatical feminism 62
fantasy 43, 90, 93, 94, 97, 142, 146, 147
Fat Lady Dances: Margaret Atwood's Lady Oracle, The (Fee) 35
Fee, Marjorie 36
  Fat Lady Dances: Margaret Atwood's Lady Oracle, The 35
Feminine Mystique, The (Friedan) 10
feminism 11, 25, 31, 92–4, 119, 121
  in 1980s 61–3
  fanatical 62
  power 92, 93
  second-wave 10, 50, 61–3, 93, 97, 136
  victim 93
Fiennes, Joseph 53
Financial Times, The 148
Findlay, Timothy 3
Fire with Fire (Wolf) 93
Food, Consumption and the Body in Contemporary Women's Writing (Sceats) 19
Foster, Joan 60
Foucault, Michel 87
Frankenstein (Shelley) 126
French, Marilyn 42
Freud, Sigmund 104
Friedan, Betty
  Feminine Mystique, The 10
Frye, Northrop 4, 16
Fukuyama, Francis 128
'Future Tense: Making History in *The Handmaid's Tale*' (Davidson) 71

gendered futures 134–6
gender politics 134
genre fiction 1
'Gertrude Talks Back' (Atwood) 127
Gibert, Teresa 147

Gibson, Eleanor Jess 3
Gibson, Greame 3, 11
Gilbert, Sophie 150
Gileadean Studies 70, 150
Globe and Mail, The 133
goddesses 36–9
God's Gardeners Oral Hymnbook, The (Atwood) 132
Goldman, Marlene 105
gothic, the 1, 18, 33, 37, 43, 75, 78, 80, 89, 90, 94–6, 103, 105, 108, 110, 138
  fairy-tale 15–17, 39, 88, 94
  horror 27, 146
  novel 27–8
  romance 32, 34–6, 94, 114, 146
  tale of victims and villains 113–15
Grace, Sherrill 43
  Violent Duality: A Study of Margaret Atwood 16–17, 27, 28
Graham, Martha 122
Graves, Robert
  White Goddess, The 37
Greene, Gayle 42, 63
Greer, Bonnie 132
Griffiths, Anthony 122–3
Grimm, Brothers
  'Robber Bridegroom, The' 17, 93, 94
Guardian, The 53, 122
Gulliver's Travels (Swift) 126

Hag-Seed (Atwood) 7, 145, 146, 148–9
Hamlet (Shakespeare) 127
Handmaid's Tale, The (Atwood) 5, 7, 17, 31, 42, 46, 47, 52–73, 75–7, 92, 103, 118, 120–2, 126, 135, 136, 140, 145, 150
  complicity 67–70
  early responses 56–7
  feminism 61–3
  'Feminist Utopias and Questions of Liberty: Margaret Atwood's' 62
  genre 58–60
  language 63–7
  narrative 63–7
  overview 54–6
  responsibility 67–70
  victimhood 67–70

Happy Zombie Sunrise Home (Atwood and Alderman)   150
Hartman, Mary S.
  Victorian Murderesses   104
Hawkshead   1
Heart Goes Last, The (Atwood)   7, 145–8
Hébert, Anne   3
Hengen, Shannon   122, 124, 135, 141–2
historical fiction   103–4
Hite, Molly   34, 77, 81–4, 87
Homer
  Odyssey, The   99, 115, 117, 118, 120
homo faber   130
Hoogheem, Andrew   133, 137
House of Anansi Press   3–4
Howells, Coral Ann   39, 44, 55, 58, 66, 71–3, 99, 111, 117–18, 121, 126, 135
  Cambridge Companion to Margaret Atwood, The   5, 145
  Margaret Atwood   2
  'Science Fiction in the Feminine'   58
  'True Trash: Genre Fiction Revisited in *Stone Mattress*, *The Heart Goes Last* and *Hag-Seed*'   145–6
Huggan, Graham   151
  Postcolonial Exotic: Marketing the Margins, The   150
Human Condition, The (Arendt)   130
humanism   136–7
Hutcheon, Linda   103
  Poetics of Postmodernism, A   106
Huxley, Aldous
  Brave New World   126

Ingersoll, Earl   54, 55, 81, 82, 84, 108, 110, 113, 114, 116, 117, 129
'In Search of *Alias Grace*' (Atwood)   103

Jameson, Fredric   133
Journals of Susanna Moodie, The (Atwood)   27

Klarer, Mario   64–5
Kolodny, Annette   34, 42–4, 47, 51, 52, 59
Kozakewich, Tobi
  Margaret Atwood: The Open Eye   145

Kröller, Eva-Marie   150
Kubrick, Stanley   127

Lady Oracle (Atwood)   7, 15, 19, 31–44, 46, 47, 52, 60, 83, 94, 102, 114, 151
  fairy-tale imagery   38
  goddesses   36–9
  gothic romance   34–6
  overview   32–4
  princesses   36–9
Laflen, Angela   56, 65
language   28–9
Laurence, Margaret   3
Layton, Irving   23
Le Guin, Ursula K.   58, 128, 132
Lessing, Doris   147
Lévi-Strauss, Claude   18
liberal ahistoricism   4
'Life, Liberty and the Pursuit of Normalcy' (Rule)   15
Life Before Man (Atwood)   7, 19, 31, 39–47, 52, 59, 122
  consumption   44–5
  overview   41–2
  between romance and realism   42–4
  survival   44–5
Life in the Clearings (Moodie)   101
Literary Celebrity in Canada (York)   151
Lively, Penelope   147
Living Over the Abyss: Margaret Atwood's Life Before Man (Beran)   40
Lloyd, Phyllida   116
London Review of Books   121, 133
Lopez, Maria J.   104

McCarthy, Mary   56–7
McCombs, Judith
  Critical Essays on Margaret Atwood   5
McLay, Catherine   16, 20, 52
MacLulich, T. D.   14, 18–19
  'Atwood's Adult Fairy Tale: Lévi-Strauss, Bettelheim, and *The Edible Woman*'   18
McMahon, Fiona
  Adapting Margaret Atwood: The Handmaid's Tale and Beyond   150
Macpherson, Heidi Slettedahl

Cambridge Introduction to Margaret Atwood, The 3
McWilliams, Ellen 32
MaddAddam (Atwood) 7
   after the Anthropocene 141–4
   narrative structure 139–41
   overview 138–9
   trilogy 73, 120–2, 127, 138–44, 146
Malahat Review, The 14, 15
Mandel, Eli 23–4
Man in the High Castle, The (Dick) 54
Marantz, Kate 50
Margaret Atwood (Howells) 2
Margaret Atwood (Rigney) 5, 32, 59
Margaret Atwood (Rosenberg) 50
Margaret Atwood (Wynne-Davies) 24, 31
Margaret Atwood: A Critical Companion (Cooke) 33, 40
Margaret Atwood: A Feminist Poetics (Davey) 52
Margaret Atwood and the Labour of Literary Celebrity (York) 151
Margaret Atwood: Feminism and Fiction (Tolan) 10
Margaret Atwood's Apocalypses (Waltonen) 145
Margaret Atwood's Fairy-Tale Sexual Politics (Wilson) 17, 37
Margaret Atwood Society 5
Margaret Atwood's Textual Assassinations (Wilson) 103
Margaret Atwood Studies 5, 7
Margaret Atwood: The Open Eye (Moss and Kozakewich) 145
'Margaret Atwood: The Stoic Comedian' (Smith) 15
'Margaret Atwood: The Surfacing of Women's Quest and Spiritual Vision' (Christ) 25
Margaret Atwood: Vision and Forms (VanSpanckeren) 31
Margaret Atwood: Works and Impact (Nischik) 5, 75–6
'Margaret the Magician' (Rogers) 13
Massoura, Kiriaki 79, 84–7
Michael, Magali Cornier 106–7
Middlemarch (Eliot) 39
Midsummer Night's Dream, A (Shakespeare) 148

Miller, Jane 14
Miner, Madonne 59–60, 69
misogyny 72
'Modest Proposal, A' (Swift) 126
Moodie, Susanna 102
   Life in the Clearings 101
Moore, Lorrie 127–8
Moral Disorder (Atwood) 2, 145, 147
Morning in the Burned House (Atwood) 82
Moss, Elisabeth 53
Moss, John
   Margaret Atwood: The Open Eye 145
Moss, Laura 151
multiculturalism 4, 40
Muñoz-Valdivieso, Sofía 149
Munro, Alice 3
Murray, Jennifer 103

Naipaul, V. S. 150
Negotiating with the Dead: A Writer on Writing (Atwood) 6, 13
Neuman, Shirley 61, 62, 69
New Statesman, The 132
New York Times, The 42, 53, 54, 57, 61, 126, 132
New York Times Review of Books, The 14, 22
Nietzsche, Friedrich 97
Nineteen Eighty-Four (Orwell) 54, 57, 58, 126
Nischik, Reingard M.
   Engendering Genre: The Works of Margaret Atwood 86
   Margaret Atwood: Works and Impact 5, 75–6
Northover, Richard Alan 132
Norwegian Order of Literary Merit 5

Odyssey, The (Homer) 99, 115, 117, 118, 120
Ondaatje, Michael 3, 150–1
O'Neill, John 108
On Writers and Writing (Atwood) 82
oppression 20, 46, 50, 59, 67–9, 104, 126, 139
Orwell, George
   Nineteen Eighty-Four 54, 57, 58, 126

Oryx and Crake (Atwood)   5, 7, 58, 59, 120–36, 138, 140–2
   ethical novel   129–31
   overview   123–5
   post-human future   127–9
   textual allusions in   125–7

Palumbo, Alice M.   75–6
Parker, Emma
   'Politics of Eating, The'   44–5
Parkin-Gounelas, Ruth   100
Patton, Marilyn   36, 48–50
   'Politics of the Body, The'   37
   'Tourists and Terrorists'   48
Penelopiad, The (Atwood)   7, 99, 100, 115–20, 149
   classical revisions and re-readings   119–20
   as novel   116–17
   overview   115–16
   voices, reclaiming   117–19
PEN Pinter Prize   5
PEN's Lifetime Achievement Award   6
Perrakis, Phyllis Sternberg   91
Phillips, Dana   132
Piercy, Marge   9–10, 25, 26
Pinter, Harold   5–6, 53
Plaskow, Judith   26
Plath, Sylvia
   Bell Jar, The   22
Poetics of Postmodernism, A (Hutcheon)   106
Political in Margaret Atwood's Fiction, The (Sheckels)   61–2
political realism   52, 59
'Politics of Eating, The' (Parker)   44
'Politics of the Body, The' (Patton)   37
Polk, James   3
pollution   54, 57, 59, 122
Positron (Atwood)   147
Postcolonial Exotic: Marketing the Margins, The (Huggan)   150
posthumanism   136–7
postmodernism   140, 141
Potts, Donna   89
Powell, Michael   37
power feminism   92, 93
Pressburger, Emeric   38
primitivism   23

Pratt, E. J.   5
princesses   36–9
psychological realism   120
Purdy, Al   3

Quebec separatism   4

Rao, Eleonora   95–6
Raschke, Debrah   132, 139–41, 143
Reading the Gothic in Margaret Atwood's Novels (Tennant)   34
realism   34, 39, 42–4, 47, 77, 96, 108
   political   52, 59
   psychological   120
   social   103
'Red Shoes, The' (Anderson)   37, 38
Red Shoes: Margaret Atwood Starting Out, The (Sullivan)   6
Richardson, Natasha   53
Richler, Mordecai   23
Rigney, Barbara Hill   69, 70, 93, 94, 100
   Margaret Atwood   5, 32, 59
Robber Bride, The (Atwood)   5, 7, 17–18, 75–7, 103, 119
   friendship/sisterhood/feminism   92–4
   gothic tale   94–6
   narrative authority   91–2
   overview   88–91
   Women Beware Women   85
Robber Bridegroom, The (Atwood)   49
'Robber Bridegroom, The' (Grimm)   17
Robinson, Alan   109
Robinson Crusoe (Defoe)   126
Rogers, Linda   13–14
   'Margaret the Magician'   13
romance   1, 11, 18, 20, 23, 29, 33, 39, 42–4, 47, 48, 59, 60, 83, 126, 135, 149
   comic   52
   conventions   43
   gothic   32, 34–6, 94, 114, 146
   mythic   16
   plot   15–17, 69, 134
   quest   16
   urban   32
Rosenberg, Jerome H.   51
   Margaret Atwood   50
Royal Danish Opera   53

Royal Ontario Museum   41, 43
Royal Society of Canada   5
Rozelle, Lee   123, 126, 128, 129
Rudy, Susan
   Writing in Our Time   3
Rule, Jane   12
   'Life, Liberty and the Pursuit of
      Normalcy,'   15
Rushdie, Salman   150
Russ, Joanna
   'Somebody's Trying to Kill Me and I
      Think It's My Husband'   35

Sage, Lorna   57
Sanchez-Grant, Sofia   32
Sandler, Linda   4, 11, 14, 28–9
Sceats, Sarah   45
   *Food, Consumption and the Body
      in Contemporary Women's
      Writing*   19–20
Schoene, Berthold   124, 126, 129, 131
science fiction   6, 31, 58, 109, 110, 114,
      122, 128, 139, 142
'Science Fiction in the Feminine'
      (Howells)   58
Second Sex, The (Beauvoir)   10
second-wave feminism   10, 50, 61–3, 93,
      97, 136
Selected Poems II (Atwood)   82
self-conscious storyteller   111–13
Servant Girl, The (Atwood)   101, 104
Shadow Males   34, 35
Shakespeare, W.
   Hamlet   127
   Midsummer Night's Dream, A   148
   Tempest, The   149
Shead, Jackie   102, 107–8
Shearer, Moira   37
Sheckels, Theodore
   *Political in Margaret Atwood's Fiction,
      The*   61–2
Shelley, Mary   58
   Frankenstein   126
Shields, Carol   3, 151
Showalter, Elaine   121, 122, 126
Shriver, Lionel   148
Signs   23
'Siren Song' (Atwood)   119
Smith, Philip   149

Smith, Rowland
   'Margaret Atwood: The Stoic
      Comedian'   15
Snaith, Helen   146
Snyder, Katherine V.   124, 125, 129
social realism   103
'Somebody's Trying to Kill Me and I Think
      It's My Husband' (Russ)   35
speculative fiction   1, 58
spotty-handed villainesses   75–97
'Spotty-Handed Villainesses: Problems
      of Female Bad Behaviour in
      the Creation of Literature'
      (Atwood)   76
Staels, Hilde   71, 92, 95, 108, 119, 120
Stanley, Sandra Kumamoto   101, 102
Stapleton, Patricia   68–9, 71
Stein, Karen   42–4, 75, 82, 101, 110, 114,
      115
Stoeber, Orville   150
Stone Mattress (Atwood)   7, 145–7
structural method   18
Sugars, Cynthia   27
Sullivan, Rosemary
   *Red Shoes: Margaret Atwood Starting
      Out, The*   6
Surfacing (Atwood)   2, 3, 9, 31–3, 40, 42,
      43, 122, 141
   body, the   20
   consumption   19
   early reception   13–15, 22–4
   feminist readings   24–7
   form   28–9
   gothic novel   27–8
   language   28–9
   overview   20–2
*Survival: A Thematic Guide to Canadian
      Literature* (Atwood)   3, 4, 10,
      22, 24, 27, 38
Suzuki, Mihoko   118–20

Tempest, The (Shakespeare)   149
Tennant, Colette   35
   *Reading the Gothic in Margaret
      Atwood's Novels*   34
Testaments, The (Atwood)   5, 10, 73, 120,
      121, 145, 150
Thomson, Tom   27–8
Tiffin, Helen   49

Times Literary Supplement, The 14, 57
Tolan, Fiona
  Margaret Atwood: Feminism and Fiction 10
'Tourists and Terrorists' (Patton) 48
True Stories (Atwood) 59
'True Trash: Genre Fiction Revisited in *Stone Mattress, The Heart Goes Last* and *Hag-Seed*' (Howells) 145–6

United States (US) 31
  imperialism 4
US, *see* United States

vampire fiction 146
VanSpanckeren, Kathryn
  Margaret Atwood: Vision and Forms 31
Vickroy, Laurie 90
victim feminism 93
victimhood 4, 9, 21, 22, 24, 25, 49, 52, 67–70, 79, 81, 117, 135
Victorian Murderesses (Hartman) 104
'Victory Burlesk, The' (Atwood) 147
violence 31, 50, 62, 115
  gendered 114
Violent Duality: A Study of Margaret Atwood (Grace) 17, 27, 28

Wagner-Lawlor, Jennifer A. 65–6
Wah, Fred 3
Walter, Natasha 122
Waltonen, Karma
  Margaret Atwood's Apocalypses 145
Watkins, Susan 133–5, 140, 147, 150
Ways of Seeing (Berger) 87
Weight (Winterson) 119
Wells, H. G. 58, 127
Wells-Lassagne, Shannon
  Adapting Margaret Atwood: The Handmaid's Tale and Beyond 150
White Goddess, The (Graves) 37
White Male Nostalgia in Contemporary North American Literature (Engels) 148
Wilderness Tips (Atwood) 146
will to power 97
Wilson, Sharon Rose 36, 38, 85–6, 95, 102
  Margaret Atwood's Fairy-Tale Sexual Politics 17, 37
  Margaret Atwood's Textual Assassinations 103
Winterson, Jeanette 132, 135
  Weight 119
Wisker, Gina 58, 61, 65, 132–3
Wolf, Naomi
  Fire with Fire 93
Woolf, Virginia 42
World's Wife, The (Duffy) 119
Writing in Our Time (Butling and Rudy) 3
Wyatt, Jean 93, 95
Wynne-Davies, Marion 39–40, 75–7, 81, 85, 87–8
  Margaret Atwood 24, 31

Yamamoto, Tae 60
Year of the Flood, The (Atwood) 7, 121, 122, 127, 131–8, 140, 142, 150
  gendered futures 134–6
  humanism/posthumanism 136–7
  overview 133–4
York, Lorraine 102
  Literary Celebrity in Canada 151
  Margaret Atwood and the Labour of Literary Celebrity 151
You Are Happy (Atwood) 27, 119

www.ingramcontent.com/pod-product-compliance
Lightning Source LLC
Chambersburg PA
CBHW061829300426
44115CB00013B/2302